This book offers a seminal contribution to demystify responsible leadership. It succeeds in taking the reader on a colourful journey of discovery, allowing one to gain insights from a rich pallet of diverse views and more importantly leaves one with the realisation that the responsible leadership journey has only started. If you want to participate on this journey, I suggest you make this book your starting point.

Derick de Jongh, *Professor, University of Pretoria, South Africa*

From enticing start to compelling finish, this is a book of broad and profound intellectual power. The authors – all people who know what they are talking about – inspire us with romantic hope and caution us with sceptical realism. In between, they allow space for careful, thoughtful understanding of responsibility in contemporary leadership. I wholeheartedly recommend this book to anyone concerned with the predicaments of modern organising, activism and governance.

Jonathan Gosling, *Emeritus Professor, University of Exeter, UK*

Responsible Leadership

It is time for the development of a new kind of business leadership. Global needs call for a revision of market capitalism and a move towards moral capitalism; a move 'from value to values, from shareholders to stakeholders, and from balance sheets to balanced development' (Kofi Annan).

With the challenge of this transition in mind, this book argues that it is time for a new understanding of leadership, a new romanticism which looks behind the overvalued, heroic leadership notion. The editors explore a romanticised rhetoric and situate it within current discourses of authentic, distributed, and ethical leadership, where societal, economic, and environmental challenges require us to take a collective lead towards doing good and growing well.

Exploring this dichotomy of romantic ideal and essential requirement, this book combines the insights of leading academics with those of practitioners in the field. Thought-provoking and engaging it will challenge both thinking and practice, and is essential reading for all those operating or researching in the field of leadership, particularly those who realise the overwhelming challenges of sustainability, and corporate social responsibility which the world now faces.

Steve Kempster is Professor of Leadership Learning and Development and Director of Leadership Development at Lancaster University Management School, UK.

Brigid Carroll is Associate Professor in the Department of Management and International Business and the Director of Research and a lead facilitator at the New Zealand Leadership Institute, both at the University of Auckland, New Zealand.

Routledge Studies in Leadership Research

Responsible Leadership

Realism and romanticism

**Edited by Steve Kempster
and Brigid Carroll**

LONDON AND NEW YORK

First published 2016 by Routledge

2 Park Square, Milton Park, Abingdon, Oxon OX14 4RN
605 Third Avenue, New York, NY 10017

Routledge is an imprint of the Taylor & Francis Group, an informa business

First issued in paperback 2021

Publisher's Note

The publisher has gone to great lengths to ensure the quality of this reprint
but points out that some imperfections in the original copies may be apparent.

British Library Cataloguing in Publication Data
A catalogue record for this book is available from the British Library

Library of Congress Cataloging in Publication Data
Kempster, Steve, 1961- editor. | Carroll, Brigid, editor.
Title: Responsible leadership : realism and romanticism / edited by
Steve Kempster and Brigid Carroll.
Description: 1 Edition. | New York : Routledge, 2016. |
Series: Routledge studies in leadership research | Includes
bibliographical references and index.
Identifiers: LCCN 2015041660| ISBN 9781138931299 (hardback) |
ISBN 9781315679822 (ebook)
Subjects: LCSH: Leadership. | Responsibility.
Classification: LCC HD57.7 .R4647 2016 | DDC 658.4/092–dc23
LC record available at http://lccn.loc.gov/2015041660

ISBN: 978-1-138-93129-9 (hbk)
ISBN: 978-0-367-34061-2 (pbk)

Typeset in Bembo
by Wearset Ltd, Boldon, Tyne and Wear

It goes without saying (we hope) that all contributors to this volume want to thank their partners, their children, their parents, and many close colleagues for support and encouragement.... So with that said the dedication of this book is to those in leadership roles to embrace the responsibility to use the force that is leadership to address the contemporary challenges that face humanity – large and small.

Contents

Figures

Contributors

Karen Blakeley. With over 25 years' experience of leadership development in banking and industry, Karen moved into academia in 2009,
joining Winchester Business School, one of the earliest signatories to the
UN PRME (Principles for Responsible Management Education) char-
ter. She helped establish the Hoare Centre for Responsible Management
at Winchester and is currently jointly leading an initiative to coordinate
research into responsible leadership amongst business schools around the
world. Karen has published in the area of responsible leadership and been
interviewed on TV concerning irresponsible leadership in banks. She is
also interested in the role played by spirituality in responsible leadership
development.

Brigid Carroll is an Associate Professor in the Department of Management
and International Business and the Director of Research and a lead facilitator at the New Zealand Leadership Institute, both at the University of
Auckland, New Zealand. Dr Carroll teaches organisation theory, critical
organisation issues, and leadership to undergraduates and postgraduates,
and designs, delivers, and researches leadership development using a constructionist, critical pedagogy to a range of sector and professional groups.
Her research interests lie primarily with identity work, discourse and narrative theory, and methodology, and critical leadership theory and practice
in contemporary organisations. Her work has been published in *Organization Studies*, *Organization*, *Human Relations*, *Management Communication
Quarterly*, and *Leadership*.

Sarah Gregory is Senior Teaching Fellow in the Department of Organisation, Work and Technology at the Lancaster University Management
School. With a PhD in Behavioural Ethics and MPhil in Critical Management her work explores middle manager ethical decision-making.
Recent conference papers include Management Learning Conference
2013 – 'We don't often talk about this': Exploring discourse ethics in
executive education; and ANZAM Conference 2014 – 'A moment of
truth': The development of a process model for the teaching of business
ethics.

Stefanie Gustafsson is a Prize Fellow (Postdoc) in Human Resource Management at the University of Bath, School of Management. She is interested in the lived experiences of professional work, trust in organisations, critical perspectives on HRM, and the development of qualitative research methods for research and teaching.

Eric Guthey is an Associate Professor at the Copenhagen Business School in Denmark, where he teaches leadership in the masters, MBA, and executive programmes. His current research explores the production and promotion of leadership concepts and leadership development services via the leadership industries, and analyses the connections between these competitive dynamics and the ways that leadership gets practised and understood.

Malcolm Higgs is Professor of Human Resources and Organisation Behaviour at the University of Southampton Management School. Until 31 October 2007 Malcolm was the Director of the School of Leadership, Change and HR, and Research Director of Henley Business School. He took up this position in August 2005 having for the previous four years been the College's Academic Dean. He remains a Visiting Professor at Henley Business School as well as being a Visiting Professor at Erasmus University in the Netherlands.

Veronica Hope Hailey is a Professor of Strategic Human Resource Management and Dean of the School of Management, University of Bath. Her research focuses on trust, the role of HR, employment relationships, and strategic change. She has been voted as one of the top thought leaders on trust and has featured repeatedly on the HR Most Influential list.

Marian Iszatt-White. After a successful career in financial risk management, Marian Iszatt-White moved to Cumbria as a training consultant for an educational trust, where she specialised in public sector leadership development. Whilst there, she completed an MSc in Organizational Behaviour before leaving to undertake her PhD research as part of Lancaster University's Centre for Excellence in Leadership. She is now a lecturer in the Department of Management Learning and Leadership at Lancaster and was until recently Director of the School's Executive MBA.

Brad Jackson is the Head of School of Government and Professor of Public and Community Leadership at Victoria University of Wellington. Prior to this he was the Fletcher Building Education Trust Chair in Leadership and Co-Director of the New Zealand Leadership Institute at the University of Auckland Business School. He is the former Vice-Chair of the International Leadership Association, Editor of *Leadership*, and Research Fellow of the Australian and New Zealand Academy of Management.

Steve Kempster is Professor of Leadership Learning and Development and Director of the Lancaster Leadership Centre at Lancaster University Management School. With a PhD in leadership learning he has published articles, chapters and books that explore leadership learning, entrepreneur-ial leadership development, leadership of change and leadership as purpose. He was formally a Board Director of the International Leadership Associ-ation, and is on the Editorial Boards of *Management Learning* and *Leadership*.

Sarah Lee's extensive experience in Human Resources and Project Man-agement, as a practitioner and university lecturer, has shaped her present research interest in the tensions and dilemmas of the management role. Her doctoral research at Southampton Business School used a values theory perspective to examine how managers deal with value conflicts at work. Currently based in Prague, she continues with academic work while getting to know the Czech language and culture.

Susan R. Madsen is the Orin R. Woodbury Professor of Leadership and Ethics in the Woodbury School of Business at Utah Valley University, a Distinguished Visiting Fellow of the Lancaster Leadership Centre (UK), a Visiting Fellow of the Faculty of Economics and Business at the Univer-sity of Zagreb (Croatia), and a Fellow of the Leadership Trust Foundation (England). She has written or edited five books and published nearly 100 articles, chapters, and reports on her research on women and leadership.

Ken Parry is Professor of Leadership Studies. He has held posts at various Australian and New Zealand universities. He was Founding Director of the Centre for the Study of Leadership, a joint venture with private indus-try, and Founding Editor of the journal of the Australian and New Zea-land Academy of Management. He has addressed the Senior Executive Service at the National Press Club and often gives keynote addresses at industry conferences.

Sharon Turnbull is an independent academic and is associate Head of Research at the Leadership Trust in the UK. She is Visiting Professor at the University of Gloucestershire, the University of Worcester, the Uni-versity of West of England and a Fellow of Lancaster Leadership Centre. Her research interests are global, worldly, and responsible leadership and organisational change. She is a Fellow of the International Research Insti-tute in Sustainability at University of Gloucestershire.

Emma Watton is Senior Teaching Fellow and Programme Director for the MSc in Leadership Practice and Responsibility at the Lancaster Leader-ship Centre, Lancaster University Management School. She has a MBA in Leadership and Sustainability and her current research interests are in responsible leadership. She has had conference papers and book chap-ters published in the areas of responsible leadership, developing leadership resilience, and service learning.

Sue Williams is a Senior Lecturer at the University of Gloucestershire, UK. She is a Chartered Member of the Chartered Institute for Person-nel and Development. Her current research interests are in leadership and management development and human resource development. She led the organisation of the 12th International HRD conference with a theme of 'Sustaining growth through HRD' in 2011. She has published in the areas of sustainable leadership, work-based learning, action learning, and reflective practice.

Foreword

The romance and realism of responsible leadership

Thomas Maak

When the editors approached me whether I would consider writing a foreword to this book I didn't hesitate to agree. Ten years have passed since my colleague Nicola Pless and I cautiously tried to set the stage of what we hoped would at least trigger some discussion around the responsibility of leaders in a connected world, and the role of responsible leadership in contributing to a better world. We didn't dare to dream then, that a great number of colleagues would join us in exploring the notion of responsibility in leadership.

Our attempt to map out a research agenda was born out of both frustration about the state of the discussion and curiosity as to how leaders in a connected world could lead effectively and responsibly. The initial frustration resulted from the dazzling discovery that while responsible leadership was high in demand no researchers had yet addressed the conceptual challenges of responsible leadership in a post-scandal era. Yes, there were attempts to explore leadership ethics from a humanities perspective but given the myriad of research on leadership and books on the topic no one had yet asked the question what responsible leadership in a stakeholder context and in regards to sustainable futures required.

Ten years on, the present collection of chapters marks a milestone – its authors revisit the debate and put it in perspective. It couldn't be more timely. In recent years, 'responsible leadership' has developed by and large into a discourse at the intersection of leadership, CSR, and stakeholder management. And while much progress has been made, critical questions and issues raised in the beginning still remain unanswered. For example, early commentators stressed the void of responsibility in extant leadership research, when perhaps it is not so much about filling that void but rather about developing a new paradigm of thinking about leadership – a truly relational, shared concept and thus an inherently socialised concept. Some contributions in this volume foray in that direction. Moreover, amidst the gritty realism of corporate misconduct and the global financial crisis this book encourages us to envision the ideals inherent in a strong notion of responsible leadership, such as being a key driver for pro-social behaviour and responsible decision-making in organisations, for building sustainable, mutually beneficial relationships to all legitimate stakeholders, and making this world a better, more equitable place.

Moreover, the volume's title couldn't be more appropriate, in that it directs us to the tension of romanticism and realism in responsible leadership. To be clear, responsible leadership is not a utopian concept – it is a response to both the dire straits of leadership research and its inability to incorporate a multi-level notion of responsibility. As a result, mainstream research is stuck in the classical leader-follower dyad when much of today's leadership work is either shared or focused on multiple stakeholders. In addition, it responds to the call for business leaders in particular to do better and more; better in so far as stakeholders are tired of, and increasingly cynical about, selfish behaviour in leadership positions; more in regards to the needs of communities and societies which rely on businesses' ability to tackle some of the world's toughest problems and turn them into opportunities.

Is it romantic to ask leaders to accept a broader responsibility to serve the needs of stakeholders in need? I don't believe so; I would argue that leaders have the unique privilege – and indeed many the potential – to mobilise others to become leaders in their own right in the pursuit social welfare, broadly defined. Some may consider this notion of servant leadership a romantic one. But it is that 'romanticism', or rather idealism, the idea of thinking boldly and positively about the future, and acting upon it, that will make a difference.

'Realism' in contrast suggests that the leadership project needs to be adjusted to the real world and that is certainly true. We know that leaders fail as they become corrupted by the power and privileges of their positions, and that a higher proportion of narcissistic personalities seek leadership positions. That's when critical followership becomes important to check and balance individualised leadership projects. But it is equally true and 'real' that most leaders are actually inclined to think broadly about the needs of their constituencies and will strive to leave a legacy. Realism here means confronting the social and systemic limitations of reality while pursuing a vision for the future.

Responsible leadership is not an easy to define concept, nor is it the same in the minds of all. However, even the sceptics these days agree that is needed and that we should more thoroughly investigate its features, how it is different from extant leadership concepts, and what it may take to disseminate it broadly in business and society. The contributors in this book unveil convincing pathways for future research and most importantly, compelling ideas to take responsible leadership – in research and practice – to the next level.

Acknowledgements

We have two prominent acknowledgements we wish to make. First, to thank the chapter authors for giving such energy, insight, and commitment to this project, this is much appreciated. Second, a big thank you to Josh Firth. He has provided superb support, much needed project structure, and kept the project on schedule. Josh, you are a diamond.

1 Introduction

Responsible leadership – realism and romanticism

Steve Kempster and Brigid Carroll

If you have followed leadership scholarship to any degree and are well acquainted with the tendency of leadership to arrive with new adjectives before it – transformational, authentic, ethical, relational leadership all being examples – it would be understandable to think that such a new descriptor heralds a whole new school of leadership thinking. That's not what this book is about. We would prefer that responsible leadership inserts itself as a critical stimulant to supply enough grit and intrigue to catalyse some new questions about the state of leadership thinking through its myriad forms. After all, responsibility is surely axiomatic with almost any variation of leadership theory, to the point that it is referenced constantly but almost never theorised or explored in its own right. If this book creates a critical engagement with responsibility in leadership – what it means to be responsible, who is responsible, and the relationships, dynamics, and networks that form and reform that 'who', what leadership is responsible for, what responsibility looks and feels like for the different actors involved, how responsibility is constructed, deconstructed and identified – then this book will achieve something of value.

We will be open straightaway about the drivers for this book. Responsible leadership theory has been largely driven by our colleagues in the corporate social responsibility space who quite naturally looked across to leadership research to help the progression of corporate social responsibility thinking and found precious little to work with. To be blunt, they found a body of thinking on leadership that didn't appear to be interested in the big, pressing challenges facing the world; that seemed to be narrowly focused on the dynamics between people in positions and their direct reports to meet organisational performance expectations, and that seemed over-disposed to view leadership as an offshoot of personality, character or psychological traits and their development. Yes, we are being provocative here, but we are inviting just a glimpse of the leadership body of work and community from another field who were disappointed and not satisfied with what they saw. Responsible leadership theory grew directly out of this lack and gap between a society facing challenges that require a big picture, multiple party, long-term process, and what we know about how influence, change, and movement happen in

the patterns of leading and following that occur between people with different and unequal positions, power, and passion.

It is important to say that this thinking on responsible leadership is very
much in its infancy. We call it a theory and can point to strong starting scholarly contributions; and there has been an enthusiastic embrace of it by those
who want to support corporates, particularly to engage with issues that go
beyond a traditional focus on financial bottom lines. However, in truth there
is much we do not know in this intersection of leadership, responsibility, and
whole-world challenges. In reading this book we can guarantee that you will
be drawn into the very largest of leadership questions, will meet all kinds of
assumptions about leaders and leadership given the ferment and contestation
intrinsic to the field, and you will be drawn in by cases, stories, and examples
of how responsibility is both understood and practised. Our wish is that you
leave with questions and real vigour not to take responsibility too lightly and
not to let it lie largely unexamined as it has done to date.

To aid us in this enterprise we have inserted responsible leadership
between two other movements – between romanticism and realism. We will
pick up what we mean by these in a later section but for now, we invite you
to have a feel or experience of them in this terrain of leadership and responsibility. Consider the following from Derick de Jongh, Director of the Centre
for Responsible Leadership (2005, p. 47):

> Just Imagine. Imagine a world where harmony, equity, social cohesion,
> ethical conduct, a sustainable environment and a just society dominate the
> thoughts and minds of all leaders, business, government and civil society....
> Imagine leaders who translate these personal ideals into standard business
> practice.... Imagine leaders who take personal interest and commit them-
> selves emotionally to the real world we want to create...

Pause a moment, not to reflect on that passage exactly, but your response to
that passage. Of course there will be a whole raft of responses to such words
but we think there will be two strong clusters of responses that loosely translate to our terms of 'romanticism' and 'realism'. The first would be characterised by an excitement and idealism on reading those words. Strong in such an
idealism would be notions of possibility, a sense of values or morals or ethics,
and something we could call belief or hope that is associated with seeing
something other than what is. We want to call that 'romanticism'. Another
response, however, looks roughly the opposite and could feel like a sense of
déjà vu or cynicism coloured by disbelief, experience, or what we might call
a reality check. Strong in that is a desire to see more than powerful words and
statements and an understanding that profound shifts and changes belie
enormous complexity and the navigation through difference, conflict, and
clashing assumptions. We would like to call this 'realism'. We argue that not
only does responsible leadership inherently risk these two responses, but it
needs them as vital points of reference in its quest to engage leadership in

larger more meaningful issues, at the same time as bringing the complexity of collective and collaborative dynamics in the pursuit of solving them. In this introductory chapter we work on 'laying the table' of responsible leadership amidst the settings, flavours, and 'tools' of romanticism and realism.

So much discussion on the theme of responsible leadership assumes, rightly in our view, that great change is required in the practices and responsibilities associated with leadership. Calls for leadership to embrace a broader and deeper kind of responsibility should set in motion a real examination of the shortfalls of traditional ways of thinking about leadership, alongside new possibilities for its redefinition and redevelopment. Working this between our poles of romanticism and realism should result in a treatment of responsible leadership not simply as 'utopian' but as 'realistic utopian' (Rawls, 1999, p. 127). We need to remember Meindl's seminal work on the 'romance of leadership' as an exploration of the tendency (both within the literature and in organisational settings) to overestimate the significance of leadership and its impact on organisational success. Developed by Meindl (1995), the phrase itself refers to the follower tendency to attribute responsibility for company performance to organisational leaders. We have much sympathy with this view when seen through a narrow, heroic, and individualistic lens. We would wish, however, to reintroduce the romanticised rhetoric to situate it within current leadership discourses regarding authentic, distributed, and ethical leadership where the societal, economic, and environmental challenges do require us to collectively take the lead in moving forward towards doing good and growing well. In this way, we see the need for both perspectives of realism and romanticism to be embraced.

In the remainder of this chapter we wish to sketch out responsible leadership, romanticism, and realism in turn in very broad brushstrokes as a way of representing the central concerns, questions, and discourses of the turns and twists that each chapter will provide. We then briefly introduce the chapters that follow and attempt to represent some of the remaining trajectory of this book.

Responsibility in leadership?

Whilst responsible leadership is termed a theory, we don't wish to present it as a body of thinking that has gained any real closure yet. Rather we view this as a perspective or lens that is very much work in progress, that enables another way in which to debate and examine leadership. Our perspective is to assume that responsibility is axiomatic to leadership. The emphasis then is on the nature and manifestation of such responsibility (or irresponsibility) within the practice of leading that requires attention. Attention in the sense of developing insight, understanding, explanation, and theorising in order to have impact on responsibility in leading. That is the broader objective of this volume.

Placing orientation on responsibility within leading rather than the development of the theory of responsible leadership is not to devalue the very helpful arguments and expositions of theories of 'responsible leadership' that will be explored by authors in this volume. This work provides many useful frames to examine the context, antecedents, processes, and outcomes of what enables/disables the manifestation of responsibility in the practice of leading. It offers up helpful guidance towards an appreciation of a variety of dimensions of responsibility in leadership. However, in itself it does not bring enough theoretical and empirical weight to the construct of responsibility, which like all constructs has a legacy of psychological, sociological, philosophical, historical, and literary thinking that can only enrich our understanding and practice of leadership. Hence we welcome an engagement with responsibility in its fullest form. To this end, we offer here ten propositions alongside ten questions that we see as shaping the development of responsible leadership at and beyond the present time.

First, is its attention and even commitment to social responsibility and the related field of CSR (Waldman & Balven, 2014).

What assumptions have driven the definition and meaning of responsibility in the social responsibility and CSR fields, and how do these confront, clash with, and extend responsibility in leadership?

Second, it seems willing to assume applicability to multiple levels of responsibility – the individual, the team, the department, the organisation, and broadly societal (Doh & Quigley, 2014; Voegtlin, Patzer, & Scherer, 2012).

Given that leadership tends to operate between levels, then what processes and practices are required to enact responsibility between people and groups with different power, position, and privilege? What paradoxes, insights, or mysteries arise when each of these levels becomes the focal point for responsible leadership?

Third, it seeks to go beyond a shareholder perspective to embrace a stakeholder perspective (Maak & Pless, 2006a; Waldman & Galvin, 2008).

Given the less direct and more networked relationship between stakeholders, then what kind of leadership engages and mobilises parties with very different interests, agendas, and institutional narratives? What assumptions, discourses, and histories shape the priorities given to competing stakeholders? Why, how, and where does responsible leadership challenge and unsettle these priorities?

Fourth, is its reliance on ethical assumptions to do no harm and do good (Ciulla, 2006; Stahl & Sully de Luque, 2014) connected with notions of duty – duty of care, duty of assistance, and duty of justice (Maak & Pless, 2009).

What kind of relationship exists between leadership, responsibility, and ethics? What kinds of questions, practices, and identities would help those in leadership hold the kind of conversations where competing ethical principles could be aired? What assumptions, discourses, and histories have driven the notions of duty and ethics within organisations and how do they shape what it means to lead responsibly?

Fifth, it tries to be sensitive to global intercultural sensitivity (Miska, Stahl, & Mendenhall, 2013), a global citizen orientation and a call to cosmopolitanism (Maak & Pless, 2009), as well as Turnbull, Case, Edwards, Schedlitzki, & Simpson's (2011) notion of 'worldly' leadership.

What tensions and paradoxes arise in a globalised world, and what does it mean to lead responsibly amid these? How is leadership challenged and stretched by responsible global citizenship, and what does it mean to lead in such a dispersed, diverse, and distributed context?

Sixth, it pursues an outcome orientation to responsibility that, for example, addresses Elkington's (1997) notion of the triple bottom line, but additional to the economic, societal, and ecological it encourages a humanitarian perspective (Maak & Pless 2009).

What tensions, conflicts, and paradoxes do corporates particularly encounter when they attempt to 'balance' financial, environmental, social, and humanitarian possibilities?

Seventh, it engages with processes of sense-making and sense-giving strongly linked with questions of purpose (Kempster, Jackson, & Conroy, 2011).

If responsibility emerges between people in interactions (as opposed to being intrinsic to someone a priori in any situation) then how do moments of giving and making sense co-create what it means to be responsible? What is the role of purpose in sustaining, driving, and connecting responsible leadership across time and boundaries?

Eighth, responsible leadership implies a shared orientation (Pearce, Wassenaar, & Manz, 2104); a collaborative and relational approach to leading that connects stakeholders together (Fairhurst & Connaughton, 2014; Maak & Pless, 2006b; Pless, Maak, & Waldman, 2012).

Why does responsible leadership imply a shared orientation? What are the limits and blindspots when approaching it with an individual orientation? What is opened up by bringing the collective into the picture of responsible leadership?

Ninth, and perhaps fundamentally, responsibility embraces notions of the use of resources: notably material, human, and financial (see, for example, Orlitzky, Schmidt, & Rynes, 2003; for a useful typology, see Voegtlin, 2015, pp. 14–15).

What types of spaces, artefacts, discourses, and technologies facilitate responsible leadership and how do they do so? What assumptions, discourses, and histories enable and constrain the use of resources, where do these need to be disrupted, and what might disruption look like?

Tenth, and finally, how responsibility is framed within short- or long-term perspectives; in a sense a focus on shareholder value has been historically short-term, while achieving stakeholder value is over the long-term (Waldman & Galvin, 2008).

How do collectives work between short-term or immediate responsibilities and long-term or more distant responsibilities? What tensions, conflicts, and processes mediate between these different levels of responsibilities?

For the purposes of this introduction, we have attempted to capture this extensive range of dimensions and questions into an image or metaphor; in part to help understanding, but also to illustrate the sheer scope of the nature of leadership responsibilities. While we do not want to package responsible leadership theory as a matter of chance, we do want to indicate the multiple ways that responsibility crosses and connects multiple levels of analysis. The convergence and integration of multiple stakeholders to examine, make decisions, and take action on challenges that systemically impact all is a vital process and one which advocates of responsible leadership suggest is an approach that has unique applicability (Waldman & Balven, 2014, p. 224). If responsible leadership theory is to redefine the kind of leadership required to sustain movement on challenges that belong to no-one, but impact many if not all of us, then it does need the capacity to track with multiple, concurrent, and mutually constructed responsibilities between individuals, groups, institutions, and networks and we hope this image conveys something of the multi-dimensional nature of this.

We seek to illustrate such systemic interaction linked to multiple levels of analysis in Figure 1.1 (which draws on a suggestion of Kempster & Watton, 2014; Voegtlin *et al.*'s levels of analysis, 2012, p. 5; and the kaleidoscope model of change from Balogun & Hope-Hailey, 2008).

Drawing on Balogon and Hope-Hailey's insightful use of the kaleidoscope metaphor (in the context of change management), Figure 1.1 seeks to represent a dynamic of issues configuring to generate distinctive and unique combinations for each institutional context. The outer ring represents levels of analysis while the inner ring represents the dimensions of responsibilities in leadership. Unique combinations come together each time the wheel is spun and a card selected. Now imagine that the kaleidoscope is not working properly and each

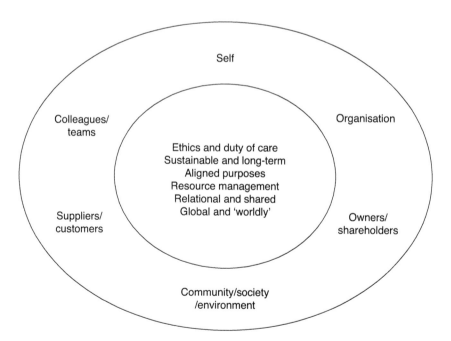

Figure 1.1 Responsibilities of leadership – a systemic perspective.

turn does shift the dimensions but not seamlessly, so that gaps and unconfigured areas are present in the midst of each configuration. To us the questions underneath each of the dimensions points to places that the kaleidoscope cannot yet assemble. Our incomplete kaleidoscope points to a body of work that is partial, ill-formed, and very much emergent in terms of understanding. In many ways we suggest it is a beginning that points to depth and complexity but not yet with enough of the pieces to create full configurations – far from a complete theory.

The image, in a novel way, speaks to Voegtlin's (2015) notion of developing a responsibility orientation. So, taking our lead from Balogun and Hope-Hailey, we suggest that approaches to researching and developing responsibility in leadership would anticipate complexity through situational variety and a focus on critical reflection that seeks to develop responsible judgement to leadership decisions and action. In this way we anticipate that theory development that generates normative ideal models of the responsible leader will at best provide useful if limited stimulus to the practising 'leader'; but at worst an idealised myth akin to becoming the 'romance' of responsible leadership. The assumption through this volume is more associated with seeing the critically rich complexity of context and contingency of outcomes.

For us then, the tension between individual and collective understandings of leadership are most salient here. Recent research and subsequent commentaries on leadership give voice to an orientation away from essentialist qualities of an individual, and toward relational, contextual, and processual perspectives of leadership. Brigid Carroll's work (Carroll, Levy, & Richmond, 2008) on leadership-as-practice most helpfully gives structure to this situated orientation of leadership. From a leadership-as-practice ontology, the focus is meaning and activity informed through participative engagement between individuals. It allows additional dimensions of materiality and history to inform meaning and action (Chia & McKay, 2007). We also are drawn to Drath and colleagues' (Drath, McCauley, Palus, Van Velsor, O'Connor, & McGuire, 2008) notion of leadership as an outcome. They speak of direction, alignment, and commitment as generating leadership from a range of activities. This may be the prominent person in the accepted role as 'leader'; but also may be the relational outcome of collective, shared, and distributed activity. It may also be in part the consequence of activity shaped by materiality and discourse. In addition Parry and Hansen have offered up a convincing and highly plausible case for leadership as a narrative 'where people follow the story as much as they follow the storyteller' (2007, p. 281). Taken together, notions of leadership as process and leadership as outcomes should greatly extend the scope of responsibility for purpose and activity beyond the few. Arguably a relational, situated perspective of engaging and working with stakeholders on aligned purposes of shared value (Porter & Kramer, 2006) will become increasingly the norm (Maak & Pless 2006a), particularly with respect to addressing the grand challenges (Malgrande, 2015) that face us – societal, ecological, and humanitarian. That is the real invitation to responsible leadership theory from both the questions and the incomplete kaleidoscope image.

To look beyond the individual as leader and extend exploration of how to develop responsibility as a relational phenomenon appears most central if leadership is to make its most necessary mark on addressing such grand challenges. Such expression begins to lean towards the romanticism that is in part the energy behind this volume, why the authors have come together. Yet the authors are also mindful of the realism that impacts on the respective aspect they will speak about – more on this very shortly. You will note the desire to break away from leader-centric notions of leadership in many of the chapters in this book, but at the same time a difficulty in doing so. Our overall sense is that the two frames of romanticism and realism go some way to shed light on this dilemma and to these we will now turn.

Romanticism

Romanticism probably is most identified with a movement that became prominent from the late eighteenth century, when it was a reaction against the enlightenment and associated notions of objectivity, control, restraint, logic, and rational behaviour. It gave emphasis to emotion, inspiration, subjectivity, imagination, and beauty. Romanticism seemed to hold much in store in understanding the past and the important link to nature. Friedrich Schlegel appears to be the first to have used the term 'romantic', describing literature depicting emotional matter in an imaginative form (Stone, 2005). Others prominent to the romantic movement were Shelley, Keats, Coleridge, and Wordsworth. Our actual usage of the construct comes from the recent *Developing Leadership Capacity Conference* held at Lancaster Leadership Centre (July 2014) which drew heavily on the work of Simon Bainbridge. He acted as co-host, providing a thread through the conference helping to frame the conference theme 'the new romantics of responsible leadership'. Many colleagues will be aware that it was the discussions and insights at this conference that became the inspiration for this book.

So in this spirit we authors have sought to draw on a central tenet of romanticism, that of the free and imaginative expression of the feelings of the artist. To this end authors were encouraged to draw on Wordsworth's view that writing should begin as 'the spontaneous overflow of powerful feelings [that] the poet can then mould into art'. Such liberation is seen to enable 'a new and restless spirit, seeking violently to burst through old and cramping forms, [...] for perpetual movement and change, an effort to return to the forgotten sources of life'. By a 'return to forgotten sources of life' (Berlin, 1965, p. 92) this is towards a closer connection to humanity and a closer ecological connection to nature and the environment. Yet we also recognise here a caution against a nostalgia for aspects of society that are quite unwarranted to the current prescient circumstances.

Following further conversation with Simon Bainbridge, we understand that the essence of romanticism is as a utopian movement imagining a better world and seeking to build a better world. Nancy Adler's recent work on leading beautifully (2011) echoes romanticism; although she does not overtly position her thesis as drawing from this. Citing the poet Donogue she brings an evocative attention to the need for beauty to be reclaimed: 'Our trust in the future has lost its innocence [...] it is because we have so disastrously neglected the *Beautiful* that we now find ourselves in such a terrible crisis' (2011, p. 208, emphasis added). Innocence and beauty are central romantic tenets. Romanticism sought to resist the rationalising objectivity and productivity of the enlightenment project. Adler's argument seeks to give voice to beauty alongside objectivity, with passion and emotion alongside reason. She evocatively critiques notions of 'progress' by discussing ugliness and beauty. Romanticism's quest was (and perhaps still is) to give attention to the industrial ugliness of mankind over nature and seek to reassert nature over mankind. Goldsmith spoke of the ugliness of industrialisation at the cost of the lost beauty of the romantic idyll of rural life:

> Sweet smiling village, loveliest of the lawn,
> Thy sports are fled, and all thy charms withdrawn;
> Amidst thy bowers the tyrant's hand is seen,
> And Desolation saddens all thy green...
> Around the world each needful product flies
> For all the luxuries the world supplies
> While thus the land adored for pleasure all
> In barren splendour feebly waits the fall.
>   (Extract from Oliver Goldsmith's 'The Deserted
>   Village', 1770)

In a way, Goldsmith described the prescient future of nature dominated by humanity, where we have lost something beautiful through our connection with nature. Many romanticist painters depicted this loss through contrasting nature with industrialisation. Our interpretation of Adler is that she is encouraging an awakening of excitement and emotion through rediscovering beauty in the acts and deeds of our endeavours. Her keynote presentations (Academy of Management, 2015; International Leadership Association, 2013) are rooted in pictures of nature and through the joy of music generating imagination of possibilities: a thoroughly romantic project. What is being argued for is that the arrogance of the enlightenment project and its offspring, modernity, be moderated by romanticism. Bainbridge suggests that this was in the mind of Wordsworth, that romanticism is not unfettered though as, even erratically, romanticism sought to unite itself with realism – Wordsworth argues in 'The Prelude' it is...

> Not in Utopia – subterraneous fields, Or some secreted island, heaven know where –
> But in the very world which is the world
> Of all of us, the place in which, in the end,
> We find our happiness, or not at all.
>   (X, 723–727, quoted in Bainbridge, 2007)

Wordsworth's phrase 'the very world which is the world/Of all of us' connects to notions of realism. He is arguing that ultimately it is in this world of realism that we will find 'our happiness, or not at all'. It is a mistake then to read romanticism as an alternative to realism: romanticism is better understood as complementing and supplementing realism. What use after all is pragmatism without possibility, logic without emotion, rationality without imagination? As we argue here and throughout the volume this real world needs the injection of imagination if we are to find movement, novelty, and aspiration in challenges that defy existing knowledge and expertise.

So the romanticism of hope and imagination needs to be grounded in the realism of context. It is here in the 'very world [...] of all of us' that we need to introduce the balance of realism to the arguments and crafting of chapters.

Realism

The primary interest of realism is in the actual or real or situated understanding of facts. It is important, however, that realism is not seen as prosaic and dull. Realism should mean confronting reality or engaging with how things really are as opposed to how one might like or imagine them to be. In such a sense, then, realism is courageous and bold, given one of the most challenging things we surely do is learn to strip away rose tinted spectacles, our own prejudices and pretence, and take a good long look at ourselves, others, and our context. Those who call themselves realists – artists or otherwise – take their inspiration and direction from what is present in life and not idealised or abstracted. Realism can have a grittiness, power, and honesty that can help us face up to what we most might want to evade about ourselves, our thinking, and our action or inaction. In such a vein, we would consider realist writers such as Charles Dickens, George Eliot, and Mark Twain who turned attention to what we could call ordinary characters deeply embedded in social relationships and structures in their accomplishment of everyday life. At its best realism has a political and social character to it where difficult realities – poverty, injustice, corruption – are seen as deserving of attention as anything else. We argue that rather than being drawn to 'just imagine' (the romanticist request of us), those in leadership need to be grounded to using their senses, being fully in the present and not flinching at inconvenient or messy 'truths'. There are few absolutes in realism so truth is a continuum and the accent is on seeking to accurately reflect a reality that will be uncertain and emergent.

Our stance then is that responsible leadership involves a reawakening to the realities of a world that demands we claim our leadership starting point from how it is experienced by the myriad of those involved. Realism focuses on context and social relations – a sense of the 'here and now'. In contrast to romanticism and its focus on the rural idol, realism focuses on urbanisation – reflecting the reality of its time. In Steve Kempster's work with Ken Parry (Kempster & Parry, 2011) the argument of a critical realist orientation to leadership research was offered that outlines the case of seeking to explain the realism of the local here and now. Drawing on Bhaskar (1978) the gritty reality is seen as composed of events, empirical experience, concepts, and language – transitive aspects of reality – and these transitive elements interact with under-lying structures – intransitive aspects of reality. As we seek to make sense and reveal the reality of our experiences and on-going practices in and of the world, these have an on-going correspondence with knowledge, meaning, and truth. We draw here on Andrew Sayer's powerful treatise on realism and social science (1992, 2000). He explicates an argument for practical adequacy of truth claims as opposed to a correspondence reduction of truth:

> truth might better be understood as 'practical adequacy', that is in terms of the extent to which it generates expectations about the world and about results of our actions which are realized. Practically adequate different parts of our knowledge will vary according to where, [when,] and to what they are applied.
>
> (Sayer, 2000, p. 43)

Set within this notion of realism our practical endeavours, relationships, assumptions, and meanings are shaped by embedded structures. Yet structures also become transitive through sufficient passage of time (Archer, 1995). So rather than truth claims being proven/not proven, truth (as a transitive form of reality) should be seen as a continuum (Dean, Joseph, Roberts, & Wight, 2006, p. 53). For example, 'certain', 'obvious', 'evident', 'beyond reasonable doubt', 'probable' on the one hand; through 'probably false', 'clear to disbe-lieve', 'reasonable to disbelieve', 'evidently false', 'obviously false', and 'cer-tainly false'. So a realist perspective seeks to offer up accounts that have verisimilitude, providing a window to the real; yet accepts that such accounts are only a kind of truth. Reality is too complex to capture – hence a contin-uum of truth claims. So what does this all mean to the discussion on respons-ible leadership: realism and romanticism?

The romantic perspective offers up imagination of what might be. It gives a lead to energy, passion, and excitement to possibilities of desirable futures. Attention to the aesthetic beauty of what we are seeking to create gives impetus to enhancing practices for collective effect. A rebalancing for nature in harmony with humankind. Romanticism gives emphasis to the heroic individual to make change occur – both a strength and a weakness: a strength in terms of energy and commitment to change the status quo, and a weakness with the limitations of the heroic leader model.

This individual orientation is different from the realist perspective which places emphasis on social relations. It emphasises an examination of why things are as they are; seeking attention to the detail of understanding situated events, relationships, motives, and power. The emphasis is on providing a glimpse of truth accounts which are assumed to be fallible as a result of reality emergence. Realism assumes deep complexity to reality. Its strength is the attention to contextual detail, description, and contingent explanation of how reality occurs. Its weaknesses are a tendency towards determinism – a sense of lacking the visionary and emotive energy and excitement of romanticism. Realism accepts limits on imagination and the possible. The gritty and often grim ordinariness of reality makes it less appealing than the romantic trope of the hero's journey and the quest to find again the loss of connection to a utopian ideal. To enable a movement toward responsible leadership is not simply a claim for imagination of possibilities or more emotional and exciting visions. Rather it is finding an intersection between an engagement with everyday experiences and expectations, and the potentiality of very different norms, practices, and expectations with the potential to transform relationships, structures, and practices.

Statement of aims and structure of the book

The aim of this book is to bring together a selection of high quality papers in a volume which helps readers navigate their understanding of responsible leadership using both realist and romantic points of reference. That is, the *romanticism* for change in practices of leadership that may address societal, ecological, and humanitarian challenges through everyday organisational activity set alongside the *realism* of such contexts and antecedent influences that may contemporaneously limit scope for action. Our intentions were deliberately expansive and we invited colleagues to explore themes of responsibility from a very broad canvas. We desired that authors would be driven by their own engagement with gritty current realities and idealistic future passions to craft and present scholarly arguments. After all, Coleridge spoke of the artist/thinker not being constrained by artificial rules that might limit imagination and limit the 'romantic originality'. Hence we have sought to give authors their voice and you will find a wide range of theoretical, empirical, critical, confirmatory, pedagogical, and action orientated voices in this volume. While we have invited Eric Guthey to give concluding voice, all chapters provide arguments that seek to provoke and move on the debate around leadership and responsibility. The chapters have been grouped into three thematic parts, as detailed below.

Part I Interrogating, critiquing, and strengthening responsible leadership theory

Chapter 2 Mapping the terrain of responsible leadership: something old, something new, something borrowed, something green

Following on from the broad canvas outlined in Chapter 1, in Chapter 2 Marian Iszatt-White makes that case that much has been written in recent years concerning the need for responsible leadership to move us 'from value to values, from shareholders to stakeholders, and from balance sheets to balanced development' (Kofi Annan, 14 October, 2002). Attempts have also been made to arrive at a consensus definition of the construct and to compare this emergent understanding of the characteristics of responsible leadership with related extant leadership theories. This is clearly a work in progress with much still to be done. In this chapter the author aims to contribute to this work of 'bricolage' by further developing the mapping process (and critiquing what has gone before) and by weaving in some thoughts in relation to the micro-level behaviours required of anybody (individual or organisation) who wishes to appear credible in proclaiming the wider 'responsible' agenda. The suggestion here is that, actually, we do need to 'sweat the small stuff' as well as striving for the big stuff!

Chapter 3 From responsibility to responsibilities: towards a theory of co-responsible leadership

Brigid Carroll explores more deeply the nature of responsibility as a phenomenon in Chapter 3. She outlines an argument for redefining responsibility: from individual attribute to collective capacity. Whilst leadership theory, practice, and development has, and is, making a slow but steady shift from an individual to a collective construct, understandings of responsibility in the leadership terrain have barely moved. This chapter critically examines notions of collective responsibility (Jonas, 1984) and co-responsibility (Apel, 1993) and asks whether either can provide a sufficient redefinition of responsibility that would facilitate collective and participatory forms of leadership. Of particular interest is how to redefine the discursive, identity, social, and political dimensions of responsibility substantively in order to achieve more relational and distributed leadership dynamics.

Part II Connecting responsible leadership theory to practice

Chapter 4 This green pastoral landscape: values, responsible leadership, and the romantic imagination

Sarah Lee and Malcolm Higgs raise three key questions for responsible leadership and practice, which emerge from an examination of the personal values concept and its application to organisational settings. By exploring the theoretical foundations of values research, they make links between personal values theory and the practice of leadership in organisations that espouse a strong, values-based culture. The chapter suggests practical ways to approach the issues raised while adding to contemporary debates on responsible leadership and to the agenda for future research.

Chapter 5 Leadership responsibility and calling: the role of calling in a woman's choice to lead

Recent research has continued to find that low numbers of women are found in top leadership positions in nearly all industries and countries. Although progress has been made, there remain many barriers that arise from within the complex team and organisational environments (external) and also within women themselves (internal). In this chapter, Susan Madsen contends that in finding ways to better prepare women for leadership, one of the most important and foundational areas of emerging research focuses on understanding women's aspirations and motivations to lead. In most cases, these aspirations and motivations appear to be significantly different for women than for men, with initial studies finding that a powerful motivator for many women who have stepped forward to lead is a sense of 'calling'. After becoming aware of their own giftedness and then understanding this call to lead, it appears that, among other things, their self-efficacy and ability to become more resilient seem to increase. These are, the author suggests, key characteristics needed for women to step forward to take on positional leadership roles. In this chapter, she shares research, cases, and personal experiences, and passions to help explore this multifaceted phenomenon and its applications to the leadership research, theory, and practice.

Chapter 6 Responsible leadership: a radical view

If Steve Jobs was the business icon of the late twentieth century, Unilever's current CEO, Paul Polman, could be viewed as today's equivalent. This quintessentially responsible leader is Vice-Chairman of the World Business Council for Sustainable Development and serves on the Board of the UN Global Compact. Polman's powerful position at the apex of a transnational corporation with a unique culture and heritage raises an important question as to whether we can all be responsible leaders whatever our organisations, contexts, and roles within the system. In this chapter, Karen Blakeley challenges particularly corporates and multinationals – and those leading in them – to claim their own complicity and power in the most significant challenges of our time. She argues that such issues require new partnerships and alliances of those who are powerful and marginalised to engage increasingly more diverse networks of stakeholders with the true complexities of such issues. She sees a real difference between radical responsible leadership theories pursuing systems-wide progress and transformational leadership approaches orientated at offering too quick but simplistic answers. This chapter avoids falling into the latter category of offering simple answers but instead calls for leadership partnerships that transcend sectors and institutions to set ethical agendas, humanistic values, democratic structures, moral character, and the fundamental transformation of systems.

Part III Developing responsible leadership

Chapter 7 Responsible leadership, trust, and the role of Human Resource Management

In this chapter Stefanie Gustafsson and Veronica Hope Hailey examine how Human Resources (HR) processes and practices may enable the development of trustworthy leadership. While studies to date have made important contributions to our understanding of trust, leadership, and Human Resource Management (HRM), none thus far has empirically investigated how organisations may either explicitly or implicitly develop trustworthy leadership through HR practices and processes. This gap is filled by the authors' own research, presented here and showing how through various HR practices and processes organisations may select, develop, and assess trustworthiness in their leaders, either explicitly or implicitly. Their findings suggest that organisations more readily make use of practices that build the ability and predictability of their leaders using well-established performance metrics, rather than practices which develop integrity and benevolence, which are seen to be more challenging because dependent on personal judgements resulting from social interactions. Instead, these were more implicitly and informally developed and often seemed to require a sense of courage in order to be explicitly addressed.

Chapter 8 Promoting responsibility, purpose, and romanticism in business schools

This chapter seeks to differentiate leadership responsibility from leadership accountability. In this chapter leadership is seen as *responsible* for generating shared sense-making whilst *accountable* for organisational outcomes. Ken Parry and Brad Jackson argue that business schools have largely focused on developing accountability for outcomes at the detriment of developing the capacity of leadership to build trust, create dialogue, and pursue ethical and sustainable solutions. This inability of business schools to develop a more nuanced interdependence between responsibility and accountability is a significant contributor to the loss of ethical and moral leadership with which the contemporary business environment can be charged. They propose that, beyond calls for new business school curricula, a new business discourse is required which develops the capacity of future business leaders to be reflective, interdisciplinary, creative, and connected to broader philosophical and cultural understandings than they currently are.

Chapter 9 Developing responsible leadership through discourse ethics

The use of case studies in the teaching of business ethics has been seen as a process to stimulate discourse ethics. However, many case studies ask students to consider abstract and sometimes hypothetical situations and, whilst these can have pedagogical value in catalysing such discourse, they have limited resonance with the milieu of everyday managerial context – they lack the necessary nuance of lived experience which is provided by live cases. In this chapter, Steve Kempster, Sarah Gregory, and Emma Watton explore how live cases can be created within management education through the use of the critical incident technique. Specifically, the chapter explores the notion of linking leadership learning lived experience (Kempster, 2006, 2009), ethical dilemmas from such lived experience using the critical incident technique in the classroom, with the primary goals of stimulating discourse ethics and interrelated management learning. In so doing, the authors seek to elaborate the theoretical argument of why such an approach of live cases in the classroom may gain greater traction than abstract cases.

Chapter 10 Developing 'next generation' globally responsible leadership: Generation Y perspectives on global responsibility, leadership, and integrity

In 2011 Daimler's Corporate Academy invited 125 next-generation leaders from across the globe to contribute essays on the theme of 'What does globally responsible leadership and integrity mean to you?'. In 2012–13, the University of Gloucestershire incorporated a final-year undergraduate module on 'Global Responsible Leadership' in which students were asked to write a similar essay; the top 22 essays were selected for analysis. In this chapter, Sharon Turnbull and Sue Williams focus on the crucial role of developing Generation Y leaders in building a responsible global society for the future, recognising that without a significant shift in business school curricula, as well as leadership development agendas, it will not be possible to break with the individualistic short-term behaviours of today's organisations and businesses. The chapter examines the discourses of globally responsible leadership embedded in the essays, and asks what underlying meaning and assumptions about the economic and social world, the planet, and the nature of responsibility and integrity are found within these discourses and how these agendas can be further developed.

Chapter 11 Romanticism, antimodernism, and a pluralistic perspective on responsible leadership

In the concluding chapter, a recognised commentator in the field of responsible leadership, Eric Guthey, brings together the chapters in a new twist on the realism/romanticism theme. Through a compelling historical lens and approach, he tosses antimodernism into the mix as a type of romanticism particularly attuned to the leadership mandate. His concern in this last chapter is, fittingly, the capacity of responsible leadership theory to be genuinely transformative and a real force for mobilising change. He argues that if responsible leadership theory relies too much on conventional and particularly individualistic notions of leadership then it will risk unwittingly reinforcing the status quo more than it would like. He concludes by calling for a fundamental reconceptualisation of leadership as a social, collective, and interactive activity that functions more as a social movement than a personal challenge or quest.

References

Adler, N. (2011). Leading beautifully: The creative economy and beyond. *Journal of Management Inquiry, 20*(3), 208–221.

Annan, Kofi, (2002). Speech mat at the MIT Sloan School of Management, Cambridge, Massachusetts on 14 October 2002. As cited in Global Responsible Leadership Initiative [no specific author stated – report said to be the 'shared thoughts and beliefs of all founding members of the GRLI'] (2005) Globally Responsible Leadership: A call for engagement. EFMD.

Apel, K.-O. (1993). How to ground a universalistic ethics of co-responsibility for the effects of collective actions and activities? *Philosophica, 52,* 9–29.

Archer, M. (1995). *Realist social theory: The morphogenetic approach.* Cambridge: Cambridge University Press.

Bainbridge, S. (2007). Wordsworth and Coleridge: Theological ways of reading literature. In A. Haas, D. Jasper, & E. Jay (Eds.) *Oxford handbook of literature and theology.* Oxford: Oxford University Press.

Balogun, J., & Hope-Hailey, V. (2008). *Exploring strategic change* (3rd edn). Harlow: Pearson Education.

Berlin, I. (1965). The AW Mellon Lectures in the Fine Arts, Washington. In H. Hardy (Ed.) *The Roots of Romanticism* (2013, second edition). Princeton, NJ: Princeton University Press.

Bhaskar, R. (1978). *A realist theory of science.* New York: Harvester Press.

Carroll, B., Levy, L., & Richmond, D. (2008). Leadership as practice: Challenging the competency paradigm. *Leadership, 4*(4), 363–379.

Chia, R., & MacKay, B. (2007). Post-processual challenges for the emerging S-as-P perspective: Discovering strategy in the logic of practice. *Human Relations, 60*(1), 217–242.

Ciulla, J. (2006). Ethics: The heart of leadership. In T. Maak & N. M. Pless (Eds.), *Responsible leadership.* London: Routledge.

de Jongh, D. (2005). *Globally responsible leadership: A call for engagement.* Brussels: European Foundation for Management Development.

Dean, K., Joseph, J., Roberts, J. M., & Wight, C. (2006). *Realism, philosophy and social science.* London: Palgrave Macmillan.

Doh, J., & Quigley, N. R. (2014). Responsible leadership and stakeholder management: Influence pathways and organizational outcomes. *Academy of Management Perspectives, 28*(3), 255–274.

Drath, W. H., McCauley, C. D., Palus, C. J., Van Velsor, E., O'Connor, P. M. G., & McGuire, J. B. (2008). Direction, alignment, commitment: Toward a more integrative ontology of leadership. *The Leadership Quarterly, 19*(6), 635–653. doi:10.1016/j.leaqua.2008.09.003.

Elkington, J. (1997). *Cannibals with forks: The triple bottom line of 21st century business.* Oxford: Capstone.

Fairhurst, G. T., & Connaughton, S. L. (2014). Leadership: A communicative perspective. *Leadership, 10*(1), 7–35.

Goldsmith, O. (1770). *The deserted village.* London: W. Griffin.

Jonas, H. (1984). *The imperative of responsibility: In search of an ethics for the technological age.* Chicago: University of Chicago Press.

Kempster, S. (2006). Leadership learning through lived experience: A process of apprenticeship? *Journal of Management & Organization, 12*(1), 4–22.

Kempster, S. (2009). *How managers have learnt to lead: Exploring the development of leadership practice.* Basingstoke: Palgrave Macmillan.

Kempster, S., & Parry, K. W. (2011). Grounded theory and leadership research: A critical realist perspective. *The Leadership Quarterly, 22*(1), 106–120.

Kempster, S., & Watton, E. (2014). Experiential development of sustainable and responsible leadership practices. *16th Annual International Leadership Association Global Conference,* San Diego.

Kempster, S., Jackson, B., & Conroy, M. (2011). Leadership as purpose: Exploring the role of purpose in leadership practice. *Leadership, 7*(3), 317–334.

Lutz, A. (1998). The politics of reception: The case of Goldsmith's 'The deserted village'. *Studies in Philosophy, 95*(2), 174–196.

Maak, T. (2007). Responsible leadership, stakeholder engagement, and the emergence of social capital. *Journal of Business Ethics, 74*(4), 329–343.

Maak, T., & Pless, N. M. (2006a). *Responsible leadership.* London: Routledge.

Maak, T., & Pless, N. M. (2006b). Responsible leadership in a stakeholder society: A relational perspective. *Journal of Business Ethics, 66*(1), 99–115.

Maak, T., & Pless, N. M. (2009). Business leaders as citizens of the world: Advancing humanism on a global scale. *Journal of Business Ethics, 88*(3), 537–550.

Malgrande, M. (2015). Grand challenges: Implications for management and organizations. *Academy of Management Journal,* Call for papers, 15 May–15 July, 2015.

Meindl, J. R. (1995). The romance of leadership as a follower centric theory: A social constructionist approach. *The Leadership Quarterly, 6*(3), 329–341.

Miska, C., Stahl, G. K., & Mendenhall, M. E. (2013). Intercultural competences as antecedents of responsible global leadership. *European Journal of International Management, 7*(5), 550–569.

Orlitzky, M., Schmidt, F. L., & Rynes, S. (2003). Corporate social and financial performance: A meta-analysis. *Organization Studies, 24*(3), 403–411.

Parry, K. W., & Hansen, H. (2007). The organizational story as leadership. *The Leadership Quarterly, 3*(3), 301–324.

Pearce, C. L., Wassenaar, C. L., & Manz, C. C. (2014). Is shared leadership the key to responsible leadership? *Academy of Management Perspectives, 28*(3), 275–288.

Pless, N. M., Maak, T., & Waldman, D. A. (2012). Different approaches toward doing the right thing: Mapping the responsibility orientations of leaders. *Academy of Management Perspectives,* November, 51–65.

Porter, M. E., & Kramer, M. R. (2006). Strategy and society: The link between competitive advantage and corporate social responsibility. *Harvard Business Review, 84*(12), 78–92.

Rawls, J. (1999). *The law of peoples.* Cambridge, MA: Harvard University Press.

Sayer, A. (1992). *Method in social science: A realist approach.* London: Routledge.

Sayer, A. (2000). *Realism and social science.* London: Sage.

Stahl, G. K., & Sully de Luque, M. (2014). Antecedents of responsible leader behavior: A research synthesis, conceptual framework, and agenda for future research. *Academy of Management Perspectives, 28*(3), 235–254.

Stone, A. (2005). Friedrich Schlegel, romanticism, and the re-enchantment of nature. *Inquiry: An Interdisciplinary Journal of Philosophy, 48*(1), 3–25.

Turnbull, S., Case, P., Edwards, G., Schedlitzki, D., & Simpson, P. (Eds.). (2011). *Worldly leadership: Alternative wisdoms for a complex world.* London: Palgrave Macmillan.

Voegtlin, C. (2015). What does it mean to be responsible? Addressing the missing responsibility dimension in ethical leadership. *Leadership* (online first, doi:10: 1177/1742715015578936).

Voegtlin, C., Patzer, M., & Scherer, A. G. (2012). Responsible leadership in global business: A new approach to leadership and its multi-level outcomes. *Journal of Business Ethics, 105*(1), 1–16.

Waldman, D. A., & Balven, R. M. (2014). Responsible leadership: Theoretical issues and research directions. *Academy of Management Perspectives, 28*(3), 224–234.

Waldman, D. A., & Galvin, B. M. (2008). Alternative perspectives of responsible leadership. *Organizational Dynamics, 37*(4), 327–341.

Part I

Interrogating, critiquing, and strengthening responsible leadership theory

.

2 Mapping the terrain of responsible leadership

Something old, something new, something borrowed, something green

Marian Iszatt-White

Introduction

> I don't believe there is any choice about this. Either we see business as a restorative undertaking, or we, business people, will march the entire race to the undertaker. Business is the only mechanism on the planet today powerful enough to produce the changes necessary to reverse global environmental and social degradation.
>
> (Hawken, 1992, pp. 94–95)

Much has been written in recent years concerning the need for responsible leadership to move us 'from value to values, from shareholders to stake-holders, and from balance sheets to balanced development' (Kofi Annan, 14 October 2002). Attempts have also been made to arrive at a consensus definition of the construct and to compare this emergent understanding of the characteristics of responsible leadership with related extant leadership theories. This is clearly a work in progress with much still to be done. It is the aim of this chapter to contribute to this work of 'bricolage' by further developing the mapping process (and critiquing what has gone before) and by weaving in some thoughts in relation to the micro-level behaviours required of anybody (individual or organisation) who wishes to appear credible in proclaiming the wider 'responsible' agenda. My suggestion here is that, actually, we do need to 'sweat the small stuff' as well as striving for the big stuff! Both my opening quotation and this somewhat mundane plea locate me firmly at the 'realism' end of the romanticism-realism spectrum which this volume seeks to explore. Whilst it is clearly important to be inspired by great ideas – and in the present context, Romanticism's orientation towards beauty and nature seem particularly fitting – it is equally important to focus on the practicalities that turn such dreams into a reality and to be pragmatic about the limitations of human heroism (especially when it comes to being asked to abandon some of our deeply entrenched materialistic comforts in favour of a more sustainable lifestyle or to abide by the requirements of best-practice human rights when these have material costs). Being a realist does not make me without hope, however, but does lead me to focus on 'bottom up' responsibility rather than 'top down' – to recognise that it needs each of us to contribute our individual 'drops' if collectively we are to constitute an 'ocean'. In pursuing this theme, I have structured my musings by drawing on a traditional rhyme more usually associated with what a bride should wear at her wedding to ensure good luck and to ward off the 'evil eye'. Whilst not entirely 'fit for purpose', and hence requiring a little licence and adaptation on my part, the four 'somethings' I touch upon are intended to offer some 'handrails' (my thanks to Brigid Carroll for this delightfully apt phrase) to guide the reader through my reasoning and to give focus to the elements of bricolage I am seeking to bring together.

This sense of focus is, I think, important. Whilst bricolage assembles disparate things into the same space without any attempt to provide an organising framework – and there are certainly elements of this in the make-up of this chapter – I would hope that the end result here is clear in its message about the need for individual action at the micro level, and the need for ongoing work from a number of different perspectives if the whole is to add up to more than the sum of the parts. Hopefully the 'somethings' framework also reflects the processes going on within this work of bricolage. For researchers it is about working bits of old, new, borrowed, and 'green' theories together in order to stretch and pull responsible leadership theory into new corners and edges of our thinking. As practitioners it may be about honouring the existing policy initiatives at the same time as pushing for further change – and turning bottom-up thinking into action by getting actively involved in change at the level of career and identity. For academics and practitioners alike it is about seeing responsible leadership as starting with us.

'Something old'

For the bride on her wedding day, wearing 'something old' was traditionally seen as an antidote to covetousness – wearing something old counterbalances the other finery in which the bride is decked out – and hence aligns with one of the ten commandments of Christian religion. For the responsibility agenda, we might perhaps see this in the light of recycling and the avoidance of needless consumerism. In the structuring of this chapter, the 'something old' refers to existing theory in relation to responsible leadership – the acknowledged core of theories seeking to define the construct and delineate the domain. Whilst the notion of responsible leadership is still relatively young in itself, Nicola Pless and Thomas Maak (e.g. 2011) stand as the elders of this genre of writing and thought, and it is their definition which serves as the root construct for much of what has followed, as it does for what follows in this chapter. Thus referring to their work as 'something old' is a somewhat tenuous use of the word 'old', but hopefully allowable in the spirit of reworking a familiar framework as the basis for building on what has gone before.

Central to our understanding of the responsible leadership construct, then, are definitions such as that it is:

> a values-based and thoroughly ethical principles-driven relationship between leaders and stakeholders who are connected through a shared sense of meaning and purpose through which they raise one another to higher levels of motivation and commitment for achieving sustainable values creation and social change.
>
> (Pless, 2007, p. 438)

Enactment of responsible leadership is said to require a change in mindset by the leader, in order to incorporate a much broader view of the stakeholders to whom they are answerable and the 'others' with whom the responsible leader should be concerned (Pless & Maak, 2011). In positioning it against the existing leadership literature, responsible leadership is portrayed as a paragon of all the best of transformational (Avolio, Waldman, & Yammarino, 1991), authentic (Avolio & Gardner, 2005), servant (Greenleaf, 2002; Russell & Stone, 2002), ethical (Brown & Treviño, 2006; Ciulla, 2004), and charismatic (Conger & Kanungo, 1987) leadership but better specified and aimed at a wider range of stakeholders. This seems at once unrealistic and something of a disservice to past attempts to define and enact leadership. Waldman (2011), in suggesting some caveats with which researchers should be concerned as they proceed to develop the construct, also seeks to position responsible leadership within the greater body of leadership theory and research, at once seeing it as a 'unique and beneficial construct' (Waldman, 2011, p. 80) and comparing it (somewhat inconclusively) with ethical leadership (Brown & Treviño, 2006). Elsewhere in the literature, attempts have been made to map responsible leadership against the '4Is' model of transformational leadership and to demonstrate the link between leader stakeholder values and transformational leadership and leader economic values and transactional leadership (Groves & LaRocca, 2011). The mapping here seems somewhat tenuous, and the broader premise seems to ignore the later additive 'full range leadership' model (Avolio, 2011) within which both transformational and transactional leadership are now understood. Since the outcomes tested here are also internal to the organisation (follower corporate social responsibility (CSR) beliefs and follower organisational citizenship behaviours) the conclusions are at best flawed. It does nonetheless represent an important attempt to operationalise an otherwise largely philosophical construct.

'Something new'

In relation to our traditional bridal rhyme, it is hard to find any reference to the purpose of wearing 'something new', although perhaps the desire to wear a new frock on a day of celebration is too deeply ingrained in at least 50 per cent of the population to need further explanation or justification! In the context of responsible leadership and for the purposes of the current chapter, I am using this element to refer to more recent interpretations or theoretical contributions that seek to build on the original core in order to develop a more nuanced exposition of what it means to be a responsible leader. In seeking to move the study of responsible leadership forward from its original specification, authors have attempted to enrich the construct by adding new dimensions or nuances. For example, the idea of replacing the 'essentialist self' with the 'poetic self' (Freeman & Auster, 2011) as a project for seeking to live authentically is suggested to be an important component of responsible leadership. Whilst this proposal is interesting, it draws attention to what Hartman (1988) refers to as the 'problem of authenticity', namely that we can get caught between not knowing our values and not knowing whether our values are realisable through action. Freeman and Auster (2011) suggest our values rest on our ability to choose and that it is through the conscious reali- sation of our choices in a particular project that the real meaning of authen- ticity lies. In this context, values are seen as inherently relational, with the 'poetic self' existing at the intersection of our values, our past, our set of con- nections to others, and our aspirations. Whilst this extension of the construct offers an interesting parallel to ideas of authentic leadership, it appears to con- flate ethics with authenticity and to ignore both socially constructed and attri- butional approaches. In another attempt to move the construct forward, Cameron (2011) offered a fourth definition (where definitions one and two are recognisable as based on economic accountability and definition three is the now widely accepted stakeholder theory approach) in terms of the ability/ inclination to act appropriately or virtuously. In this context, virtuousness is contrasted with ethics in that it is said to be more unchanging and hence to offer the only 'fixed point' in leader decision-making. Here again, the premise appears problematic whilst the attempt to make responsible leader- ship more operationalisable is to be applauded.

In addition to defining more closely what we mean by 'responsible', there may also be the need for a paradigm shift in our conceptualisation of leader- ship (du Toit & Woermann, 2012) and a requirement for leaders to re- inscribe their understanding of themselves in this role. Du Toit and Woermann draw on Hawken's (1992) insistence on the need for a 'restora- tive economy' – and hence restorative leadership – if business is to reinvent itself in response to the current ecological crisis. Within this new paradigm, the previous alignment of responsible leadership with transformational leader- ship is critiqued as coming from an atomistic rather than a systemic view- point, and Western's (2010) 'ecoleadership' is proposed as an alternative to the more established Messianic models. Restorative leadership is thus much closer to forms of distributed leadership (Gronn, 2003) in its embeddedness and fluidity, rather than a reliance on positional power and authority. Finally, in another move to operationalise the doing of responsible leadership, Voegt- lin, Patzer, and Scherer (2012) draw on Habermas to propose deliberative practice and discursive conflict resolution as a pragmatic approach to the daily practice of leadership that centres on communicative engagement with a broad range of stakeholders. In so doing they seek to bridge the gap between the macro level of corporate responsibility and the micro level of leadership responsibility. This attempt and others like it are, I believe, central to the future of the responsible leadership construct. It is through the operationalisation of responsible leadership at an individual level that we must build the credibility to be heard when we call for change at the macro level. The resonance suggested with distributed approaches seems to me to align more authentically with the need for 'bottom up' activism in achieving responsibility, rather than relying on 'top down' inspiration to get the job done, and thus to perhaps bring us closer to 'real' responsible leadership.

'Something borrowed'

For the blushing bride of the traditional rhyme, the 'something borrowed' was perhaps the most important requirement in securing good luck and warding off the most usual effect of the 'evil eye' which was to render the bride barren. Traditionally, the borrowed garment should properly be the undergarment of another woman who had already been blessed with children, thus obviating the effects of the 'evil eye' by communicating fertility to the bride. In the context of the present chapter, what I am borrowing is a theory from outside the body of work relating to responsible leadership, and I am using it in the hope that the exercise of mapping out the domain of responsible leadership in relation to other leadership theories will prove fruitful in furthering our understanding of what these domain claims might actually require of practicing leaders. Specifically, I have chosen to 'borrow' – or at least use – the framework developed by Hernandez, Eberly, Avolio, and Johnson (2011), which sought to map existing leadership theories into a cohesive body according to their shared and distinguishing characteristics, using their loci and mechanisms as the underpinning dimensions. Whilst I would question whether their framework is successful in generating a 'more comprehensive view of leadership theory' (Hernandez *et al.*, 2011, p. 1165) it does, nonetheless, offer a useful common language for comparing the scope of different theories in terms of where the leadership comes from and how leadership is transmitted. The former (loci) are posited to comprise the leader, the context, followers, collectives, and dyads, whilst the latter (mechanisms) are said to be affect, cognition, behaviours, and traits. The framework illustrates the mapping of relevant theories from the original work, together with a proposed mapping of responsible leadership.

I would suggest that responsible leadership requires the addition of a further locus to reflect the emphasis on a wide range of external stakeholders (who as well as being the recipients of responsible leadership are likely to be instrumental in its enactment) and a further mechanism to incorporate the values-driven nature of responsible leadership. Including these two additions,

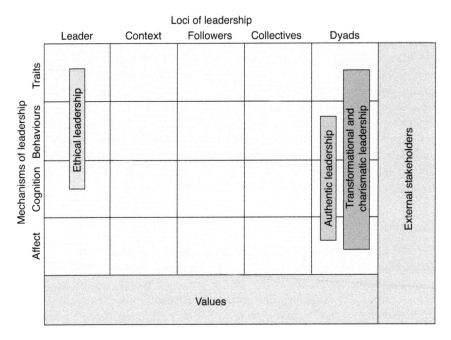

Figure 2.1 Loci of leadership (source: adapted from Hernandez *et al.*, 2011).

responsible leadership can then be seen to cover the entire area of the pro-posed framework in a truly all-encompassing feat of altruism. Alternatively, the mapping exercise could be seen as suggesting that responsible leadership is not a new and different form of leadership, but a manner of undertaking whatever other form of leadership we choose to adopt. It is a stance which permeates the content of our leadership interventions as well as (rather than?) a form of leadership in its own right. At the same time, if the responsible leadership 'elephant' truly is this large and all-encompassing, then we really do need to start thinking about the much smaller (and more personal) ways in which we can eat it one bite at a time!

'Something green'

With that in mind, I want to turn to the need for individual 'responsible' behaviours – what I refer to as 'sweating the small stuff' – in a slight colour twist on our traditional bridal recipe. In the context of the present chapter, this is perhaps the most tenuous link, and the one requiring most indulgence by the reader. First, having changed the original 'blue' of the rhyme to 'green', the associations of fidelity arising from phrases such as 'true blue' are immediately lost. In addition, in the context of the responsibility agenda the use of the word 'green' may suggest a focus purely on environmental issues which will not be the case in what follows (although like many others, I suspect, this was where my 'responsible' musings began). To justify the licence taken here, the word 'green' may perhaps be seen as suggesting a growing metaphor, and the way in which small initiatives may grow into major influences – a green lawn providing coverage through the amalgamation of millions of individual blades of grass. Thus what I am seeking to pull together with my 'something green' are the individual acts of responsible leadership which collectively add up to dramatic changes in individual and organisational practice or provide the catalyst for wider policy initiatives. At the same time, I want to explore the apparent disconnect between these individual grass-roots practices and the 'big picture' visions, aspirations, and policy-level initiatives. Consensus appears to be developing and gaining momentum around the 'big idea' of the pursuit of the 'triple bottom line', which balances social, environmental, and economic value at the same time as moderating the satisfaction of today's needs in order to allow for the needs of tomorrow. But it is less clear how this translates into individual day-to-day practices, insignificant in themselves but cumulatively important and with the power to influence both governments and corporates. So how do we get from the Global Compact to responsible leadership practice and back again?

Top down?

If we start at the top of the pyramid, we have such high-profile, boundary spanning initiatives as the 'millennium development goals' (www.globally-responsibleleadership.net, accessed 1 August 2014) and – more specifically business-focused – the Global Compact. Developed at the UN Millennium summit in 2000 with a deadline for achievement of 2015, the millennium development goals focused on such major issues as eradicating extreme poverty and hunger; ensuring environmental sustainability; and reducing child mortality (at the same time as improving maternal health). Other goals related to the promotion of gender equality and the empowerment of women; combating HIV/AIDS, malaria and other diseases; and achieving universal primary education, with the recognition that a spirit of global partnership would be needed for these goals to be met. Whilst we have no doubt moved some way towards meeting these goals, we are certainly not there yet and the proposed 15-year time-period proposed at the outset for their achievement now seems ludicrously optimistic.

Convened as a policy platform and practical framework for companies committed to sustainability and responsible business practices, the Principles of the UN Global Compact (www.globallyresponsibleleadership.net, accessed 1 August 2014) fall into the following four categories: human rights, labour standards, the environment, and anti-corruption. Under the banner of human rights, the Compact states that businesses should support and respect the protection of internationally proclaimed human rights and make sure that they are not complicit in human rights abuses. The labour standards category requires businesses to uphold the freedom of association and the effective recognition of the right to collective bargaining; to eliminate all forms of forced and compulsory labour; to bring about the effective abolition of child labour; and to eliminate discrimination in respect of employment and occupation. In safeguarding the environment, businesses are called upon to support a precautionary approach to environmental challenges; to undertake initiatives to promote greater environmental responsibility; and to encourage the development and diffusion of environmentally friendly technologies. And finally, businesses should work against corruption in all its forms, including extortion and bribery. Once again, there is clearly more work to be done under all of these headings.

Taken together, these headline goals are nonetheless important in setting the agenda for and raising the profile of sustainability and responsibility-related issues, but there is a significant amount of translation work required if they are to fulfil their objectives. The Globally Responsible Leadership Initiative, founded in 2004 and comprised initially of senior representatives from 21 companies, business schools, and centres for leadership learning, sought to collectively flesh out the leadership challenges represented by the Global Compact. Formulating these challenges in terms of the need for organisational leaders to think and act in a global context, to broaden their corporate purpose to reflect accountability to society around the globe, to put ethics at the centre of their thoughts, words, and deeds, and to transform their business education to give corporate global responsibility the centrality it deserves, they then circulated a broad-based call for engagement in this initiative with the aim of 'harness[ing] the power of the global network and add[ing] new members to it' (GRLI, 2005: 41). It now operates as a worldwide partnership of companies and business schools/learning organisations (currently 52 of each) working together in 'a laboratory of change to develop the next generation of globally responsible leaders' (www.globallyresponsibleleadership.net, accessed 1 August 2014). As such, it sees itself as 'a partner organisation, a foundation, an advanced laboratory and a movement' which is engaged in 'thought leadership, advocacy, and projects to achieve measurable impact' (www.globallyresponsibleleadership.net, accessed 1 August 2014).

The potential for corporates to take a leading role in initiatives aimed at the responsibility agenda is subject to mixed support, however. Lehmann, Toh, Christensen, and Ma's (2010) case study of the Danfoss Group presents an example of a business 'at an advanced stage of CSR development focusing on products and processes and employee relations' (2010, p. 153). In this instance, responsible behaviours are seen as integral to the organisation's identity and not just window dressing aimed at wooing customers through the creation of good public relations (PR). This is what Lehmann *et al.* refer to as the 'third wave' of CSR activities, such that there is close alignment between the CSR activities undertaken and the core business of the organisation itself. They also identify a number of modes of engagement with CSR, ranging from the establishment of not-for-profit foundations through to direct sponsorship of worthy institutions.

By contrast, the mini-scandal surrounding the questionable online postings of John Mackey, founder and CEO of Whole Foods Market Inc. (WFM) (in which he anonymously bad-mouthed a competitor organisation, thus adversely affecting its share price, for which WFM subsequently made a takeover bid) show how a seemingly 'virtuous' organisation 'visibly committed to environmentally sound strategies and other responsible business practices' (Manz, Anand, Joshi, & Manz, 2008, p. 385) can still fall foul of unethical leadership practices.

Thus we are left with the vexed question of who do we trust to take the lead on these important issues? As we have already seen, Hawken (1992) would tell us that businesses are the only entities with the power to initiate change on this scale in a modern society. In contrast, Brownlee and Kueneman (2012), building on the work of Peter Barnes, suggest that commons trusts are the most feasible means of safeguarding our natural resources. They maintain, however, that Barnes did not go far enough when he saw commons trusts as being a useful counterbalance to corporate capitalism: instead, they see the need for a wholesale overhaul of capitalist institutions (amongst which they would include the state) and a transition to a post-capitalist economy. In so saying, they are casting doubt on both the state and corporate big business as trustworthy stewards of our future, and trusting instead to members of the general public as the ultimate stakeholders. What seems to be ignored here is that it is the same 'general public' who created capitalism and drive consumerism who are now to be seen as the movers behind this new world order, with only a need for 'ecological literacy' (Brownlee & Kueneman, 2012, p. 68) to create a 'strong, organised, and informed public' (ibid., p. 71) capable of achieving the commons trust agenda. Research into environmentalists' attributions of responsibility for addressing climate change (Stoddart, Tindall, & Greenfield, 2012) suggest that this may be somewhat optimistic. Even those at the heart of environmental activism seem to lay the responsibility on governments to take the lead here, with individuals playing a supporting role through 'political consumerism' and 'environmental citizenship' (Spaargaren & Mol, 2008) through which corporates and governments might be pressurised into taking action. That the environmentalists surveyed for this research don't name their own organisations as leading forces for change in this context serves to reinforce the problem of 'phenomenal dissociation' (Worthy, 2008) noted by Brownlee and Kueneman (2012, p. 69), under which modern institutions and organisational structures are seen as generating an increasing 'lack of immediate engagement with the consequences of our everyday actions' such that it is always somebody else who needs to do something to solve these problems, never ourselves!

Bottom up?

It is easy to feel that our individual acts are too small to have an impact on climate change, sustainable development, or social inequality, but arguably without them nothing will ever change. And if, as Hawken (1992) claims, business is the driver of restorative economics, then by changing the decisions we make concerning our patterns of consumption and the like (what and how much we buy, where we buy it, and from whom, how we consume and/or recycle/reuse it, and so on), then we are the drivers of business. Whilst each of us – and each decision we make – may be only a drop in the ocean, how else can we create a tidal wave if not by a steady accumulation of drops? To return to the realism versus romanticism theme which runs through this volume, our actions might be guided by big ideas – and ideals – but we still have to enact them day by day, and minute by minute, if they are ever to be more than just ideas.

Thus the pursuit of the 'triple bottom line' at a business level, which balances social, environmental, and economic value at the same time as moderating the satisfaction of today's needs in order to allow for the needs of tomorrow, can be expected to require a little personal sacrifice at the individual level as well as some big ideas. In her book, *The sustainable MBA: A manager's guide to green business*, Giselle Weybrecht (2010) offers a number of suggestions for how we can 'green' both our offices and our lives. We are all used to the sight of recycling bins in our corridors and in our homes, but it is surprising how few of us car-share our journey to work; print (if at all) on both sides of our paper; take a washable mug to the cafeteria instead of using disposable ones; turn our lights off when we leave our offices; and skype when we used to travel. Turning to broader, social issues, if we *all* bought Fairtrade goods and refused to buy from businesses whose suppliers had poor labour practices or whose countries of origin had questionable human rights, the weight of influence to be exerted on business practice would be huge. But it takes effort to find out about such practices and self-denial to restrict our consumption to within 'responsible' parameters: to learn to read and annotate documents on screen; to forgo our favourite blend of coffee; or to pay an environmentally sustainable price for our air travel. Small things all, but if we aren't prepared to endure a little personal inconvenience then it seems likely that all our grand ideas of 'restorative leadership' are likely to remain unfulfilled because we will always be expecting someone else to follow where we aren't actually prepared to lead.

Once again, this raises the issue of 'ecological literacy' (Brownlee & Kueneman, 2012, p. 68), without which our good intentions may result in minimal or even negative impact on the issues we are trying to address. In illustration of this, I would like to recount a small incident from my own 'ecological literacy' journey – a journey that is still, very much, ongoing. The ideas presented in this chapter were originally presented at the 6th Developing Leadership Capacity Conference, with the theme of 'The new romantics of responsible leadership'. In concluding my session, I put up a slide suggesting some actions we as individuals could take to collectively impact on environmental issues, one of which was to hold such conferences as webinars rather than to fly round the world and meet face to face. This generated some interesting contributions from the floor, which serve to illustrate the difficulties of being responsible and of achieving 'ecological literacy'. The dialogue went something like this:

ME: So as a concluding thought, I wonder why we are not holding this conference virtually, rather than travelling to a shared location. Surely that would be the environmentally friendly option?
SPEAKER 1: Actually, using skype or the internet has a worse impact on the environment than air travel.
ME: Really? I didn't know that.
SPEAKER 2: And actually, we should all become vegetarians and stop keeping pet dogs.
ME: I assume we should become vegetarians because cows give off methane, but why should we stop keeping pets?
SPEAKER 2: Because a significant percentage of livestock are reared to be turned into pet food.
ME: Yes, I guess so. I hadn't thought of that either.

This somewhat bizarre and unexpected exchange prompted me to explore beyond the 'big headline' rhetoric of climate change, fed to us all via the media, to understand whether my fellow conference participants were really better informed or were just promulgating their own pet theory. My investigations (and I confess that these did begin with a trip to Wikipedia!) suggested there is some truth on both sides. For example, the burning of fossil fuels (including those used to power airplanes) is one of the leading sources of anthropogenic greenhouse gases. According to the United Nations Environment Programme the dramatic rise in global tourism – accounting for around 50 per cent of traffic movements – is a significant contributor to the increasing concentrations of greenhouse gases in the atmosphere, with rapidly expanding air traffic contributing about 2.5 per cent of the production of carbon dioxide (CO_2). The number of international travellers is expected to increase from 594 million in 1996 to 1.6 billion by 2020, adding greatly to the problem unless steps are taken to reduce emissions. (www.unep.org/resourceefficiency, accessed 31 July 2014). So score one for the idea of a virtual conference, but what about the computer usage that underpins the alternative of a virtual conference? Most computers create 40–80 grams of greenhouse gas emissions per hour through their electricity usage (depending on electricity source and computer type), so the aggregated greenhouse gas emissions just from computers is quite sizable, never mind the servers and fibre optic lines. Sources suggest that the internet accounts for 3 per cent of US electricity consumption and 2 per cent of global CO_2 emissions (www.treehugger.com, accessed 1 August 2014). Whilst it would be hard to calculate the directly comparable figures for a virtual versus face-to-face conference, these numbers do suggest that my conference interlocutors may have a point!

So what about vegetarianism and the family pet? The issue raised here related to the methane gas produced by ruminant livestock. Enteric fermentation, along with paddy rice farming and covered vented landfill emissions, are responsible for significant increases in methane atmospheric concentrations. Methane emissions are an important contribution to global greenhouse gas emissions, with the Intergovernmental Panel on Climate Change (IPCC) reporting that methane is more than 20 times as effective as CO_2 at trapping heat in the atmosphere, thus counterbalancing the fact that it is produced in substantially smaller amounts. Other agricultural activities, including the use of fertilisers that lead to higher nitrous oxide (N_2O) concentrations, are also significant contributors to the problems of greenhouse gases. So score one for my conference colleagues. At the same time, however, changes in land use, mainly due to deforestation, account for up to one-third of anthropogenic CO_2 emissions (http://ipcc.ch, accessed 14 July 2014) with tropical deforestation alone responsible for approximately 20 per cent of world greenhouse gas emissions. And yet this was not on their agenda. To be fair, it wasn't on mine either! My aim here is not actually to see which of us was more ecologically savvy, but to illustrate some of the pitfalls of sifting through the available information in order to become so. And as noted elsewhere in this chapter, the agendas of governments and corporations may not always be transparent or unbiased in helping us on this quest. I leave it to individual readers to decide what this means for the future of the family pet!

More broadly, it is not just through lifestyle changes that individuals can engage with the responsible agenda. Tams and Marshall (2011: 110) draw attention to the growth of 'careers that respond to wider societal debates through the professionalisation and institutionalisation of responsible business practices across a variety of sectors and in the spaces beyond organisational boundaries' and hence the development of what they term 'responsible careers'. They characterise such careers as being protean – or self-directed and values-based (Hall, 2004) – and boundaryless, such that they require physical and psychological mobility (Sullivan & Arthur, 2006). Those who pursue such careers do so in an attempt to have an impact on societal challenges through undertaking CSR and similar type roles, as well as through managing their careers according to responsible values. Tams and Marshall identify six career practices adopted by those pursuing responsible careers – namely, that their work is an expression of themselves and their values; that they connect with affirming others; that they seek to construct their contribution by defining how their expertise can be applied to responsible business fields; that they act to embed or legitimise responsible practices in established organisations; that their activities serve to redefine and shape established patterns of operating; and that they engage positively with systemic initiatives rather than protesting against perceived ills. At the same time, the development of these practices is said to be influenced by four learning dynamics around orientation to 'shifting landscapes', biographical and systemic reflexivity, and exploration.

In an alternative take on the idea of responsible careers, Ketola (2010) suggests having recourse to identity theory – and specifically the work of psychologist Erik Erikson – to understand how individuals find their 'responsible leadership identity' amidst the uncertainties and pressures of a chaotic world. Ketola identifies six areas of difficulty to be addressed by the would-be responsible leader. These relate to:

- taking personal responsibility for one's actions based on espoused values,
- maintaining a healthy self-image, in balance with one's external image,
- achieving balance between short- and long-term time perspectives,
- experimentation with different roles to find out which ones feel like a good fit,
- anticipation of achievement and an internal locus of control, and
- willingness to be both leader and follower.

These individual level issues are recognised as being located in wider organisational and societal contexts, with similar issues needing to be addressed at each level. Whilst it is acknowledged that responsible leadership can be either supported or thwarted by the milieu in which it is undertaken – Ketola suggests that both responsibility and irresponsibility are contagious – attention is also drawn to courageous individuals who, in Ketola's words, take up the challenge and 'care and dare' (2010, p. 173).

The pursuance of responsible careers – of caring and daring – is not without its problems, however. 'Good' managers or leaders are usually seen as those who generate effective organisational performance rather than those who strive for 'morally sustainable leadership, i.e. leadership with an awareness of both light and dark sides contained in the role of leader' (Kociatkiewicz & Kostera, 2012, p. 861). In their narrative collage study of social actors from a range of different age groups and organisational backgrounds, Kociatkiewicz and Kostera found that participants were sceptical of the idea of goodness in management or leadership, and disenchanted with the 'false front' which leaders in their experience presented to them. This dystopian view of leadership archetypes raises, amongst other questions, the issue of whether 'good' leaders will be believed in a world where they are perceived to be so rare!

Somewhere in between?

What seems to be emerging here is the need for integration between levels on the one hand, and the potential for the initiative to come from any level on the other. In an interesting action research project with leaders in South African SMEs, Hind and Smit (2012) observed both the need for integration and the power of personal learning journeys demonstrated by participating organisations over a 12-month period. At an individual level, the leaders reported increased awareness, mindfulness, and personal accountability. At the same time there was evidence of engagement with sustainability challenges at three organisational levels:

- Macro level – e.g. business legitimacy, stakeholder engagement, and social capital development;
- Mid level – e.g. brand identity, organisational culture/climate, and performance measures; and
- Micro level – e.g. personal interactions and impact on followers' behaviours, attitudes, knowledge, motivation, and job satisfaction.

(Hind & Smit, 2012, p. 82)

Study participants also noted that implementing sustainability into their businesses required a high level of specificity and focus about what actually needed to be done, by whom, and when, as well as real commitment from individuals to do things differently. In terms of the premise of this chapter, they really did need to 'sweat the small stuff'!

In another take on the need for integration, Waldman and Galvin (2008) offer a series of best practices within the context of a broader, more comprehensive definition of responsible leadership. Instead of eschewing an economic perspective and considerations of effectiveness in favour of a values-driven stakeholder perspective, they contend that some balance between the two is required. The best practices they arrive at are aimed at operationalising a thoughtful approach to the challenges thus thrown up, in terms of the tension between authenticity and calculative behaviours, the balancing of organisational and societal concerns, and the more complex managerial motivations which ensue. Whilst the premise here is good, the best practices themselves are woefully vague: 'leading by example' and 'incorporating stakeholder values into core purpose and vision' (Waldman & Galvin, 2008, p. 335) tell us nothing about how to really deliver responsibility on the ground. Similarly 'using intellectual stimulation to help followers implement stakeholder values' and 'the demonstration of employee empowerment' are at best problematic. Perhaps closer to the mark is Pless, Maak, and Stahl's (2011) study of responsible leadership learning through international service-learning programmes. The learning areas evidenced by study participants – namely responsible mindset, ethical literacy, cultural intelligence, global mindset, self-development, and community building – come somewhat closer to putting some practical 'meat' on the bones of what it is to do 'being a responsible leader'. The study also stands testament to the work of becoming a responsible leader through resolving cultural and ethical paradoxes, constructing new life-worlds, and making sense of the emotions experienced during these processes. This more competence-based approach offers real developmental potential, albeit with all the difficulties attaching to the removal of managers from the workplace in order to undertake significant and lasting learning.

Conclusion

So where does this leave us? For me, the dilemma of who is responsible for taking the lead on responsible leadership remains complex and unresolved. At the same time, it seems obvious (to me at least) that those who wish to have credibility in promulgating the 'big ideas' of responsibility must also be willing to practice the everyday components, however insignificant they might seem in isolation. This brings me full circle, to my original belief that it really is important to 'sweat the small stuff'. To quote Richard Bolden (2013, p. 4) from a Business Leadership Review editorial challengingly entitled 'Change the world or go home', 'in a complex and uncertain world the only way to make a difference is to do something'.

References

Annan, Kofi, (2002) Speech mat at the MIT Sloan School of Management, Cambridge, Massachusetts on 14 October 2002. As cited in Global Responsible Leadership Initiative [no specific author stated – report said to be the 'shared thoughts and beliefs of all founding members of the GRLI'] (2005) Globally Responsible Leadership: A call for engagement. EFMD.

Avolio, B. J. (2011). *Full range leadership development* (2nd ed.). Thousand Oaks, CA: Sage.

Avolio, B. J., & Gardner, W. L. (2005). Authentic leadership development: Getting to the root of positive forms of leadership. *The Leadership Quarterly, 16*, 315–338.

Avolio, B. J., Waldman, D., & Yammarino, F. (1991). Leading in the 1990s: The four I's of transformational leadership. *Journal of European Industrial Training, 15*, 9–16.

Bolden, R. (2013). Editorial: Change the world or go home. *Business Leadership Review, 10*(2), 3–4.

Brown, M. E., & Treviño, L. K. (2006). Ethical leadership: A review and future directions. *The Leadership Quarterly, 17*, 595–616.

Brownlee, J., & Kueneman, R. (2012). Transitioning from endgame to sustainability: Revisiting the commons trusts model. *Organization and Environment, 25*(1), 59–75.

Cameron, K. (2011). Responsible leadership as virtuous leadership. *Journal of Business Ethics, 98*, 25–35.

Ciulla, J. B. (Ed.). (2004). *Ethics: The heart of leadership* (2nd edn). Westport, CT: Praeger.

Conger, J. A., & Kanungo, R. N. (1987). Towards a behavioural theory of charismatic leadership in organisational settings. *Academy of Management Review, 12*(4), 637–647.

Du Toit, L., & Woermann, M. (2012). When economy becomes ecology: Implications for understanding leadership. *Reflections on responsible leadership: 2nd International conference in responsible leadership.* Pretoria. 18–21 November 2012.

Freeman, R. E., & Auster, E. R. (2011). Values, authenticity, and responsible leadership. *Journal of Business Ethics, 98*: 15–23.

Greenleaf, R. K. (1977/2002). *Servant leadership: A journey into the nature of legitimate power and greatness* (25th Anniversary Edition). Mahwah, NJ: Paulist Press.

GRLI (Global Responsible Leadership Initiative) (2005) *Globally responsible leadership:*

A call for engagement. [No specific author stated; the report is said to be the 'shared thoughts and beliefs of all founding members of the GRLI'.] Brussels: European Foundation for Management Development.

Gronn, P. (2003). Leadership: Who needs it? *School Leadership and Management, 23*(3), 267–290.

Groves, K. S., & LaRocca, M. A. (2011). Responsible leadership outcomes via stakeholder CSR value: Testing a values-centred model of transformational leadership. *Journal of Business Ethics, 98,* 37–55.

Hall, D. T. (2004). The protean career: A quarter century journey. *Journal of Vocational Behaviour, 65*(1), 1–13.

Hartman, E. M. (1988). *Conceptual foundations of organization theory.* Cambridge, MA: Ballinger.

Hawken, P. (1992). The ecology of commerce. *Inc, 14*(4), 93–100.

Hernandez, M., Eberly, M. B., Avolio, B. J., & Johnson, M. D. (2011). The loci and mechanisms of leadership: Exploring a more comprehensive view of leadership theory. *The Leadership Quarterly, 22*(6), 1165–1185.

Hind, P., & Smit, A. (2012). Enabling sustainability through responsible leadership: An action research project with SMEs. *Reflections on responsible leadership: 2nd International conference in responsible leadership.* Pretoria. 18–21 November 2012.

Ketola, T. (2010). Responsible leadership: Building blocks of individual, organisational and societal behaviour. *Corporate Social Responsibility and Environmental Management, 17*(3), 173–184.

Kociatkiewicz, J., & Kostera, M. (2012). The good manager: An archetypal quest for morally sustainable leadership. *Organization Studies, 33*(7), 861–878.

Lehmann, M., Toh, I., Christensen, P., & Ma, R. (2010). Responsible leadership? Development of CSR at Danfoss, Denmark. *Corporate Social Responsibility and Environmental Management, 17*(3), 153–168.

Manz, C. C., Anand, V., Joshi, M., & Manz, K. P. (2008). Emerging paradoxes in executive leadership: A theoretical interpretation of the tensions between corruption and virtuous values. *The Leadership Quarterly, 19*(3), 385–392.

Pless, N. M. (2007). Understanding responsible leadership: Role identity and motivational drivers. *Journal of Business Ethics, 74*(4), 437–456.

Pless, N. M., & Maak, T. (2011). Responsible leadership: Pathways to the future. *Journal of Business Ethics, 98,* 3–13.

Pless, N. M., Maak, T., & Stahl, G. K. (2011). Developing responsible global leaders through international service-learning programs: The Ulysses experience. *Academy of Management Learning & Education, 10*(2), 237–260.

Russell, R. F., & Stone, A. G. (2002). A review of servant leader attributes: Developing a practical model. *Leadership and Organisational Development Journal, 23*(3), 145–157.

Spaargaren, G., & Mol, A. P. J. (2008). Greening global consumption: Redefining politics and authority. *Global Environmental Change, 18*(3), 350–359.

Stoddart, M. C., Tindall, D. B., & Greenfield, K. L. (2012). 'Governments have the power?' Interpretations of climate change responsibility and solutions among Canadian environmentalists. *Organization and Environment, 25*(1), 39–58.

Sullivan, S. E., & Arthur, M. B. (2006). The evolution of the boundaryless career concept: Examining physical and psychological mobility. *Journal of Vocational Behaviour, 69*(1), 19–29.

Tams, S., & Marshall, J. (2011). Responsible careers: Systemic reflexivity in shifting landscapes. *Human Relations, 64*(1), 109–131.

Voegtlin, C., Patzer, M., & Scherer, A. G. (2012). Responsible leadership in global business: A new approach to leadership and its multi-level outcomes. *Journal of Business Ethics, 105*, 1–16.

Waldman, D. A. (2011). Moving forward with the concept of responsible leadership: Three caveats to guide theory and research. *Journal of Business Ethics, 98*, 75–83.

Waldman, D. A., & Galvin, B. M. (2008). Alternative perspectives of responsible leadership. *Organizational Dynamics, 37*(4), 327–341.

Western, S. (2010). Eco-leadership: Towards the development of a new paradigm. In B. W. Redekop (Ed.), *Leadership for environmental sustainability* (pp. 36–54). New York and London: Routledge.

Weybrecht, G. (2010). *The Sustainable MBA: A manager's guide to green business.* Chichester: Wiley.

Worthy, K. (2008). Modern institutions, phenomenal dissociations, and destructiveness towards humans and the environment. *Organization and Environment, 21*(2), 148–170.

3 From responsibility to responsibilities

Towards a theory of co-responsible leadership

Brigid Carroll

Introduction

> EU should shoulder responsibility in Syrian refugee crisis says commissioner.
> (*Daily News*, 10 May 2015)

> Ed Miliband says election bloodbath is 'my responsibility alone' as he looks set to resign.
> (*Mirror*, 8 May 2015)

> Exclusive: JK here to stay

> 'Being a successful team doesn't happen straight away. It's not about individuals. It is about creating an environment where there is collective responsibility and we think that is the right way to go.'
> (*New Zealand Herald*, 9 May 2015)

Above you find media headlines for three stories that featured strongly while this chapter was being written. These in fact were only a tiny selection of the stories and reports about issues and events which evoked a call, claim, or denial of leadership responsibility. It is in fact difficult not to encounter a constant barrage of what we could call responsibility discourses linked to leadership. This chapter will use these three headlines and stories to ask some critical questions about responsibility: What it is? Is it singular or plural? What or who it is for? Most of all, who might be responsible in the name of leadership?

If we spend even a cursory amount of time thinking about the three contexts underneath our chosen headlines then we can see how complex responsibility really is.

The refugee story is arguably one of the biggest and most internationally complex challenges facing our world today. Europe has become the frontline of much of this challenge, but the sources of refugee flight belong with multiple sites of conflict where past legacies and current realities have created conditions where sustainable, healthy, and peaceful lives are all but impossible. This phenomenon sits therefore in a complex intersection of global, cultural, economic, and political forces well beyond the sole responsibility of single individuals or even collectives – such as the EU.

The 2015 UK election would on the surface of it be an easier event in which to apportion responsibility. Certainly it is not uncommon for leaders of losing parties to claim responsibility and fall on their sword voluntarily or be ousted soon after the event in a mass clamour for the visible manifestation of responsibility. Yet the 2015 UK election is quite an extraordinary event. No fewer than three leaders have resigned due to unexpectedly dire results, while a new political force (the Scottish Independence Party) rises from seemingly nowhere to herald a potential reconfiguration of the British Union. What has happened appears to be an upheaval in the political landscape which has seen a rise and fall of political parties at the expense of each other. Such interdependence of outcomes and contextual uncertainty raises yet another set of issues to do with responsibility.

Finally we turn to our third context in New Zealand – a country where rugby is often likened to a national religion. The 'Blues' rugby team based in New Zealand's largest city, Auckland, in the third year of its rebuild under iconic coach Sir John Kirwan was suffering not only a consistent string of defeats but also visible player and team inadequacies. Fans were staying away in droves and even the most passionate die-hard supporter could but wince at the poor strategy and performance frequently on display. Media were building up to what was seemingly becoming the inevitable climax of this sorry saga and the resignation of Sir JK (as he is known). That in fact has now happened, but the lure of this thing called collective responsibility was hard for many to give up, delaying both a decision and action for months.

With the help of these three examples, we intend to put responsible leadership theory to the test. First of all we explore and critique responsible leadership theory applying it to these three examples to assess the contribution it makes to our understanding of responsibility. Then we turn to philosophy and sociology especially to find alternative ways of thinking about responsibility that go beyond individual and positional ways of thinking about leadership and also apply those to these three examples. Of particular interest here are alternatives to individual notions of responsibility, namely co-responsibility or collective responsibility. What we are seeking to address here is a mis-match between complex, ambiguous multi-stakeholder challenges and traditional leader-centric notions of responsibility which rely on an individual. The hypothesis of this chapter is that responsibility in such challenges would need to be moved amongst a series of connected individuals and groups throughout the network of stakeholders. That would seem more like thinking in terms of responsibilities than responsibility. For this to happen, complex interpersonal, relational, and system dynamics need to be understood in the pursuit of such leadership and such capacity needs to shape the call and development of responsible leadership theory.

Responsible leadership theory

Encountering responsible leadership theory involves a number of caveats right from the start. So many leadership 'theories' enter with an adjective in front of them as if that makes them theoretically distinct in themselves. To its credit responsible leadership theory resists such an approach. It makes it clear that it builds off transformational, authentic, servant, and ethical leadership theories (Waldman & Galvin, 2008, p. 327) but provides a correction to these in bringing responsibility into the foreground. Accordingly Pless and Maak (2011, p. 4) characterise responsible leadership as 'a multilevel response to deficiencies in existing leadership frameworks and theories'. While uncharacteristically modest in its claims, it does seek to create a focus and contribution in terms of responsibility hitherto lacking.

Responsible leadership theory is defined by two key theorisations: its 'amalgamation' (Waldman, 2011, p. 75) of social responsibility with leadership and its broadening of a leader's attention beyond followers, organisational members, and shareholders to stakeholders. At the core of it we could argue is both a desire to move *away* from a sense of corporate and executive leaders having or exercising less than robust ethics and to move *towards* the host of major global, social, environmental, and cultural issues that beset the contemporary world. It appears then to invite a more expansive mindset beyond what can seem narrow financial, productivity, and performance concerns. Equally it seems to address a broadening of gaze in leadership with an orientation to both internal and external constituencies. On a surface level it would seem to widen, enlarge, and refocus leadership in ways that many have been calling for.

Underneath such a surface, responsible leadership theory appears often a far less radical shift than one might hope. I note particularly that much of it remains a leader-centric theory with an assumption that responsibility lies in 'the inner theatre' (Pless, 2007, p. 437) or 'good character' (Waldman, 2011, p. 75) of an individual, usually with formal positional authority in an organization. Additionally responsibility is frequently talked about as 'a balancing act' (Waldman & Galvin, 2008, p. 330) amongst the various stakeholder concerns indicating that a too simple harmony and consensus might be underlying drivers of this theory.

Responsible leadership theory also lacks some vital theoretical dimensions. For instance, it generally lacks a definition of 'responsible' and appears to assume that what it means to be responsible is singular and self-evident. Commonly it speaks of responsible in terms of other related 'synonyms', such as accountable or ethical or moral, thus we lack a theoretical exploration of what it might mean to be responsible as opposed to ethical and accountable, and what different definitions might rule in and rule out. Indeed, responsibility is often represented as something one either has or not, and very few clues are given in terms of how it actually works.

An exception to such theoretical underdevelopment are the few articles not taking a mainstream, individualistic perspective, such as Pless and Maak (2011) and Voegtlin, Patzer, and Scherer (2012). Pless and Maak (2011) take a relational view of responsible leadership theory and argue that if 'relationships are the centre of leadership' (p. 4) then responsible leading involves being a 'weaver in and among a network of relationships' (p. 11). Put succinctly, responsible leadership happens 'in social processes of interaction' (Maak & Pless, 2006, p. 103) where stakeholders connected in a challenge construct a 'values-based and thorough ethical principles-driven relationship'. Even more specifically Voegtlin *et al.* (2012, p. 4) take a discursive approach to responsible leadership theory where it is 'discursive conflict resolution' that offers a process to mediate between diverse and presumably often conflicting interests. Even in these, however, stakeholders seem largely shadowy, background figures in a landscape still dominated by a few designated leaders.

This chapter asks if responsible leadership theory really does answer what it sets out to in terms of 'to whom or what should leaders be responsible and how will responsibility be demonstrated' (Waldman & Galvin, 2008, p. 328) by going back to our three headlines and stories at the beginning of this chapter and interpreting them through the lens of responsible leadership theory.

The refugee crisis is a tough challenge for responsible leadership theory right from the start. The EU is a confederation/federation of multiple stakeholders (28 separate countries), it has a complex and confusing structure (seven institutions), and who 'leads' is an impossibly complex answer ('Brussels or Berlin?' is the popular riddle). While it certainly does attempt to operate as a collective, member nations with their separate leaders are never far from their own individual interests and agendas. One would imagine that every challenge and issue it looks at would be one of social, cultural, and economic responsibility with a vast and interdependent array of stakeholders. This refugee issue is particularly complex given that a few countries are bearing the brunt of refugee arrivals (Greece and Italy) but their flow through to the rest of Europe is uneven to say the least. It is hard to characterise what responsibility actually is for in this case: preventing tragedy? equitable spread of implications of decisions? protecting the EU? humanitarian rights? criminal liability of people traffickers? However we might answer, it seems impossible to reduce responsibility down to an individual character or even a range of individuals. Nor does balancing stakeholder interests seem desirable or relevant.

The defeat of the British Labour Party and Ed Miliband's subsequent resignation seems a textbook conventional treatment of responsibility that on the surface does not require a reading through responsible leadership theory at all. While all dimensions of the defeat presumably cannot be laid at the feet of Ed Miliband, responsibility can. His resignation is both sacrificial and symbolic: in one swoop the failure of the campaign is focused on one person and the party is allowed to fight another day. Responsibility in this case is synonymous with blame. Not surprisingly since the defeat, narratives of blame have been constructed around Ed Miliband in terms of his focus on the poor (as opposed to the middle-classes) of the UK, his fairly benign personal presence, and his inability to attract broad-based support. These retrospectively build the required 'Ed Miliband is responsible for this defeat' narrative. Yet different and equally compelling narratives perhaps point to a more complex picture of responsibility. The dramatic, and seemingly unforeseen, resurgence of the Scottish National-ist Party, the equally unforeseen demise of the Liberal Democrats, and the relatively 'high vote–few seats' predicament of the anti-immigration United Kingdom Independence Party together appear to have created a whole new voter terrain. Whoever takes responsibility for the British Labour Party will have a complex conversation with future stakeholders to build a platform that will identify, articulate, and act on the social, cultural, environmental, and political issues of the age. It is not clear whether responsible leadership theory can offer much insight prospectively for this set of challenges.

Our Blues story seems to offer a set of circumstances that further tests responsible leadership theory in an interesting and contemporary way. The Blues Board is itself a combination of stakeholders, with half the board representing business/commercial interests and half representing rugby. While one would imagine that performance and success on the field is in everyone's interest, other aspirations such as region/franchise identity, profile, profitability, sponsorship, development, and relationship to the community are also understood as important. Media report that the business/commercial half of the Board understand Sir John Kirwan as having come through strongly on identity, profile, and community relationships, whilst the rugby half is most concerned with the striking lack of results. Add to this the quest for what they are calling collective responsibility that has put in more complexities with a concerted desire to grow a different relationship between Board, coaching staff, players, local clubs, and community that will take sustained culture change and time. The simple blame of a sacrificial and symbolic 'responsible' individual seems to miss the wider intricacies in terms of responsibility that weave in and out of this scenario.

All three of our contemporary stories affirm the importance of responsibility and its centrality to leadership at the same time as making visible its limits and constraints. Responsible leadership theory seems correct in broadening the leadership sphere to embed stakeholders and refocusing leadership on broader social, cultural, and political issues, but in staying predominantly with well-established leader, influence, and balance assumptions it does not seem to provide the theoretical or practice sophistication to enable its own theorisation. This chapter will attempt to extend responsible leadership theory in three ways: (1) the nature of responsibility; (2) co- or shared responsibility; and (3) practices that enact responsibilities (a more multi-dimensional understanding of what it means to be responsible).

Defining responsibility

If we accept that responsibility is most commonly 'a fashionable slogan, as it is commonly used, but rarely conceptualized and analysed thoroughly' (Snell, 2009, p. 17) and 'a vague and polyvalent term' (McCarthy & Kelty, 2010, p. 406), then we need to pause and do some work on what we mean by responsibility. Looking up the word in the dictionary will not supply much of a start here given that most of the definitions of responsibility take one straight to the state of being responsible, and in turn the definitions of responsible take one straight back to having responsibility. The few definitions that escape the responsible–responsibility circle go immediately to synonyms such as account-able, answerable, and reliable. It seems important then to canvas the meaning around the word and its meaning particularly when associated with leadership. In terms of leadership let's also pay attention to McCarthy and Kelty's (2010) directive that 'responsibility must be constructed and understood as something novel, interesting not bureaucratic' if it is to bring something fundamentally different to our understandings of leadership.

One starting place is to agree with Caruana and Crane (2008, p. 1495) that researchers fall too readily into seeing responsibility as 'an objectively identifi-able trait' that speaks to an assumed universal reality, and new possibilities could emerge from approaching responsibility 'as an essentially contested dis-course' (ibid.) where different interpretations and meanings of responsibility are in circulation in our world today. The intent of this section is to test out different discourses in terms of what they might bring to responsible leader-ship theory. There are two discursive 'contests' that seem particularly important to defining responsibility:

1   causal, legal, and moral responsibility;
2   backward- and forward-looking responsibility.

If I take on responsibility for something I directly did then I am causally responsible. Few of us would argue with this, I suspect, or want that connec-tion between doing something and feeling responsible ever lessened. However, this is usually not the form of responsibility that leadership takes although those in leadership are certainly not exempt from being responsible for what they do. That would need to be a given. In none of our three stories is there a straightforward and linear connection between what anyone in leadership actually did and responsibility. Alternatively, legal responsibility is more about obligation and duty under the law. This is the same as saying that we are required to do certain predefined things. Given these requirements are legal then they are set down and, while they can be argued in any context, are comparatively clear-cut (compared to other forms of responsibility). It would be safe to assume that anyone in leadership in our three stories had legal and contractual responsibilities, but that these did not constitute the struggles or challenges around responsibility in any of the three stories.

This leaves moral responsibility. Moral responsibility is not direct like causal responsibility or predefined like legal responsibility. Isaacs (2011, p. 13) defines moral responsibility as 'blameworthiness and praiseworthiness' and argues that moral responsibility differs from the others in terms of the range of things for which one can be responsible and in its enforceability. It is moral responsibility (in the widest sense of 'moral') that seems to be the type of responsibility most at stake in responsible leadership theory. So let us assume that leaders, like everyone else, can expect to be responsible for what they do and, as leaders or part of leadership collectives, are liable legally for certain responsibilities or duties which they take on knowingly with any leadership role. That leaves moral responsibility as the big challenge. In our stories, the EU, the Labour Party, and the Blues franchise all have moral responsibilities that seem to require a different way of thinking about responsibility than if it was as simple as being responsible for what they directly do or are required to do legally.

However, both blame and praise are backward-looking forms of responsibility. By definition they can only be assessed or attributed retrospectively. Snell (2009, p. 26) defines backward-looking responsibility as 'being liable for a deed that has happened'. She contrasts this with forward-looking responsibility, defined as 'being accountable for the future consequences of one's actions' (p. 26). She sees both as inevitable given the 'dual but entangled meaning' (p. 25) of responsibility in both assumptions of causing something and being liable for it. We are well used to notions of backward-looking responsibility and leaders receiving blame or praise after an event. Indeed this would be the most dominant discourse of responsibility and one which two of our stories – the resignation of Ed Miliband and the struggles over Sir John Kirwan's reappointment – directly speak to. However, our EU story clearly invites a forward-looking responsibility and the capacity to think into and own future consequences. Interestingly the Blues story seemed to be fighting for the right to view responsibility as forward- not backward-looking at this juncture. I would argue that the ability to view moral responsibility going forward would appear to offer something crucial to responsible leadership theory.

To reflect here, then, definitional exploration of responsibility poses real challenges and possibilities for responsible leadership theory. At the very least it needs to stop talking about responsibility as if it is a self-evident and non-problematic term. This chapter argues that there is no responsibility but *responsibilities* (causal, legal, and moral) that come into play with social, cultural, and political issues, and disentangling or tracking these should help us gain more precision and power in our explorations. This section has zeroed in on moral responsibility as offering particular potential to stretch us to grappling with complex problems distributed across multiple stakeholders. Wrestling with moral responsibility means wrestling with whether we can or should in fact attribute blame or praise to any single or grouping of individuals in what are essentially networks of leadership. In fact, we should be questioning whether *leaders* in fact are the unit of analysis for responsible leadership at all. One further issue we have encountered in this section is the difficulty of being able to recognise responsibility in the present or looking forwards as to date we have relied as a scholarly field and society on attributing responsibility retrospectively.

I would like to build on these propositions – responsibility as having a moral dimension, responsibility as forward-looking, and responsibility as shared – in the next section, which offers the concept of co-responsibility as a way of stepping out of a too individualistic paradigm and engaging with responsibilities as sitting between people in both routine and exceptional interactions and hence able to be relationally and socially developed and understood.

Co-responsibility

A shift to moral and consequence inevitably brings others into the picture. In fact Isaacs (2011) argues that morality only really makes sense in the context of interaction where the intents and actions of an individual are changed by the intents and actions of others. Out of such interaction comes moral (or not) outcomes. That would make a collective frame for responsibility essential, and in fact Issacs argues that 'denial of collective prevents us, as individuals, from seeing our own moral effectiveness' (p. 9). This would be supported by Strydom (1999, p. 66), who heralds a sociological shift from understanding responsibility in individual terms to grappling with 'the macro-dimension of humankind's fragile existence on the finite earth'. Likewise McCarthy and Kelty (2010, p. 409) argue that 'responsibility cannot be approached through the decisions of individual actors even if it is not clear where else to look' and that 'the creation of new forms of responsibility' are becoming vital. Other scholars do not agree. In an oft-quoted comment French (1972, p. 143) stated that 'where all are responsible no one is responsible', which speaks to the biggest fear around co-responsibility: that responsibility becomes diluted and benign as soon as individuals are no longer its focus. This section will explore the construct of co-responsibility and ask whether it can pull responsible leadership theory beyond its leader-centric assumptions yet still remain potent and meaningful.

Co-responsibility is one of three forms of responsibility in Strydom's (1999) three-fold typology, alongside traditional or individual responsibility and post-traditional responsibility (a form of responsibility where responsibility is attached to knowledge and expertise more than to roles as with traditional responsibility). Strydom draws predominantly on the sociologist Apel in his construction of co-responsibility. Apel (1993, p. 9) saw a need for a concept of responsibility that was neither traditional nor post-traditional that 'neither can be reduced to individual accountability nor allows for the individuals unburdening themselves from personal responsibility by shifting it into institutions or social systems'. Like other contemporary theorists (Jonas, 1984; McCarthy & Kelty, 2010; Strydom, 1999), Apel (1993, p. 10) saw a strong link between risk and responsibility given the complexity of designs, technologies, and processes that rely on disparate experts, managers, and frontline workers in 'interconnected socio-cultural processes', meaning decision-makers rely on others in ways that stretch way beyond what traditional or individual forms of responsibility tend to take into account. This appears to speak straight to the contexts where 'old problems have reached a novel moral quality and [...] classical solutions are no longer morally satisfactory' (ibid., p. 9), which surely are also significant drivers of responsible leadership theory.

For Apel, co-responsibility marks an imperative for humanity to take responsibility for collective actions. Co-responsibility rests on a discourse ethics where individuals accept they are integral to different communication communities or what he sometimes calls 'argumentation communities' (ibid., p. 24). That means taking up the responsibility to be active in the issues that present to these communities requiring collective reflection, exploration, debate, and choices/decisions. The preference is for those affected directly to construct solutions but within the meta-conversation of the broader communication communities. This is not a picture of some kind of giant United Nations forum but a 'network of formal or informal dialogues and conferences, commissions and boards on all levels' (ibid., p. 24).

Strydom (1999, p. 69) calls this 'a mobilizable form of responsibility' in the sense that those in leadership and indeed stakeholders in any issue can seize the responsibility to communicate to their communities in ways that invite people to have a voice or stake in the discussion and argumentation that will be required. In linking co-responsibility to framing, Strydom is bringing co-responsibility right into a leadership space where 'intense framing contests' (McAdam, McCarthy, & Zald, 1996, p. 17) are indicative of the political and strategic efforts of collectives, institutions, and nations to shape the meaning and understanding of an issue. Popke (2003, p. 300) terms such framing contests as 'an ethics of encounter without a commitment to resolution or closure'. In discourse ethics, then, leadership is about creating and holding the discursive spaces where groups and institutions wrestle with the framing and meaning they bring to issues. One could charge a utopian quality to co-responsibility but Issacs in particular sees it as offering meaningful power and hope to individuals who want to accept their part in solving issues and challenges that go beyond the responsibility of any one individual or grouping to own. To this effect she claims:

> when we reorient ourselves in relation to others and take the broader perspective of collective action, new moral possibilities present themselves, and our contributions, small though they may be, gain greater significance from the collective contexts in which they take place.
>
> (Isaacs, 2011, p. 20)

Let's see how co-responsibility might work in our three stories

Essentially the EU is a communication/argumentation community. It relies on co-responsibility and the capacity of member nations to claim and exercise a voice. This doesn't make it an ideal communication community by any means, but indicates a set of assumptions that those affected by shared issues and possibilities need to wrestle with, questioning and understanding them in order to arrive at action. Those in the EU are also part of other communication communities, such as NATO and the United Nations, and in this way take part in a series of overlapping conversations attempting to engage with an issue. Co-responsibility theory reminds us however that the EU doesn't own the refugee problem and that the nations from where the refugees are coming constitute the most affected, and need a central voice in the resolution of the issue. Oddly enough, however, it is another group of stakeholders who are very influential here and that is the population of those across Europe and beyond who live in the countries who have the bulk of the resources to help in one way or another. Those in leadership – meaning multiple people and groups across multiple contexts – have the task of listening, reflecting, framing, and reframing this issue, so that more and more people become a voice in the discourse of refugees and migration/resettling. In becoming a voice those people influence what this issue means and meaning ultimately will influence action. The EU, then, outside of its routine management activities, needs to understand itself in leadership terms as a framing and boundary-testing body with the power to set and frame problems and challenges in a way that invites others to work with it. Its task is to mobilise the kind of engagement and responsibility that will create some kind of movement for those stuck in entrenched understandings and approaches.

The Labour Party and its new leadership have a similar task in gathering and sifting through the different understandings of what it has meant to be Labour and what it will mean to be Labour in the future. Leadership after all is about meaning work. A co-responsible frame would assume that the failure of the Labour Party in this election is the result of many stakeholder groups failing in their responsibilities to each other. Such responsibilities are likely to include the lack of voice, dialogue, robust conversation with contested topics and forging of new understandings and action between the myriad of sub-groups and institutions that have formed the Labour tradition. Some of those conversations must be with those who do not choose to call themselves Labour at the moment, including the new United Kingdom Independence Party. 'Stakeholder' in this context has a complex meaning as who the stakeholders are in political movements and organisations in a moving, fluid, and ambiguous endeavour at best. To be honest, who is or is not a stakeholder is not as clear-cut and static as responsible leadership theory seems to assume. It is precisely this kind of discourse process that is most difficult for political parties to work through and sustain. In all likelihood if it cannot then the Labour party will seek another individual to take responsibility: one who might have the face, presentation, and words that will either win (or lose) a new generation of 'Labour'. Why though would the future of a party or movement be seen as the responsibility of an individual?

Our third story of the Blues rugby team proves itself to be a story of co-responsibility in action. Undoubtedly it shows the messiness and divisiveness of trying to create meaningful responsibility between stakeholders. On reading that story many will feel individual responsibility has a much more clear-cut and straightforward appeal. In a sense that would be correct. However, the prize for the Blues and rugby in general lies long beyond the results of one team over this particular season. Is it actually possible for the players to share responsibility and leadership of their aspirations and performance with coaching staff and Board? Is a different professional sports culture based on co-responsibility, shared community, and conversations even possible? Is it possible and desirable to transform the identity of coach, player, and Board member so that they become a different conversation community? Sir John Kirwan may be correct in asserting that the middle of such a paradigm change is no place to make a definitive call. The lure of defaulting back to far more traditional and individual notions of leadership is far too great where Sir John Kirwan would really only have one choice – resign like Ed Miliband – and indeed this is exactly what happened.

Co-responsible leadership in discourse, mindset, and practice

Co-responsible leadership requires a commitment to a new discourse, mindset, and set of practices. This section will detail what those could look like as a step to moving co-responsibility from theory to practice. The first step to doing this is to supply some new concepts and language with which to talk about co-responsibility. Earlier in this chapter we discussed the importance of being moral and forward-thinking to responsible leadership. One of the challenges we can put to co-responsibility is how it might characterize and action moral and forward-thinking. In order to do this we will turn back to sociology (Isaacs, 2011) and applied ethics (May & Hoffman, 1992).

Both Isaacs (2011) and May and Hoffman (1992) start their discussion with a relational ontology and the understanding of what being in community means. Isaac's (2011, p. 9) starting place is that 'we need to start understanding ourselves in relation to others, as members of communities who can act together as moral agents', while May and Hoffman explore community as a constitutive of an individual's identity, role, and action. Being moral if one's starting place is relationship or community takes on a different meaning. Joining a collective and choosing a community are moral acts in themselves. One cannot belong to a collective or community without having to engage with what that community thinks, voices, and acts. For Isaacs (2011, p. 9) this is a positive thing and she advocates 'we urgently need to start thinking of ourselves as implicated' in the understanding that 'an apathy permeates much of what we do; it is grounded in our inability – or perhaps our refusal – to see our actions in the broad context of the actions of others'. May and Hoffman (1992) don't believe such an engagement should be directly heroic, in the sense of having the direct responsibility to voice what those in power might not be inclined to hear. However, we all have the responsibility of not only being moral people with the capacity to voice what we need to but to create moral structures and institutions that will hear and work with counter perspectives. Co-responsibility then is not just directed at acts and other people but also at the constitution and change of our very systems which means it has a wide and powerful leadership mandate. Put simply, co-responsibility actually should have the effect of increasing leadership responsibility.

May and Hoffman (1992) draw on existentialism to involve the concept of metaphysical guilt as a core assumption of co-responsibility. Metaphysical responsibility arises from the very identity and membership of being implicated in a community. However, metaphysical responsibility is radically different from blame (or by association praise) because it is not 'based on a narrow construal of what one does, but rather on the wider concept of who one chooses to be' (May & Hoffman, 1992, p. 241). Who we choose to be involves not only what we do but what we don't do, how we feel or don't feel, and how we make sense or don't of what is happening. It means taking responsibility for who we are in a group, situation, or society and our stance to what is happening. Interestingly for leadership scholars and practitioners they evoke a much beloved construct in the leadership lexicon in the notion of authenticity to indicate responsibility for the overall way one approaches self in the world. Likewise Fillion (2004, p. 122) talks about responsibility as 'response-ability' to indicate an openness to experience that is forward-looking as opposed to 'account-ability' which is backwards-looking. 'Response-ability' invites each of us to view the nature of our response (or lack of response) as integral to any of the challenges and responsibilities we are part of by virtue of being a member of a group, team, organisation, sector, community or society. Our response or lack of it makes us complicit in the trajectory or an issue. If we feel the power of our own responses moment by moment then we cannot lay accountability elsewhere – it lies with our choices. As a rule of thumb, to live by 'response-ability' invites us into the leadership of what affects us. Imagine if we could live into such leadership?

We have moved a long way away from blame or praise as appropriate responses to metaphysical responsibility, but May and Hoffman (1992, p. 251) propose the word 'taint' as a word capable of carrying a sense of our complicity in anything connected to our community. Isaacs (2011, p. 145) further loads the dice by taking us through scenarios where individual bystanders might have a case for 'deciding not to act' but collectives of bystanders tend not to have any excuse. 'Failure to take action' Isaacs (2011, p. 145) is not excusable when one is tainted by one's choice to identify with a particular collective or community and, with others, doesn't contribute a voice or stance or action. Such an interpretation of taint and its associated co-responsibility would appear to speak directly to distributed and shared leadership where anyone in theory could and should lead by inserting themselves into the conversation and action that they are involved in.

Snell (2009, p. 13) sheds light on such a dynamic when she talks about 'responsibility chains' which show how responsibilities are distributed amongst people in connected endeavours. This work is important here because co-responsibility exists alongside traditional and post-traditional forms of responsibility as a set of responsibilities people tend to innately feel and exercise. Her work draws on a qualitative research project involving scientists and characterises four kinds of responsibility they articulated as being involved in:

1   role-bounded responsibility – a formal and technical form of responsibility related to whatever role they might have;
2   extended responsibility – responsibilities attributed to things beyond a role such as power, influence, or knowledge;
3   dispersed responsibility – responsibility for collective as opposed to individual activity;
4   challenging responsibility – a form of macro attention to the flow, dynamics, and framing of responsibility throughout an organisation or system.

Snell finds that people experience *responsibilities* (as opposed to *responsibility*) that invite them to engage in responsibility from individual, relational, and systems perspectives. There is something intuitively powerful about a multi-faceted experience of responsibility that calls multiple ways of being in leadership amongst a collective or community. This would appeal as a strong and meaningful platform on which to contemplate responsible leadership.

If we return to our three stories for one more time then we can show the impact of a more expansive and nuanced understanding of *responsibilities* that might provide something through which to look forward.

For instance the refugee crisis, while impacting European space now, should not be treated as a European crisis. It is a crisis which the EU is at the forefront of and needs to accept responsibility for leading forward on, but in itself it cannot be solved by either the EU or Europe. EU can and needs to mobilise a greater mass of stakeholders in order to build more possibilities and strategies for resolution. If the only possible responsibility is rejecting or accepting refugees then there is too constrained a leadership space. Other stakeholders need to be mobilised to shut down the people-smuggling trade, to provide a safe, unified pathway from flight to resettlement, to speed up the processing of people in refugee camps, to investigate safe zones or terrains within conflicted territories or to create temporary, fluid communities/ societies/citzenship who can cluster and contribute to societies needing new expertise, energy, and rejuvenation whilst they are unable to remain in their current homes. Such a strange mixture of concurrent responses require all manner of people, institutions, agencies, and societies to recognise and claim multiple responsibilities in this challenge. There is work for individual leaders in this, but within a connected network holding the leadership of the whole system or challenge. One could imagine Greece taking responsibility for the people smuggling gangs, the UK developing a speedy processing system regardless of whatever camp a refugee ended up in, and Jordan setting up a collaboration responsible for a safe zone in the conflict terrain.

The British Labour Party has acted on one of Snell's four responsibilities: role-bounded responsibility. Engaging with the other three holds the promise of radically redefining its 'responsibility chain'. Attention to power, influence, and knowledge will help them understand dynamics of responsibility that aren't visible if one apportions responsibility just to those in positions. Attention to co- or dispersed responsibility will reveal a myriad of moments where those not choosing to speak or act narrowed down the possibilities for party action too much. Attention to challenging responsibility holds the hope of building a party structure or system that constitutes a different paradigm of what it means to be

Labour and who is heard in that. It is time to stop searching for the right leader and instead search for what it means to be Labour now and in the future in the very grassroots of the political terrain. Youth may do so through virtual discussion boards, party faithful through committees and meetings, 'agnostic' voters through media and so on. 'A' leader seems a poor option compared to distributed responsibility in multiple stakeholders.

Sir John Kirwan and the Blues have the nightmare of intense media scrutiny and what amounts to a public trial of their experiment in collective responsibility. Their challenge perhaps is integrating both forward-looking response-ability and backwards-looking accountability. Missing from public accounts at any rate is any visibility of the player voice on which movement to co-/collective responsibility depends. They need to assess that they have a structure and community which enables that voice. Other voices, particularly development and community voices, seem too quiet as well. Snell (2009) points out that responsibilities get fragmented where there is no strong and articulated vision and aspiration which focuses responsibilities. What is their vision of rugby in the future that invites a different kind of responsible leadership? What responsibilities could players take outside of their own performance? Given coaching teams operate around head coaches then what would coaching team responsibilities look like? What are the integration mechanisms that bring together aspirations in terms of identity, culture, finance, performance, development, and community reach? Winning games may be non-negotiable but what needs to come together from increasingly corporate looking enterprises to constitute that winning? Who is the contemporary coach co-responsible with?

Conclusion

This chapter has aimed to take responsible leadership seriously and assess its potential to refine and extend what must be one of the most important constructs in leadership in responsibility. Understanding leadership in relation to stakeholders and complex societal issues seems bold, audacious, and a real shift in how leadership has been approached and understood. Yet embarking on such a shift with traditional and leader-centric notions intact seems too limiting of the theoretical and experiential complexity associated with responsibility. Consequently this chapter has tried to develop and extend responsible leadership theory through attention to philosophical and sociological definitional debates of responsibility, typologies of responsibilities, particularly co-responsibility, and new discourses, mindsets, and practices that enact responsibility. At the very least the movement from responsibility to responsibilities over the course of this chapter could provide a richer, more textured, and challenging terrain for responsible leadership theory into the future.

In the overall tension weaving through this book between romanticism and realism then this chapter possibly zig zags between both. It doesn't seem realistic, given both the complex and often ambiguous nature of contemporary challenges and issues and attention to multiple stakeholders, to view leadership predominantly as the province of leaders – particularly leaders designated by position. In bringing in stakeholders one is creating a multi-leader scenario where leadership needs to be understood in more sophisticated relational, network terms. However, there is something about communitarian notions of morality, metaphysical guilt, co-responsibility, and being defined by what one doesn't say or do that surely does seems romantic. Perhaps responsible leadership is a rare phenomenon in which realism and romanticism need to be intertwined? Hopefully that is the overall effect of this chapter: first, a reality check on a theory which needs to be more courageous in rethinking some of the assumptions it has taken through from previous leadership schools; and second, dare we say it, more ideals that take seriously the distributed nature of networks and stakeholder interactions and create a language, mindset, and set of assumptions that might enable a different way of leading responsibly for those involved.

References

Apel, K.-O. (1993). How to ground a universalistic ethics of co-responsibility for the effects of collective actions and activities? *Philosophica, 52*, 9–29.

Caruana, R., & Crane, A. (2008). Constructing consumer responsibility: Exploring the role of corporate communications. *Organization Studies, 29*(12), 1495–1519.

Fillion, R. (2004). Freedom, responsibility, and the 'American Foucault'. *Philosophy & Social Criticism, 30*(1), 115–126.

French, P. (1972). *Individual and collective responsibility: The massacre at My Lai.* Cambridge, MA: Schenkman.

Isaacs, T. L. (2011). *Moral responsibility in collective contexts.* Oxford; New York: Oxford University Press.

Jonas, H. (1984). *The imperative of responsibility: In search of an ethics for the technological age.* Chicago: University of Chicago Press.

Maak, T., & Pless, N. M. (2006). Responsible leadership in a stakeholder society: A relational perspective. *Journal of Business Ethics, 66*(1), 99–115.

May, L., & Hoffman, S. (1992). *Collective responsibility: Five decades of debate in theoretical and applied ethics.* Savage, MD: Rowman & Littlefield.

McAdam, D., McCarthy, J. D., & Zald, M. N. (1996). *Comparative perspectives on social movements: Political opportunities, mobilizing structures, and cultural framings.* Cambridge, UK; New York: Cambridge University Press.

McCarthy, E., & Kelty, C. (2010). Responsibility and nanotechnology. *Social Studies of Science, 40,* 405–432.

Pless, N. M. (2007). Understanding responsible leadership: Role identity and motivational drivers. *Journal of Business Ethics, 74*(4), 437–456.

Pless, N. M., & Maak, T. (2011). Responsible leadership: Pathways to the future. *Journal of Business Ethics, 98*(1), 3–13.

Popke, E. J. (2003). Poststructuralist ethics: Subjectivity, responsibility and the space of community. *Progress in Human Geography, 27*(3), 298–316.

Snell, K. (2009). *Social responsibility in developing new biotechnology: Interpretations of responsibility in the governance of Finnish biotechnology.* PhD, University of Helsinki, Helsinki.

Strydom, P. (1999). The challenge of responsibility for sociology. *Current Sociology, 47*(3), 65–82.

Voegtlin, C., Patzer, M., & Scherer, A. G. (2012). Responsible leadership in global business: A new approach to leadership and its multi-level outcomes. *Journal of Business Ethics, 105*(1), 1–16.

Waldman, D. A. (2011). Moving forward with the concept of responsible leadership: Three caveats to guide theory and research. *Journal of Business Ethics, 98*(1), 75–83.

Waldman, D. A., & Galvin, B. M. (2008). Alternative perspectives of responsible leadership. *Organizational Dynamics, 37*(4), 327–341.

Part II

Connecting responsible leadership theory to practice

4   This green pastoral landscape

Values, responsible leadership, and the romantic imagination

Sarah Lee and Malcolm Higgs

In many ways, values represent a concept dear to the romantic writers' hearts – one that corresponds with their emphasis on the personal, the ideal, and the transcendent. The aspirational nature and content of values is in tune with the romantic optimism and belief in the possibility of progress and improvement, both for individuals and for society. Perhaps ironically, the thrust of contemporary values scholarship has been towards the scientific definition, operationalisation, and measurement of this elusive concept: the aim of social psychological research on values has been to bring the 'fuzzy' nature of values (Cha & Edmondson, 2006, p. 71) into sharper focus, in order to demonstrate their utility to our understanding of individual and collective behaviour. More broadly, personal and societal values – or the lack of them – are the frequent subject of media attention and popular debate. Rallying cries for a return to 'traditional' values are made with scant insight into the nature and development of values and the complexities of values change in practice.

In the organisational context, similar paradoxes emerge. Writers in the 'culture-excellence' tradition regard shared values as a powerful lever in the development of a cohesive culture. Peters and Waterman (1982) specifically refer to values as representing the core of corporate culture, and they associate (shared) values with corporate success. For Collins and Porras (1996, 2000), values of visionary organisations are characterised as timeless guiding principles, which reflect how the organisation 'should' behave, albeit according to the organisation's own definition of what is right. On the one hand, values may be regarded simply – and cynically – as normative devices deployed in culture management programmes to focus employee effort on organisational success, measured by stakeholder return. At the same time, values that are publicly stated and, crucially, personally enacted by organisational leaders may equally represent a genuine commitment to 'do good' behaviour (Stahl & De Luque, 2014, p. 238) directed at a range of stakeholders. Such discretionary and principled behaviour is regarded as a facet of 'integrative' responsible leadership (Pless, Maak, & Waldman, 2012). For employees, the prospect of working for an organisation whose values and working practices align with personal values and standards is an attractive one, promising a sense of mutuality, purpose, and identity at work (O'Reilly, Chatman, & Caldwell, 1991).

Values have also become a familiar part of leadership discourse, not only in those leadership forms that may be loosely coupled under the popular term *values-based leadership* (Kraemer, 2011), such as ethical and authentic leadership (Brown & Treviño, 2006; Gardner, Cogliser, Davis, & Dickens, 2011), but also in connection with the burgeoning literature on corporate social responsibility (see Aguinis & Glavas, 2012). Values appear equally relevant to responsible leadership, and yet questions remain about the nature of personal and organisational values and their role in 'real world' responsible leadership development and practice.

In this chapter we explore these aspects through an examination of the personal values concept and its application to organisational settings. In the course of the discussion, we make links between personal values theory and the practice of leadership in organisations that espouse a strong, values-based culture. In exploring the theoretical foundations of values research, we draw out three key questions for responsible leadership development and practice. In particular:

1   How far does responsible leadership involve enabling employees to fulfil their personal values at work?
2   How can responsible leaders equip managers to deal with value conflicts?
3   How can responsible leaders foster organisational integrity, and how should they respond when integrity breaches occur?

We conclude by suggesting possible ways to approach these issues, thereby contributing a values perspective to contemporary debates on responsible leadership development and research.

It is beyond the scope and intention of this chapter to re-examine the concept of responsible leadership, which has been explored in detail by our fellow contributors in this volume. Suffice to say that we lean firmly towards the 'extended stakeholder' view of responsible leadership identified by Waldman and Galvin (2008), which includes consideration of the needs of a range of constituencies inside and outside the organisation. We also include discretionary, welfare-enhancing activities (Stahl & De Luque, 2014) in our conception of the term, while accepting the *sine qua non* that the organisation must remain economically viable. Like Crilly, Schneider, and Zollo (2008), we consider that while responsible leadership may be based on moral idealism, it is equally based in 'the capacity to take realistic decisions given various situational constraints' (Crilly *et al.*, 2008, p. 176) – a marrying of the romanticist and the realist.

The 'reality' of personal values

Values are popularly conceived as timeless, guiding principles, linked in some way to behaviours and feelings, and fundamental to our understanding of what it is to be human (Rohan, 2000). A person's idiosyncratic set of value priorities may be regarded as in some way expressive of his or her identity, giving a sense of coherence over time and across situations. Indeed, Maslow (1962) states that the search for identity is effectively a search for one's intrinsic and authentic values. Values are experienced as 'deeply propriate' (Allport, 1961, p. 454) even though they are socially patterned and communicated. However, the self-expressive nature of values is only one facet of the values concept. Schwartz and Bilsky (1987) list five characteristics of values commonly found in the psychological literature: they (1) are cognitive concepts or beliefs, (2) refer to desirable end states or behaviours, (3) transcend specific situations, (4) guide the selection and evaluation of behaviour and events, and (5) are ordered by relative importance. As 'criteria or standards of preference' (Williams, 1979, p. 16) values guide people's judgement about desirable or undesirable ways of behaving, and about the desirability or otherwise of general goals.

Experimental research has identified a connection between value preferences and preferred courses of action (Feather, 1995, 1996), and yet the relationship between values and behaviour remains controversial. Influential values scholar Rokeach (1968, 1973) argued that values constitute the organising principles for thousands of beliefs and attitudes, and that they have a direct influence on attitudinal and behavioural outcomes. His contemporary, Williams (1979), commented however that *only a maniac or a saint* will always act consistently in terms of a simple, prearranged hierarchy of value preferences. Although the idea of values as guiding forces for behaviour is intuitively appealing, it remains difficult to demonstrate empirically (Kristiansen & Hotte, 1996). Like Robertson and Callinan (1998), we regard values as one of a number of elements involved in cognitive-affective mediating processes which, together with a contingent combination of other situational factors, influence behaviour. Nevertheless, as we explain later in the chapter, the idea that values shape attitudes and behaviour has captured the imagination of writers on organisational culture and leadership, whether in pursuit of profit maximisation or wider ethical concerns.

An ongoing challenge for values researchers is that values, like personality, are latent constructs; they are not observable. Therefore, we can only make inferences about values manifested in action, or rely on people's conscious awareness of their values and their ability or willingness to articulate them. A further challenge is that values are used as socially or personally acceptable ways of justifying actions: people use them to convince themselves and others that they are acting in accordance with sound moral or ethical principles, thereby addressing the fundamental self-motive of self-esteem maintenance or enhancement (Sedikides, 1993). When asked to account for their behaviour in value-based terms, people often fall back on platitudes or truisms which lack cognitive support (Maio, Olson, Allen, & Bernard, 2001). This perhaps reflects the way in which values are taught from infancy as moral absolutes.

Although generally conceived as cognitive structures, it is clear that values have strong, positive emotional associations. Kluckhorn (1951, p. 400) speaks of 'the union of reason and feeling inherent in the word value' and, more recently, Hitlin (2003, p. 132) describes values as 'emotion-laden conceptions of the desirable'. We *feel* attached to our values, and indeed inducing people to consider logically the *reasons* why they place importance on a particular value can result in value change (Maio & Olson, 1998). Moreover, the pure and aspirational nature of values speaks to the romantic imagination and desire for freedom of expression, as evoked in Wordsworth's 'Lines Composed a Few Miles above Tintern Abbey':

> ... to recognize
> In nature and the language of the sense,
> The anchor of my purest thoughts, the nurse,
> The guide, the guardian of my heart, and soul
> Of all my moral being.
> (Wordsworth, 1798, p. 201)

For example, Rokeach's (1973) list of terminal values – those which reflect desirable end states of existence – includes items such as a world at peace; equality; mature love; and a world of beauty, nature, and the arts.

The romanticist rejection of rationality and scientific dogma is far removed from the dominant paradigm in values research, which is based on the use of quantitative methods, survey instruments, and experimental approaches. We suggest that the *meaning* that values hold for individuals, and the operation of values in real-life contexts, may have been overlooked as a consequence of this positivistic approach. Nevertheless, values research has been hugely facilitated and given impetus by the development and validation of a universal structure of values and associated measures (Schwartz, 1992). In Schwartz's theory, values are classified into ten types, each representing a cluster of single values, based on the overarching motivational goal they express. His model, shown in Figure 4.1, represents the value types in a circular structure, which depicts the relationships between them. Values which express complementary motives are placed in adjacent positions, and values that express conflicting motives are placed opposite each other.[1]

Two motivational dimensions are also shown in Figure 4.1, which express conflict between opposing, higher-order value types or orientations. One dimension contrasts self-enhancement values, which promote self-interest, with self-transcendent values, which emphasise the welfare of others. The second contrasts conservation values, which focus on certainty and the status quo, with openness values, which are concerned with pursuit of self-directed interests in unpredictable or uncertain directions. Although the *structure* of values is universal, people differ in the *priority* they assign to particular values.

Having delved into the values concept in some detail, we now focus on three specific aspects of values theory and indicate their relevance to organisational membership and leadership. These are: (1) the relationship between values, needs fulfilment, and optimal functioning; (2) the conflicting nature of

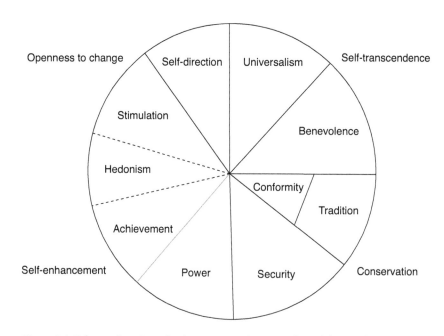

Figure 4.1 Schwartz's universal value structure (source: adapted from Schwartz, 1992).

values; and (3) organisational values and integrity. We use the discussion of these areas to identify three particular and significant challenges for responsible leadership development and practice that are generally neglected in broader discussions of organisational values, social responsibility, and ethics.

Values, needs fulfilment, and optimal functioning

Interestingly, given the underlying positivist assumptions of psychological values research, Schwartz's operationalisation of the values system concept was informed by Maslovian humanist theory, which is based on the idea of a growth–oriented self and the inherent human drive to satisfy basic, universal needs. Indeed, Maslow describes his theory as 'a theory of the ends and ultimate values of the organism' (1970, p. 35), and states that people's value priorities relate to their needs priorities in the hierarchy. According to Rokeach (1973), values do represent needs and yet they also represent societal or institutional demands, which are internalised through socialisation and cognitively transformed into values. That is, values incorporate external normative influences but they are experienced as personally owned. More broadly, adopting the value priorities of a group or institution can be regarded as means of maximising the opportunity for (socially sanctioned) advancement and recognition, while also deriving sense of security and acceptance.

It is notable that Rokeach appears to differentiate between the motivational drive to satisfy needs, and the cultivation of self-esteem – 'the sentiment of self-regard' (Rokeach, 1968, p. 132) – even though the latter is itself defined as a fundamental human need (Maslow, 1943):

> The ultimate function of values is to provide us with a set of standards to guide us in all our efforts to satisfy our needs and at the same time maintain, and, in so far as possible, enhance self-esteem, that is, to make it possible to regard ourselves and to be regarded by others as having satisfied societally and institutionally originating definitions of morality and competence.
>
> (Rokeach, 1979, p. 48)

This emphasis on values as essentially self-serving devices seems, at first glance, to be directly at odds with the notion of values as noble, higher principles. Indeed, it is the opposing, altruistic idea of self-transcendence – putting the needs and welfare of others before one's self-interest – which is often tacitly assumed in the leadership and organisational values literature (see Argandona, 2003).

Self-determination theory (SDT; Ryan, 1995; Ryan & Deci, 2002) shares Maslow's (1970) conception of the self as actively seeking to fulfil its potential and to satisfy its innate, motivational needs. Focusing on psychological rather than physiological needs, an essential proposition of SDT is the desirability of behaviours that arise from natural inclinations and interests, and goals that are pursued for their own sake (*intrinsic* motivation) rather than for reasons external to the self (*extrinsic* motivation). Intrinsically motivated behaviour represents a prototype of *self-determined behaviour*. It best fulfils the three psychological needs of competence, relatedness, and autonomy,[2] and is associated with healthy psychological functioning and 'true' self-esteem (Ryan & Deci, 2003). There is a parallel here with Rohan's (2000, p. 264) contention that personal value systems are a means of ordering the requirements or desires which are more or less important to *best possible living*: one's value priorities represent a personal view of what it means to live 'as pleasantly and productively as possible', and they function to guide activity towards this aspiration. Waterman (1993) associates best possible living with fulfilling one's potential and optimal psychological functioning, rather than merely meeting basic survival needs and avoiding pain. As such, it relates to the Aristotelian concept of *eudaimonia*, which Waterman interprets as achieving self-realisation and personal expressiveness: 'What is considered worth desiring and having in life is the best within us or personal excellence' (ibid., p. 678). The idea of optimal functioning is found elsewhere within humanist psychology as self-actualisation (Maslow, 1962) and full functioning (Rogers, 1961), and is a key tenet of positive psychology (Seligman, 2003). Thus, in a sense, enacting one's values priorities represents the kind of Utopia which exists only in the romantic imagination, where:

...neither evil tongues,
Rash judgements, nor the sneers of selfish men,
Nor greetings where no kindness is, nor all
The dreary intercourse of daily life,
Shall e'er prevail against us, or disturb
Our cheerful faith, that all which we behold
Is full of blessings.

(Wordsworth, 1798, p. 201)

Of course, reality intervenes, and individuals rarely have complete freedom to choose their activities – particularly in organisational settings (Gagné & Deci, 2005). Extrinsically motivated behaviours are conceived in SDT as varying in the extent to which they are experienced as autonomous and authentic. The most autonomous behaviour occurs when external rules and norms are internally assimilated through a process of internalisation, so that they become self-regulated and ultimately integrated into the individual's sense of self and personal values. At the other end of the continuum, behaviour is regulated by intra-psychic means – to avoid guilt or anxiety or to maintain a positive self-view – or undertaken to comply with external demands in order to avoid sanction or to gain (extrinsic) reward or recognition. SDT also emphasises the importance of the social context (e.g. the organisation) in helping or hindering the individual's ability to act with autonomy and self-integrity. Thus, SDT explains why acting in accordance with personal values, in an environment that is conducive to doing so, leads to positive outcomes for the self.

This brings us to our first challenge for responsible leadership development and practice:

How far does responsible leadership involve enabling employees to fulfil their personal values at work?

Safeguarding the health and safety of employees is, of course, at its basic level, a legally defined obligation for organisations and their leaders. However, in the context of our discretionary conception of responsible leadership, the theoretical and empirical linkages between values fulfilment and psychological wellbeing suggests a deeper level of responsibility to engage with employees *at the level of their personal value priorities*. This has immediate implications not only for managers in the context of skills and career development discussions with reportees, but also for organisation-wide human resource management processes.

The conflicting nature of values

Conflict between values is inevitable. Schwartz's values structure represents 'the relations of conflict and compatibility among values' (Schwartz, 1992, p. 3), and the higher level dimensions (openness to change/conservation and self-interest/self-transcendence) represent polar opposite orientations. In formulating a personal value system, the individual must make choices about the relative importance of different and potentially competing values, and these choices represent trade-offs or concessions – giving priority to a particular value at the expense of another (Tetlock, 1986). The notion of a relatively stable personal value system, which guides behaviour and decision-making, often without awareness (Sagiv & Schwartz, 1995), perhaps belies the reality of everyday decisions and dilemmas, which have value-based implications and cannot easily be resolved. Schwartz (1996, p. 2) suggests that values are likely to be activated and to enter awareness in the presence of values conflicts. However, this does not necessarily mean that the conflict can be dissipated with no personal cost: confronting values conflicts may involve making a choice supportive of one or more values but opposed to others, which are also important to the individual.

It may be intuitively appealing to act in accordance with higher principles, which represent best possible living and ideal self-standards, but in reality, normative pressures and other situational factors intervene. When faced with a difficult decision and multiple, competing pressures, values, as *abstract* conceptions of the desirable (Kluckhorn, 1951), may not suggest a clear way forward. What might be desirable in theory may not be viable in practice: a fundamental tension between the *romanticist* and the *realist*.

Importantly for this discussion, conflict between values may result from a discrepancy between an individual's personal value priorities and his or her perception of the value priorities of others – termed *social value systems* (Rohan, 2000). While people have only one personal value system, they are likely to have multiple social value systems, such as work team and organisation. Discrepancies between one's own and others' values are essentially conflicts between two cognitions, resulting in dissonance or unpleasant psychological tension (Festinger, 1957). Faced with such a conflict, people must decide whether to conform to others' expectations (social value system priorities) or to their personal value system priorities. This is neither a new nor a tractable problem: Allport (1955, p. 39) described the reconciliation of 'the personal' and 'the tribal' as an ongoing process.

In addition to the personal and situational factors that bring value conflicts to the fore, we consider that role and organisational structure are highly relevant to an individual's experience of value conflicts and to his or her choice of responses. This is particularly the case for those in first-line and middle management roles, who occupy a 'betwixt and between' (Hallier & James, 1997, p. 707) position in the organisational hierarchy, between their reportees and senior leaders. Indeed, the need to reconcile conflicting forces, interests, and ideals is a recurrent feature of management literature over a number of decades (Barnard, 1938; Hill, 2003; Watson, 1994). Managers have to make difficult decisions, often based on incomplete information, which have unpredictable (and moral) consequences (Illies & Reiter-Palmon, 2008; Mintzberg, 2009). At the same time, managers' accountabilities to a wide range of stakeholders inside and outside of the organisation inevitably involve trade-offs between different values and expectations. For instance, managers are expected to endorse and implement organisational strategies and policies, which may be at odds with their personal value priorities or have negative implications for their team. They need to be able to assess what is the 'right' thing to do (Caldwell, 2010) with reference to their personal values as well as the values and normative expectations of the organisation, higher-level managers, peers, and reportees. Therefore, we suggest a second challenge for responsible leadership development and practice, which is especially relevant to *senior* leaders:

How can responsible leaders equip managers to deal with value conflicts?

There is little doubt that the psychological consequences of managers' decisions, such as guilt and emotional distress, raise moral concerns of their own in terms of a responsible leader's obligations to this important stakeholder group. Managers' concerns about the potential detrimental personal and career consequences of not conforming to organisational demands can result in value conflicts being left unresolved over a period of time. Ultimately, unreconciled value conflicts may lead to 'value crisis' (Hermans & Oles, 1996), with deleterious psychological consequences.

However, as well as highlighting a concern for the psychological effects of dealing with value conflicts, our challenge has implications for responsible leadership practice at all levels of the organisation. Shared or distributed conceptions of leadership (Gronn, 2002; Pearce & Conger, 2003; Pearce, Manz, & Sims, 2008) have contributed to a shift in emphasis away from leadership as the sole preserve of top executives (Avolio, Walumbwa, & Weber, 2009) towards the idea of leadership as a social process (Pearce & Conger, 2003). Indeed, most managers regard leadership as a necessary component of their role (Hill, 2003; Mintzberg, 2009; Watson, 1994), specifically concerned with facilitating and influencing peoples' effective functioning in support of organisational goals. As close or nearby leaders (Alimo-Metcalfe & Alban-Metcalfe, 2001; Shamir, 1995), managers are role models for employees 'whether they like it or not' (Pearce & Manz, 2014, p. 222), and thus their responses to value conflicts will, in turn, influence behaviour throughout the organisation.

Writing about managers and morality, Watson (2003, p. 177) refers to one manager's comment that you cannot be ethically pure in management work: 'you just have to make the best of things, given the circumstances and given your own moral values'. Arguably, managers represent a marrying of idealism and pragmatism, in the very fact that they *have* to become adept at making decisions, often under time pressure, that inevitably have moral implications even if they are not perceived as major ethical dilemmas. As Watson (2006, p. 272) points out:

> Managers' own values and their 'theories' about what will 'work' in the managerial context have been shown to be very closely connected:

morality and pragmatism are tightly interrelated in the way managers 'think'.

However, for organisations that wish to develop a consistent stance towards ethical and (socially) responsible decision-making at all leadership levels, it is insufficient to leave managers to find their own brand of pragmatic morality.

Organisational values and integrity

While we, along with a number of others (e.g. Morgan, 1986; Reichers, 1985; Smircich, 1983), question the unitary assumptions of much of the organisational culture literature, undoubtedly there is widespread acceptance of the normative functions of organisational culture and values. According to Schein (1997) the personal values of an organisation's founder or top leader are transformed into shared values through collective experience of their effectiveness, and these may over time be incorporated into shared basic assumptions. The normative powers of shared (ethical) values are also a feature of the ethical leadership and corporate governance literatures. These tend to contrast 'values-and-integrity' approaches with those based on compliance or 'command-and-control', although Treviño, Weaver, Gibson, and Toffler (1999) noted that the majority of Fortune 1000 companies combine both approaches. Verhezen (2010, p. 190) contrasts a *culture of compliance* with a *culture of integrity* and argues for the desirability of moving from the former to the latter:

> A movement beyond a purely compliance oriented *modus operandi* is important: mandates may achieve compliance, but such a compliance that may remain half-hearted, foot-dragging, and resentful. Cooperation is realized more enduringly and more fully by fostering commitments to shared moral values.

In many ways, an organisation's stated or *espoused* values represent a statement of its aspirations – a romantic, idealised vision of a better way of working and engaging with stakeholders and, in many cases, with wider society. *Values-based* decision-making has become synonymous with socially responsible decision-making (Urbany, Reynolds, & Phillips, 2008), and Collins and Porras (1994, pp. 73–74) notably describe an organisation's values and purpose as its core ideology: guiding principles that are not compromised for the sake of short-term expediency or financial gain, and fundamental reasons for existence beyond just making money – 'a perpetual guiding star on the horizon'. However, leaving aside the rhetoric of the romantic imagination, it is clear that, in practice, the organisation's *espoused* values all too often differ from the values implicit in day-to-day organisational decisions and actions – the *enacted* values (Argyris, 1990; Rohan, 2000).

A number of authors question whether formal values statements have any bearing on management decision-making (Johnson, Scholes, & Whittington,

2008; Murphy, 1995; Shapiro, 1995). Indeed, published lists of values often serve more of a symbolic role as part of an externally oriented public relations strategy (Stevens, Steensma, Harrison, & Cochran, 2005). Organisational values statements may give rise to employee cynicism and expose senior management to accusations of hypocrisy when they are perceived as failing to live up to these values (Urbany, 2005). Moreover, organisations that fail to enact their stated values are likely to undermine the credibility of the values themselves in the eyes of employees, diminishing their anticipated positive effects on outcomes such as employee commitment and motivation. Cha and Edmondson's (2006) research in an advertising firm found that employees made attributions of hypocrisy when they perceived the CEO had acted inconsistently with his espoused values, and the authors suggested that the results of this 'negative sensemaking' (ibid., p. 73) process were likely to undermine the positive effects of strong organisational values that have been indicated by charismatic leadership research.

Consistency between espoused and enacted values perhaps *feels* desirable because it is associated with the concept of *integrity*, which is generally regarded as 'a good thing' (Audi & Murphy, 2006; Koehn, 2005). Indeed, integrity is the value most frequently included in corporate values statements and is found regularly in company mission statements and codes of conduct (Audi & Murphy, 2006). Leader behavioural integrity has been linked conceptually with trust formation (Simons, 2002), and found empirically to have a strong positive correlation with trust (Simons, Friedman, Liu, & Parks, 2007) and employee attitudes such as job satisfaction and organisational commitment (Davis & Rothstein, 2006). We adopt Palanski and Yammarino's (2009) definition of organisational integrity as *word-action consistency*, which specifically includes enacting stated values and keeping promises. There is thus a double irony should an organisation that includes integrity in its formal values statement then fail to live up to its own values (see Chapter 6 in this volume, for discussions on such examples).

The issues outlined above point to the need for responsible leaders to consider the effect on stakeholders of (perceived or actual) mismatches between espoused and enacted values. These represent breaches of integrity and, as such, risk undermining credibility and trust. Therefore, our third and final challenge for responsible leadership development and practice is as follows:

How can responsible leaders foster organisational integrity, and how should managers respond when integrity breaches occur?

As in the previous discussion of value conflicts, role and organisational structure are highly relevant here. Lack of organisational integrity has particular implications for first-line and middle managers, who are intermediaries between the organisation (personified by its executive leaders) and non-managerial employees. These managers typically operate with limited autonomy and little influence over the actions and decisions of senior leaders or the way in which these are communicated. Nevertheless, their role involves a form of sense-making for employees, interpreting seeming inconsistent events to create coherence and meaning (Balogun & Johnson, 2004; Beck & Plowman, 2009; Weick, 1995). Indeed, Palanski and Yammarino (2009, p. 418) suggest that it is often first-line and middle managers who are responsible for resolving 'cross-level integrity conflicts', choosing whether to prioritise their own integrity above defending that of the organisation.

Values and leadership frames of reference

The personal values of leaders, and the way in which these are used to shape the values of the organisation and the behaviour of employees, are common features of a number of strands of literature, particularly in connection with leadership influencing processes (Lord & Brown, 2001; Shamir, House, & Arthur, 1993; Sosik, 2005). In charismatic leadership, for example, the values invoked by (top) leaders form part of their compelling vision of the organisation, motivating followers, and enhancing trust, commitment, and performance (Bass & Steidlmeier, 1999; Boal & Bryson, 1988; Conger, Kanungo, & Menon, 2000). Conceptualisations of ethical leadership typically emphasise the personal values, principles, and moral character of leaders (Brown & Treviño, 2006), and how, as *moral managers* (Treviño, Hartman, & Brown, 2000) or *ethical stewards* (Caldwell, Hayes, Karri, & Bernal, 2008), they enact and embed them in organisational settings.

Personal values feature, too, in models of authentic leadership (Avolio & Gardner, 2005; Gardner, Avolio, Luthans, May, & Walumbwa, 2005; May, Chan, Hodges, & Avolio, 2003; Walumbwa, Avolio, Gardner, Wernsing, & Peterson, 2008): authentic leaders act in accord with their values, making balanced and principled decisions rather than acting for political ends or to conform to others' expectations (George, Sims, McLean, & Mayer, 2007; Ilies, Morgeson, & Nahrgang, 2005). Here, the emphasis is on remaining true to oneself and one's principles in order to do what is right. Similarly, Kraemer's (2011) four principles of (ethical) values-based leadership comprise self-reflection, balance and perspective, true self-confidence, and genuine humility. Role-modelling values-congruent behaviour is a key component of leadership influencing behaviour in these and a number of other leadership frameworks, including ethical and transformational leadership (Avolio & Gardner, 2005).

Authentic behaviour has been argued to be essential to success in many situations, notably in the context of change implementation (Rowland & Higgs, 2008). The components of authentic leadership include self-awareness, self-regulation, relational transparency, and a clear moral compass (Avolio *et al.*, 2009; Gardner *et al.*, 2005; Walumbwa *et al.*, 2008). These relate clearly to research that points to the importance of self-awareness as a core component of effective leadership (Higgs & Rowland, 2010; Tekleab, Sims Jr, Tesluk, Yun, & Cox, 2008) and the linkages between emotional intelligence and leadership (Goleman, 1996; Higgs & Dulewicz, 2002).

However, the prime focus of much writing on authentic leadership, along with other leadership forms, remains rooted in the 'heroic' or 'larger-than-life' (Meindl, Ehrlich, & Dukerich, 1985) archetype, in relation to executive leaders (e.g. George, 2003), although Avolio *et al.* (2009) suggest that there is a need to ensure that leadership is executed in an authentic manner within any framework. The development of shared or distributed and relational leadership models (Gronn, 2002; Pearce, Hoch, Jeppesen, & Wegge, 2011; Uhl-Bien, 2006; Yukl, 2010), and the emergent interest, noted by Kempster and Carroll in the opening chapter of this book in more situated, participatory forms of leadership practice, present a challenge for authentic leadership: unlike chief executives, those at lower levels of the organisation may not have the authority to act on their principles, nor feel the freedom to be their 'true self' at work.

Having established the significance of values for individuals, for organisations, and for leadership behaviours, we now return to the overarching theme of this book by considering the relevance of leader and organisational values to the responsible leadership construct. We then revisit the three challenges for responsible leadership identified earlier in the chapter and explore how a values perspective may help go some way in addressing them.

Personal values and responsible leadership

Whether one takes a more limited economic/strategic view or a more extended stakeholder view of the responsible leadership construct, there is little doubt that any discussion of leadership obligations and accountabilities to others involves underlying assumptions about values and morality. It is, therefore, not surprising that the leader characteristics identified by Stahl and De Luque (2014) as antecedents of responsible leadership behaviour in their theoretical model include personal values and beliefs. In drawing on ideas from the literature on ethical decision-making and ethical leadership (e.g. Ciulla, Uhl-Bien, & Werhane, 2013; De Cremer, van Dick, Tenbrunsel, Pillutla, & Murnighan, 2011; Ford & Richardson, 1994; Mumford, Helton, Decker, Connelly, & Van Doorn, 2003; Yukl, Mahsud, Prussia, & Hassan, 2013), responsible leadership includes consideration of individual level attributes, such as personality traits (Kalshoven, Den Hartog, & De Hoogh, 2011) and character (Wright & Quick, 2011) as well as behaviours and competencies (Resick Martin, Keating, Dickson, Kwan, & Peng, 2011; Treviño *et al.*, 2000). From their review of the literature, Hind, Wilson, & Lenssen (2009) identified 30 attributes of responsible leaders, which include personal qualities, such as honesty and trustworthiness; and behaviours, such as willingness to act on criticism and not making unrealistic demands on self and others. These attributes clearly relate to the Schwartz (1992) self-transcendence higher-order value type. Similarly, Crilly *et al.*'s (2008) survey of middle managers in five multinational corporations found that self-transcendence values (universalism and benevolence), along with other factors, including positive affect and moral/reputation-based reasoning, increased the propensity to engage in socially responsible behaviours. In their broad conception of global responsible leadership, Maak and Pless (2009, p. 539) emphasise that responsible leadership needs to be driven by 'ethical principles and values that enable both leader and followers to find a common meaning and purpose, such as contributing to a sustainable future or assisting the distant needy'.

Because the notion of responsible leadership has clear moral and ethical associations, by implication it draws elements from those leadership frames of reference which are concerned with acting on personal values and convictions, such as authentic leadership (Gardner *et al.*, 2011); or with service to others, wisdom and connection with humanity, such as servant and spiritual leadership (Fry, 2003; Karakas, 2010; Liden, Wayne, Zhao, & Henderson, 2008; Spears & Lawrence, 2002). These typically emphasise leader attributes such as humility, capacity for self-reflection, integrity, and respect for others. For example, servant leadership stresses personal integrity and focuses on forming long-term relationships with employees and stakeholders outside the organisation, including communities and society as a whole (Liden *et al.*, 2008). Therefore, a view emerges of responsible leadership as a fundamentally values-based form of leadership: one which involves 'knowing our core values and exercising desirable ones appropriately and consistently' (Peregrym & Wollf, 2013, p. 5).

The personal values of leaders also enter the responsible leadership discourse from the literature on corporate social responsibility (CSR), which aligns with the 'discretionary responsibility' responsible leadership mind-set (Stahl & De Luque, 2014). For example, research has linked leader deontological ethical values (i.e. altruism and universalism) with follower beliefs in the stakeholder view of CSR (Groves & LaRocca, 2011). Waldman, de Sully, Nathan, and House (2006) argue that the values used by managers use to guide their decision-making are critical for insight into CSR practices, because organisational-level actions are, at least partially, the product of managerial decisions and discretion.

Organisational values and responsible leadership

Just as *personal* values enter into the responsible leadership arena from a number of streams of literature, so do *organisational* values, because of their ascribed normative influence on employee behaviour. Stahl and de Luque (2014) propose that several organisational-level factors, including culture, ethical climate, and CEO role-modelling, operate to enable or constrain responsible leadership behaviour, and certainly all three of these elements have strong links with organisational values.

For instance, in the business ethics literature, the terms *ethical climate* and *ethical culture* are used variously (and often interchangeably) to describe collective perceptions about what constitutes 'right behaviour' – standards or norms for decision-making based on particular ethical principles – and the organisational procedures, policies and practices which reinforce them (Martin & Cullen, 2006; O'Fallon & Butterfield, 2005; Victor & Cullen, 1988). Organisational values help to establish the moral criteria through which behavioural decision are translated to actions (Cullen, Victor, & Stephens, 1989). Sims (1992) argues that an organisation's culture has a significant influence on establishing and supporting individual ethical behaviour; and that CEOs should establish an ethical climate by demonstrating that they care about ethical practices, implementing formal processes to reinforce and reward ethical behaviour, and embedding ethical norms and practices at all levels. These activities are, of course, well-known building blocks of ethical leadership (Brown & Treviño, 2006; Mayer, Aquino, Greenbaum, & Kuenzi, 2012), and research has found that ethical leadership is positively related to ethical climate; ethical climate is negatively related to dysfunctional organisational behaviours such as employee misconduct; and that it mediates the relationship between ethical leadership and employee misconduct (Kuenzi & Schminke, 2009; Martin & Cullen, 2006; Mayer, Kuenzi, & Greenbaum, 2010).

The 'top-down' approach to establishing an ethical culture tends to assume that organisational values, articulated by the top leader, can be shared by all employees in order to produce consistent responses to ethical issues. However, Pearce, Wassenaar, and Manz (2014) remark that most leaders overestimate the degree to which vision and values are truly shared. Similarly Kempster, Gregory, and Watton, in Chapter 9 of this book, speak of the limited occurrence of discourse ethics occurring in organisational contexts. Measuring the level of congruence between organisational values and employee values is central to *person-organisation values fit* research (Cable & Edwards, 2004; Chatman, 1991, Meyer, Hecht, Gill, & Toplonytsky, 2010), which is also used by some researchers as an indication of the strength of an organisation's culture (O'Reilly *et al.*, 1991). It is important to be clear about what type of fit is being measured: perceived (subjective) fit, which is the congruence between an employee's values and his or her *perception* of the organisation's values; or actual (objective) fit, which compares the employee's values with the organisation's values as assessed by a subset of its employees (Edwards & Cable, 2009). Nevertheless, empirical studies have established a positive relationship between both types of values fit and organisational citizenship behaviours, teamwork, and (self-reported) tendencies toward ethical behaviour (Kristof, 1996; Meglino & Ravlin, 1998), all of which may be regarded as desirable responsible leadership outcomes. However, such measures do not consider how far the stated or 'official' values of the organisation differ from employee (and other stakeholder) assessments of its actual or enacted values, which is equally relevant to responsible leadership development.

Encouraging employees to identify with the top leader's vision and values is a well-recognised facet of transformational and charismatic leadership behaviour (Avolio *et al.*, 2009; Conger *et al.*, 2000; Shamir *et al.*, 1993). For conceptualisations of responsible leadership that do not rely on a single, 'heroic' leader, however, fostering shared *organisational* values seem all the more important as a means of guiding (ethical and socially responsible) behaviour. Employee internalisation of organisational values is a recognised objective of socialisation processes (Ashforth & Mael, 1989; Chatman, 1991). At the same time, an organisation's values, as a manifestation of its culture, also have an outward-facing role, not least because employees are attracted to organisations on the basis of their fit with the organisation's characteristics and culture (Schneider, 1987; Schneider, Goldstein, & Smith, 1995). It seems to us, therefore, that responsible leadership involves not only developing and establishing the 'right' organisational values (which are consistent with its commitment to the wider stakeholder community and to society); but also enacting and embedding those values throughout the organisation via a combination of social influence mechanisms such as role-modelling (Bandura, 1986) and values-aligned policies and practices.

Given the relevance of personal and organisational values to responsible leadership, as outlined above, we suggest that further conceptual development and research needs to include a more systematic consideration of values, and the ways in which they can support or inhibit responsible leadership practice. In the final section of this chapter, we return briefly to the three challenges for responsible leadership development and practice proposed earlier. Continuing with the values-based perspective of this chapter, we offer some ideas on possible responses to these challenges, which we hope will add to current debates on responsible leadership development and inspire future research.

Back to reality: the three challenges for responsible leadership development and practice

We approached this chapter, and the following section in particular, with our feet firmly grounded in a (critical) realist conception of the world; as such, we share the orientation to leadership research adopted by the editors of this volume in the opening chapter. Critical realism goes beyond observable phenomena to consider often unobservable but nevertheless 'real' social structures and associated causal powers (Sayer, 1998). These structures or entities include discursively mediated elements, such as concepts, language, and beliefs, as well as structures, relationships, practices, and processes. They are considered real not because they are observable but because they have actual consequences: 'something is real if it has an effect or makes a difference' (Fleetwood & Ackroyd, 2004, p. 29). Particularly pertinent to our ensuing discussion is critical realism's acceptance that people may be *constrained or enabled* by their environment, in terms of the structures in which they are located (Lawson, 2003); and that, at the same time, human agents' interaction with these (pre-existing) social structures can sustain or – crucially – modify them (Archer, 1998).

Thus, the realist voice in us wishes to avoid platitudes and prescriptive rhetoric about what responsible leaders 'should do', which stray too far into the realms of the romantic imagination, however attractive that form of Utopia may be. Therefore, we offer suggestions relevant to those operating within existing structures, influenced by our own notions of practical adequacy (Sayer, 1992) or – as Watson (2006) puts it – *what works* in the leadership context.

In the first challenge, we posed the question: *How far does responsible leadership involve enabling employees to fulfil their personal values at work?* Concern for the values of others is highlighted by Kraemer (2011) as characteristic of value-based leaders. He connects this concern with 'balance and perspective', which, he argues, is a key principle of values-based leadership. Not only do leaders listen willingly to others' viewpoints in order to develop well-rounded opinions, but also, Kraemer (ibid.) suggests, they want to discern the personal values that lay behind their views. This raises two interesting considerations for responsible leadership.

First is the recognition that no one set of value priorities is intrinsically any better than others, and the acceptance that, within an overarching conception of shared organisational values, there is room for different personal value priorities, reflecting a range of individual aspirations and needs. Of course, taken to extreme, a desire for power, self-gratification and success at the expense of others is associated with narcissistic tendencies and the dark side of leadership (Aasland, Skogstad, & Einarsen, 2008; Conger, 2007). However, Meglino and Ravlin (1998) point out that the type of values which support interpersonal co-operation and group cohesion may be at odds with the type of values required for organisational survival. Similarly, employees with value priorities such as self-respect, influence, capability, curiosity, creativity, and ambition, all of which lie outside the 'ethically desirable' (Fritzsche & Oz, 2007; Mumford *et al.*, 2003) self-transcendence value dimension (Schwartz, 1992), have much to offer either as responsible leaders or followers.

Second is the shift in emphasis from measures that identify performance weaknesses or undesirable behaviour and attitudes, towards finding out people's values – not in order to *improve* them but rather to *understand* them. If, as Rohan (2000) suggests, people's value priorities represent their personal view of best possible living, then finding ways for employees to fulfil their potential surely involves asking about what they value and exploring ways in which they can meet their needs and aspirations at work. In addition, given the close association between values and the self (Hitlin, 2003), encouraging employees (and leaders) to reflect on their value priorities helps to develop their capacity for self-reflection and self-awareness. Self-reflection is a key principle of values-based leadership (Kraemer, 2011) and developing self-awareness or personal insight is important for authentic leadership development (Gardner *et al.*, 2005, p. 347):

> By reflecting through introspection, authentic leaders gain clarity and concordance with respect to their core values, identity, emotions,

motives, and goals … by learning who they are and what they value, authentic leaders build understanding and a sense of self that provides a firm anchor for their decisions and actions.

Despite the ideal of anchoring decisions through a sense of one's true self, the day-to-day tensions and dilemmas faced by managers, and the implications of their responses for themselves and for the organisation, are often overlooked. In our second challenge we asked: *How can responsible leaders equip managers to deal with value conflicts?* This question differs in emphasis from that more typically raised in the context of ethical decision-making: *What is the 'right' thing to do?* In practice, examples of value conflicts experienced by managers can be used in leadership development activities such as coaching. Managers are encouraged to recall such incidents in detail, for example: how they felt when faced with a value conflict; how they responded; what was going through their minds when they decided on a course of action; and what was the outcome of their response for themselves, their team, or for the organisation. This enables a wider discussion about the implications of alternative response strategies within the context of organisational values and expectations.

From our own experience of talking to managers about value conflicts, those who can draw on a sense of legitimacy and decision-making autonomy – rather than acting through fear of sanction or a sense of guilt – report more positive psychological outcomes. Likewise, they feel more able to deal with a decision that they personally disagree with when they have had an opportunity to express their views to senior management, or feel that a fair process has been followed. But what are the implications of their responses for organisations and for responsible leadership development? This relates to our final challenge:

> *How can responsible leaders foster organisational integrity, and how should they respond when integrity breaches occur?*

Earlier in this chapter we positioned integrity as keeping one's promises and acting consistently with espoused values. The practice in many organisations who wish to develop a values-based culture is (a) to try to make values meaningful to employees by expressing them as behaviours, and (b) to reinforce them by embedding them in role descriptions and appraisal objectives. However, placing a strong emphasis on organisational values in this way brings a heightened awareness of inconsistencies between organisational values and behaviour – particularly the actions and decisions of senior leaders. In the case of an actual or perceived failure by the organisation (represented by its leaders) to live up to its values, managers face the leadership challenge of interpreting and mitigating the situation for their reportees, while protecting their own behavioural integrity and dealing with the inconsistency at a personal level. For some managers, such resolution may be achieved by defending the organisation's action, accompanied by bolstering rationales, such as having no choice or fulfilling the obligations of the role. For others, choosing not to defend the organisation's action, in the pursuit of autonomy and authenticity, may leave the breach unrepaired. Either way, the fundamental cause of the breach of integrity remains unresolved.

It therefore seems crucial for responsible leaders to develop a shared sense of what organisational values – and values enactment – mean in the context of 'real world' decisions, if they are to sustain organisational integrity in the eyes of stakeholders. In practice, awareness that their actions are likely to be interpreted in value terms may encourage senior leaders to frame strategic or tactical decisions in terms of organisational values. By using this form of 'proactive sense-giving' (Cha & Edmondson, 2006, p. 75), they will help to develop shared meanings and avoid perceived or actual inconsistencies.

Finally, are senior leaders prepared to be challenged when their decisions appear to compromise organisational values and integrity? If so, facilitating the acceptance and implementation of those decisions may not constitute the 'right' thing for managers to do in the context of responsible leadership practice. Fostering shared values and enacting values-aligned behaviour need not, in our view, lead to 'moral muteness' (Bird & Waters, 1989) or 'organizational silence' (Morrison & Milliken, 2000; Verhezen, 2010); nor to the dysfunctional outcomes associated with strong or over-cohesive cultures, such as stagnation and lack of innovation (Kristof, 1996; Morgan, 1986) and groupthink (Janis & Mann, 1977). It is rather a question of *what* the organisation values, and which types of behaviours are encouraged. Thus, organisations might consider how they can develop a culture that encourages managers to challenge lapses of integrity, and how they can prepare senior leaders to respond to such challenges.

In our discussion of values and responsible leadership in this chapter we have trodden a careful path through:

> ...these steep woods and lofty cliffs
> And this green pastoral landscape.
>   (Wordsworth, 1798, p. 201)

Our aim was to demonstrate the relevance of personal and organisational values to responsible leadership, and at the same time to avoid the rhetoric that all too often features in the values discourse. In doing so, we have raised three challenges for responsible leadership, all of which have values-related issues at their core. We hope that these will add to current research and debates on 'real world' responsible leadership, while retaining the spirit and optimism of the romantic imagination.

Notes

1 Schwartz (2014, p. 247) emphasises that the circular arrangement of values in the model represents a 'continuum of motivations': the only critical constraint when partitioning the continuum is preserving the order of motivations around the circle.

Indeed, Schwartz et al. (2012) recently refined the original value theory by partitioning the circle into 19 more narrowly defined values.

2 Deci and Ryan (2002, p. 7) define these as follows: (a) Competence: feeling
effective in one's ongoing interactions with the social environment; experiencing
opportunities to exercise one's capacities; (b) Relatedness: feeling connected to
others, accepted by others and the community; and (c) Autonomy: experiencing
behaviour as an expression of the self; acting from interest and integrated values
rather than to comply with external direction.

References

Aasland, M. S., Skogstad, A., & Einarsen, S. (2008). The dark side: Defining destructive leadership behaviour. e-Organisations & People, 15(3), 20–28.

Aguinis, H., & Glavas, A. (2012). What we know and don't know about corporate
social responsibility: A review and research agenda. Journal of Management, 38(4),
932–968.

Alimo-Metcalfe, B., & Alban-Metcalfe, R. J. (2001). The development of a new
Transformational Leadership Questionnaire. Journal of Occupational and Organizational Psychology, 74, 1–27.

Allport, G. W. (1955). Becoming: Basic considerations for a psychology of personality. New
Haven, CT: Yale University Press.

Allport, G. W. (1961). Pattern and growth in personality. New York: Holt.

Archer, M. (1998). Realism and morphogenesis. In M. Archer, R. Bhaskar, A.
Collier, T. Lawson, & A. Norrie (Eds.), Critical realism: Essential readings
(pp. 356–381). London: Routledge.

Argandona, A. (2003). Fostering values in organizations. Journal of Business Ethics,
45(1–2), 15–28.

Argyris, C. (1990). Overcoming organizational defenses. Boston, MA: Allyn and Bacon.

Ashforth, B. E., & Mael, F. (1989). Social identity theory and the organization.
Academy of Management Review, 14(1), 20–39.

Audi, R., & Murphy, P. E. (2006). The many faces of integrity. Business Ethics Quarterly, 16(1), 3–21.

Avolio, B. J., & Gardner, W. L. (2005). Authentic leadership development: Getting
to the root of positive forms of leadership. The Leadership Quarterly, 16(3),
315–338.

Avolio, B. J., Walumbwa, F. O., & Weber, T. J. (2009). Leadership: Current theories, research, and future directions. Annual Review of Psychology, 60(1), 421–449.
doi:10.1146/annurev.psych.60.110707.163621.

Balogun, J., & Johnson, G. (2004). Organizational restructuring and middle manager
sensemaking. Academy of Management Journal, 47(4), 523–549.

Bandura, A. (1986). Social foundations of thought and action: A social cognitive theory. Eng-
lewood Cliffs, NJ: Prentice Hall.

Barnard, C. I. (1938). The functions of the executive. Cambridge, MA: Harvard University Press.

Bass, B. M., & Steidlmeier, P. (1999). Ethics, character, and authentic transformational leadership behavior. The Leadership Quarterly, 10(2), 181–217.

Beck, T. E., & Plowman, D. A. (2009). Experiencing rare and unusual events richly:
The role of middle managers in animating and guiding organizational interpretation. Organization Science, 20(5), 909–924. doi:10.1287/orsc.1090.0451.

Bird, F. B., & Waters, J. A. (1989). The moral muteness of managers. *California Management Review, 32*(1), 73–88.

Boal, K. B., & Bryson, J. M. (1988). Charismatic leadership: A phenomenological and structural approach. In J. G. Hunt, B. R. Baliga, H. P. Dachler, & C. A. Schriesheim (Eds.), *Emerging leadership vistas: International symposium on leadership and managerial behavior research* (pp. 11–28). Lexington, MA: Lexington Books.

Brown, M. E., & Treviño, L. K. (2006). Ethical leadership: A review and future directions. *The Leadership Quarterly, 17*(6), 595–616. doi:10.1016/j.leaqua.2006.10.004.

Cable, D. M., & Edwards, J. R. (2004). Complementary and supplementary fit: A theoretical and empirical integration. *Journal of Applied Psychology, 89*(5), 822–834.

Caldwell, C. (2010). Identity, self-awareness, and self-deception: Ethical implications for leaders and organizations. *Journal of Business Ethics, 90*, 393–406. doi:10.1007/s10551-010-0424-2.

Caldwell, C., Hayes, L. A., Karri, R., & Bernal, P. (2008). Ethical stewardship: Implications for leadership and trust. *Journal of Business Ethics, 78*, 153–164.

Cha, S. E., & Edmondson, A. C. (2006). When values backfire: Leadership, attribution, and disenchantment in a values-driven organization. *The Leadership Quarterly, 17*(1), 57–78. doi:10.1016/j.leaqua.2005.10.006.

Chatman, J. A. (1991). Matching people and organizations: Selection and socialization in public accounting firms. *Administrative Science Quarterly, 36*(3), 459–484.

Ciulla, J. B., Uhl-Bien, M., & Werhane, P. H. (2013). *Leadership ethics*. Los Angeles, CA: Sage.

Collins, J. C., & Porras, J. I. (1994). *Built to last: Successful habits of visionary companies*. New York: HarperBusiness.

Collins, J. C., & Porras, J. I. (1996). Building your company's vision. *Harvard Business Review, 74*(5), 65–77.

Collins, J. C., & Porras, J. I. (2000). *Built to last: successful habits of visionary companies* (3rd edn). London: Random House Business Books.

Conger, J. A. (2007). The dark side of leadership. In R. P. Vecchio (Ed.), *Leadership: Understanding the dynamics of power and influence in organizations* (2nd edn) (pp. 199–215). Notre Dame, IN: University of Notre Dame Press.

Conger, J. A., Kanungo, R. N., & Menon, S. T. (2000). Charismatic leadership and follower effects. *Journal of Organizational Behavior, 21*(7), 747–767. doi:10.1002/1099-1379(200011)21:7<747::aid-job46>3.3.co;2-a.

Crilly, D., Schneider, S. C., & Zollo, M. (2008). Psychological antecedents to socially responsible behavior. *European Management Review, 5*(3), 175–190.

Cullen, J. B., Victor, B., & Stephens, C. (1989). An ethical weather report: Assessing the organization's ethical climate. *Organizational Dynamics, 18*(2), 50.

Davis, A. L., & Rothstein, H. R. (2006). The effects of the perceived behavioral integrity of managers on employee attitudes: A meta-analysis. *Journal of Business Ethics, 67*(4), 407–419. doi:10.1007/s10551-006-9034-4.

De Cremer, D., van Dick, R., Tenbrunsel, A., Pillutla, M., & Murnighan, J. K. (2011). Understanding ethical behavior and decision making in management: A behavioural business ethics approach. *British Journal of Management, 22*, S1–S4. doi:10.1111/j.1467-8551.2010.00733.x.

Deci, E. L., & Ryan, R. M. (2002). *Handbook of self-determination research*. Rochester, NY: University of Rochester Press.

Edwards, J. R., & Cable, D. A. (2009). The value of value congruence. *Journal of Applied Psychology, 94*(3), 654–677. doi:10.1037/a0014891.

Feather, N. T. (1995). Values, valences, and choice: The influence of values on the perceived attractiveness and choice of alternatives. *Journal of Personality and Social Psychology, 68*(6), 1135–1151.

Feather, N. T. (1996). Values, deservingness and attitudes toward high achievers: Research on tall poppies. In C. Seligman, J. M. Olson, & M. P. Zanna (Eds.), *The Ontario Symposium: The psychology of values* (pp. 215–251). Mahwah, NJ: L. Erlbaum Associates.

Festinger, L. (1957). *A theory of cognitive dissonance.* Stanford, CA: Stanford University Press.

Fleetwood, S., & Ackroyd, S. (Eds.). (2004). *Critical realist applications in organisation and management studies.* London; New York: Routledge.

Ford, R. C., & Richardson, W. D. (1994). Ethical decision-making: A review of the empirical literature. *Journal of Business Ethics, 13*(3), 205–221.

Fritzsche, D. J., & Oz, E. (2007). Personal values' influence on the ethical dimension of decision making. *Journal of Business Ethics, 75*(4), 335–343. doi:10.1007/s10551-006-9256-5.

Fry, L. W. (2003). Toward a theory of spiritual leadership. *The Leadership Quarterly, 14,* 693–727. doi:10.1016/j.leaqua.2003.09.001.

Gagné, M., & Deci, E. L. (2005). Self-determination theory and work motivation. *Journal of Organizational Behavior, 26*(4), 331–362.

Gardner, W. L., Avolio, B. J., Luthans, F., May, D. R., & Walumbwa, F. (2005). 'Can you see the real me?' A self-based model of authentic leader and follower development. *The Leadership Quarterly, 16*(3), 343–372.

Gardner, W. L., Cogliser, C. C., Davis, K. M., & Dickens, M. P. (2011). Authentic leadership: A review of the literature and research agenda. *The Leadership Quarterly, 22*(6), 1120–1145. doi:10.1016/j.leaqua.2011.09.007.

George, B. (2003). *Authentic leadership: Rediscovering the secrets to creating lasting value.* San Francisco: Jossey-Bass.

George, B., Sims, P., McLean, A. N., & Mayer, D. (2007). Discovering your authentic leadership. *Harvard Business Review, 85*(2), 129–138.

Goleman, D. (1996). *Emotional intelligence: Why it can matter more than IQ.* London: Bloomsbury.

Gronn, P. (2002). Distributed leadership as a unit of analysis. *The Leadership Quarterly, 13*(4), 423–451.

Groves, K., & LaRocca, M. (2011). An empirical study of leader ethical values, transformational and transactional leadership, and follower attitudes toward corporate social responsibility. *Journal of Business Ethics, 103*(4), 511–528. doi:10.1007/s10551-011-0877-y.

Hallier, J., & James, P. (1997). Middle managers and the employee psychological contract: Agency, protection and advancement. *Journal of Management Studies, 34*(5), 703–728.

Hermans, H. J. M., & Oles, P. K. (1996). Value crisis: Affective organization of personal meanings. *Journal of Research in Personality, 30*(4), 457–482.

Higgs, M., & Dulewicz, S. V. (2002). *Making sense of emotional intelligence* (2nd edn). London: ASE.

Higgs, M., & Rowland, D. (2010). Emperors with clothes on: The role of self-awareness in developing effective change leadership. *Journal of Change Management, 10*(4), 369–385. doi:10.1080/14697017.2010.516483.

Hill, L. A. (2003). *Becoming a manager: How new managers master the challenges of leadership* (2nd edn). Boston, MA: Harvard Business School Publishing.

Hind, P., Wilson, A., & Lenssen, G. (2009). Developing leaders for sustainable business. *Corporate Governance: The International Journal of Business in Society, 9*(1), 7–20. doi:10.1108/14720700910936029.

Hitlin, S. (2003). Values as the core of personal identity: Drawing links between two theories of self. *Social Psychology Quarterly, 66*(2), 118–137.

Ilies, R., Morgeson, F. P., & Nahrgang, J. D. (2005). Authentic leadership and eudaemonic well-being: Understanding leader-follower outcomes. *The Leadership Quarterly, 16*(3), 373–394.

Illies, J. J., & Reiter-Palmon, R. (2008). Responding destructively in leadership situations: The role of personal values and problem construction. *Journal of Business Ethics, 82*(1), 251–272. doi:10.1007/s10551-007-9574-2.

Janis, I. L., & Mann, L. (1977). *Decision making: A psychological analysis of conflict, choice, and commitment*. New York: Free Press.

Johnson, G., Scholes, K., & Whittington, R. (2008). *Exploring corporate strategy* (8th ed.). Harlow: FT Prentice Hall.

Kalshoven, K., Den Hartog, D. N., & De Hoogh, A. H. B. (2011). Ethical leader behavior and big five factors of personality. *Journal of Business Ethics, 100*(2), 349–366.

Karakas, F. (2010). Spirituality and performance in organizations: A literature review. *Journal of Business Ethics, 94*(1), 89–106.

Kluckhorn, C. (1951). Values and value-orientations in the theory of action. In T. Parsons & E. A. Shils (Eds.), *Toward a general theory of action* (pp. 388–433). New York: Harper.

Koehn, D. (2005). Integrity as a business asset. *Journal of Business Ethics, 58*(1–3), 125–136. doi:10.1007/s10551-005-1391-x.

Kraemer, H. M. (2011). *From values to action: The four principles of values-based leadership*. San Francisco: Jossey-Bass.

Kristiansen, C. M., & Hotte, A. M. (1996). Morality and the self: Implications for the when and how of value-attitude-behaviour relations. In C. Seligman, J. M. Olson, & M. P. Zanna (Eds.), *The Ontario Symposium: The psychology of values* (pp. 77–105). Mahwah, NJ: L. Erlbaum Associates.

Kristof, A. L. (1996). Person-organization fit: An integrative review of its conceptualizations, measurement, and implications. *Personnel Psychology, 49*(1), 1–49.

Kuenzi, M., & Schminke, M. (2009). Assembling fragments into a lens: A review, critique, and proposed research agenda for the organizational work climate literature. *Journal of Management, 35*(3), 634–717. doi:10.1177/0149206308330559.

Lawson, T. (2003). *Reorienting economics*. London: Routledge.

Liden, R. C., Wayne, S. J., Zhao, H., & Henderson, D. (2008). Servant leadership: Development of a multidimensional measure and multi-level assessment. *The Leadership Quarterly, 19*, 161–177. doi:10.1016/j.leaqua.2008.01.006.

Lord, R. G., & Brown, D. J. (2001). Leadership, values, and subordinate self-concepts. *The Leadership Quarterly, 12*(2), 133–152.

Maak, T., & Pless, N. M. (2009). Business leaders as citizens of the world: Advancing humanism on a global scale. *Journal of Business Ethics, 88*(3), 537–550.

Maio, G. R., & Olson, J. M. (1998). Values as truisms: Evidence and implications. *Journal of Personality and Social Psychology, 74*(2), 294–311.

Maio, G. R., Olson, J. M., Allen, L., & Bernard, M. M. (2001). Addressing discrepancies between values and behavior: The motivating effect of reasons. *Journal of Experimental Social Psychology, 37*(2), 104–117.

Martin, K., & Cullen, J. (2006). Continuities and extensions of ethical climate theory: A meta-analytic review. *Journal of Business Ethics, 69*(2), 175–194. doi:10.1007/s10551-006-9084-7.

Maslow, A. H. (1943). A theory of human motivation. *Psychological Review, 50*(4), 370–396. doi:10.1037/h0054346.

Maslow, A. H. (1962). *Toward a psychology of being.* Princeton, NJ: Van Nostrand.

Maslow, A. H. (1970). *Motivation and personality* (3rd edn): New York: Harper Collins.

May, D. R., Chan, A. Y. L., Hodges, T. D., & Avolio, B. J. (2003). Developing the moral component of authentic leadership. *Organizational Dynamics, 32*(3), 247–260. doi:10.1016/S0090-2616(03)00032-9.

Mayer, D. M., Aquino, K., Greenbaum, R. L., & Kuenzi, M. (2012). Who displays ethical leadership, and why does it matter? An examination of antecedents and consequences of ethical leadership. *Academy of Management Journal, 55*(1), 151–171. doi:10.5465/amj.2008.0276.

Mayer, D. M., Kuenzi, M., & Greenbaum, R. L. (2010). Examining the link between ethical leadership and employee misconduct: The mediating role of ethical climate. *Journal of Business Ethics, 95*, 7–16. doi:10.1007/s10551-011-0794-0.

Meglino, B. M., & Ravlin, E. C. (1998). Individual values in organizations: Concepts, controversies, and research. *Journal of Management, 24*(3), 351–389.

Meindl, J. R., Ehrlich, S. B., & Dukerich, J. M. (1985). The romance of leadership. *Administrative Science Quarterly, 30*(1), 78–102. doi:10.2307/2392813.

Meyer, J. P., Hecht, T. D., Gill, H., & Toplonytsky, L. (2010). Person-organization (culture) fit and employee commitment under conditions of organizational change: A longitudinal study. *Journal of Vocational Behavior, 76*(3), 458–473. doi:10.1016/j.jvb.2010.01.001.

Mintzberg, H. (2009). *Managing* (1st edn). San Francisco: Berrett-Koehler Publishers.

Morgan, G. (1986). *Images of organization.* Thousand Oaks, CA: Sage.

Morrison, E. W., & Milliken, F. J. (2000). Organizational silence: A barrier to change and development in a pluralistic world. *Academy of Management Review, 25*(4), 706–725.

Mumford, M. D., Helton, W. B., Decker, B. P., Connelly, M. S., & Van Doorn, J. R. (2003). Values and beliefs related to ethical decisions. *Teaching Business Ethics, 7*(2), 139–170.

Murphy, P. E. (1995). Corporate-ethics statements: Current status and future-prospects. *Journal of Business Ethics, 14*(9), 727–740.

O'Fallon, M., & Butterfield, K. (2005). A review of the empirical ethical decision-making literature: 1996–2003. *Journal of Business Ethics, 59*(4), 375–413. doi:10.1007/s10551-005-2929-7.

O'Reilly, C. A., Chatman, J., & Caldwell, D. F. (1991). People and organizational culture: A profile comparison approach to assessing person-organization fit. *Academy of Management Journal, 34*(3), 487–516.

Palanski, M. E., & Yammarino, F. J. (2009). Integrity and leadership: A multi-level conceptual framework. *The Leadership Quarterly, 20*(3), 405–420. doi:10.1016/j.leaqua.2009.03.008.

Pearce, C. L., & Conger, J. A. (2003). *Shared leadership: Reframing the hows and whys of leadership.* Thousand Oaks, CA: Sage.

Pearce, C. L., Hoch, J. E., Jeppesen, H. J., & Wegge, J. (2011). New forms of management: shared and distributed leadership in organizations. *Journal of Personnel Psychology, 9*(4), 151–153. doi:10.1027/1866-5888/a000022.

Pearce, C. L., & Manz, C. C. (2014). The leadership disease. *Business Horizons, 57*(2), 215–224. doi:10.1016/j.bushor.2013.11.005.

Pearce, C. L., Manz, C. C., & Sims, H. P. (2008). The roles of vertical and shared leadership in the enactment of executive corruption: Implications for research and practice. *The Leadership Quarterly, 19*(3), 353–359. doi:10.1016/j.leaqua.2008.03.007.

Pearce, C. L., Wassenaar, C. L., & Manz, C. C. (2014). Is shared leadership the key to responsible leadership? *Academy of Management Perspectives, 28*(3), 275–288. doi:10.5465/amp.2014.0017.

Peregrym, D., & Wollf, R. (2013). Values-based leadership: The foundation of trans- formational servant leadership. *The Journal of Values-Based Leadership, 6*(2). Retrieved from http://scholar.valpo.edu/jvbl/vol.6/iss2/7.

Peters, T. J., & Waterman, R. H. (1982). *In search of excellence: Lessons from America's best-run companies.* New York: Harper and Row.

Pless, N. M., Maak, T., & Waldman, D. A. (2012). Different approaches toward doing the right thing: Mapping the responsibility orientations of leaders. *Academy of Management Perspectives, 26*(4), 51–65. doi:10.5465/amp.2012.0028.

Reichers, A. E. (1985). A review and reconceptualization of organizational commit- ment. *Academy of Management Review, 10*(3), 465–476.

Resick, C. J., Martin, G. S., Keating, M. A., Dickson, M. W., Kwan, H. K., & Peng, C. (2011). What ethical leadership means to me: Asian, American, and European perspectives. *Journal of Business Ethics, 101*(3), 435–457. doi:10.1007/ s10551-010-0730-8.

Robertson, I., & Callinan, M. (1998). Personality and work behaviour. *European Journal of Work and Organizational Psychology, 7*(3), 321–340.

Rogers, C. R. (1961). *On becoming a person: A therapist's view of psychotherapy.* London: Constable.

Rohan, M. J. (2000). A rose by any name? The values construct. *Personality and Social Psychology Review, 4*(3), 255–277. doi:10.1207/s15327957pspr0403_4.

Rokeach, M. (1968). *Beliefs attitudes and values: A theory of organization and change.* San Francisco: Jossey-Bass.

Rokeach, M. (1973). *The nature of human values.* New York: Free Press.

Rokeach, M. (1979). From individual to institutional values: With special reference to the values of science. In M. Rokeach (Ed.), *Understanding human values: Indi- vidual and societal* (pp. 47–70). New York: Free Press.

Rowland, D., & Higgs, M. J. (2008). *Sustaining change: Leadership that works.* Chiches- ter: Jossey-Bass.

Ryan, R. M. (1995). Psychological needs and the facilitation of integrative processes. *Journal of Personality, 63*(3), 397–427.

Ryan, R. M., & Deci, E. L. (2002). Overview of self-determination theory: An organismic dialectical perspective. In E. L. Deci & R. M. Ryan (Eds.), *Handbook of self-determination research* (pp. 3–33). Rochester, NY: University of Rochester Press.

Ryan, R. M., & Deci, E. L. (2003). On assimilating identities to the self: A self- determination theory perspective on internalization and integrity within cultures. In M. R. Leary & J. P. Tangney (Eds.), *Handbook of self and identity* (pp. 253–272). New York: Guilford Press.

Sagiv, L., & Schwartz, S. H. (1995). Value priorities and readiness for out-group social contact. *Journal of Personality and Social Psychology, 69*(3), 437–448.

Sayer, A. (1992). *Method in social science: A realist approach* (2nd ed.). London: Routledge.

Sayer, A. (1998). Abstraction: A realist interpretation. In M. Archer, R. Bhaskar, A. Collier, T. Lawson, & A. Norrie (Eds.), *Critical realism: Essential readings* (pp. 120–185). London: Routledge.

Schein, E. H. (1997). *Organizational culture and leadership* (2nd ed.). San Francisco, CA: Jossey-Bass.

Schneider, B. (1987). The people make the place. *Personnel Psychology, 40*(3), 437–453.

Schneider, B., Goldstein, H. W., & Smith, D. B. (1995). The ASA framework: An update. *Personnel Psychology, 48*(4), 747–773.

Schwartz, S. H. (1992). Universals in the content and structure of values: Theoretical advances and empirical tests in 20 countries. *Advances in Experimental Social Psychology, 25*, 1–65.

Schwartz, S. H. (1996). Value priorities and behavior: Applying a theory of integrated value systems. In C. Seligman, J. M. Olson, & M. P. Zanna (Eds.), *The Ontario Symposium: The psychology of values* (pp. 1–24). Mahwah, NJ: L. Erlbaum Associates.

Schwartz, S. H. (2014). Functional theories of human values: Comment on Gouveia, Milfont, and Guerra (2014). *Personality and Individual Differences, 68*, 247–249.

Schwartz, S. H., & Bilsky, W. (1987). Toward a universal psychological structure of human-values. *Journal of Personality and Social Psychology, 53*(3), 550–562.

Schwartz, S. H., Cieciuch, J., Vecchione, M., Davidov, E., Fischer, R., Beierlein, C., et al. (2012). Refining the theory of basic individual values. *Journal of Personality and Social Psychology, 103*(4), 663–688. doi:10.1037/a0029393.

Sedikides, C. (1993) Assessment, enhancement, and verification determinants of the self-evaluation process. *Journal of Personality and Social Psychology, 65*(2), 317–338.

Seligman, M. E. P. (2003). Positive psychology: Fundamental assumptions. *The Psychologist, 16*(3), 126–127.

Shamir, B. (1995). Social distance and charisma: Theoretical notes and an exploratory study. *The Leadership Quarterly, 6*(1), 19–47.

Shamir, B., House, R. J., & Arthur, M. B. (1993). The motivational effects of charismatic leadership: A self-concept based theory. *Organization Science, 4*(4), 577–594.

Shapiro, E. C. (1995). *Fad surfing in the boardroom: Reclaiming the courage to manage in the age of instant answers*. Reading, MA; Wokingham: Addison-Wesley.

Simons, T. (2002). Behavioral integrity: The perceived alignment between managers' words and deeds as a research focus. *Organization Science, 13*(1), 18–35. doi:10.1287/orsc.13.1.18.543.

Simons, T., Friedman, R., Liu, L. A., & Parks, J. M. (2007). Racial differences in sensitivity to behavioral integrity: Attitudinal consequences, in-group effects, and 'trickle down' among Black and non-Black employees. *Journal of Applied Psychology, 92*(3), 650–665. doi:10.1037/0021-9010.92.3.650.

Sims, R. (1992). The challenge of ethical behavior in organizations. *Journal of Business Ethics, 11*(7), 505–513. doi:10.1007/bf00881442.

Smircich, L. (1983). Concepts of culture and organizational analysis. *Administrative Science Quarterly, 28*(3), 339–358.

Sosik, J. J. (2005). The role of personal values in the charismatic leadership of corporate managers: A model and preliminary field study. *The Leadership Quarterly, 16*(2), 221–244. doi:10.1016/j.leaqua.2005.01.002.

Spears, L. C., & Lawrence, M. (2002). *Focus on leadership: Servant leadership for the 21st century*. New York: John Wiley & Sons.

Stahl, G. K., & De Luque, M. S. (2014). Antecedents of responsible leader behavior:

A research synthesis, conceptual framework and agenda for future research. *Academy of Management Perspectives, 28*(3), 235–254.

Stevens, J. M., Steensma, H. K., Harrison, D. A., & Cochran, P. L. (2005). Symbolic or substantive document? The influence of ethics codes on financial executives' decisions. *Strategic Management Journal, 26*(2), 181–195. doi:10.1002/Smj.440.

Tekleab, A. G., Sims Jr, H. P., Tesluk, P. E., Yun, S., & Cox, J. (2008). Are we on the same page? Effects of self-awareness of empowering and transformational leadership. *Journal of Leadership and Organizational Studies, 14*(3), 185–201. doi:10.1177/1071791907311069.

Tetlock, P. E. (1986). A value pluralism model of ideological reasoning. *Journal of Personality and Social Psychology, 50*(4), 819–827.

Treviño, L. K., Hartman, L. P., & Brown, M. (2000). Moral person and moral manager: How executives develop a reputation for ethical leadership. *California Management Review, 42*(4), 128–142.

Treviño, L. K., Weaver, G. R., Gibson, D. G., & Toffler, B. L. (1999). Managing ethics and legal compliance: What works and what hurts. *California Management Review, 41*(2), 131–151.

Uhl-Bien, M. (2006). Relational leadership theory: Exploring the social processes of leadership and organizing. *Leadership Quarterly, 17*(6), 654–676. doi:10.1016/j.leaqua.2006.10.007.

Urbany, J. E. (2005). Inspiration and cynicism in values statements. *Journal of Business Ethics, 62*(2), 169–182. doi:10.1007/s10551-005-0188-2.

Urbany, J. E., Reynolds, T. J., & Phillips, J. M. (2008). How to make values count in everyday decisions. *MIT Sloan Management Review, 49*(4), 75–80.

Verhezen, P. (2010). Giving voice in a culture of silence: From a culture of compliance to a culture of integrity. *Journal of Business Ethics, 96*(2), 187–206. doi:10.1007/s10551-010-0458-5.

Victor, B., & Cullen, J. B. (1988). The organizational bases of ethical work climates. *Administrative Science Quarterly, 33*(1), 101–125.

Waldman, D. A., & Galvin, B. M. (2008). Alternative perspectives of responsible leadership. *Organizational Dynamics, 37*, 327–341. doi:10.1016/j.orgdyn.2008.07.001.

Waldman, D. A., de Sully, L. M., Nathan, W., & House, R. J. (2006). Cultural and leadership predictors of corporate social responsibility values of top management: A GLOBE Study of 15 countries. *Journal of International Business Studies, 37*(6), 823–837.

Walumbwa, F. O., Avolio, B. J., Gardner, W. L., Wernsing, T. S., & Peterson, S. J. (2008). Authentic leadership: Development and validation of a theory-based measure. *Journal of Management, 34*(1), 89–126. doi:10.1177/0149206307308913.

Waterman, A. S. (1993). Two conceptions of happiness: Contrasts of personal expressiveness (eudaimonia) and hedonic enjoyment. *Journal of Personality and Social Psychology, 64*(4), 678–691.

Watson, T. J. (1994). *In search of management: Culture, chaos and control in managerial work*. London: Routledge.

Watson, T. J. (2003). Ethical choice in managerial work: The scope for moral choices in an ethically irrational world. *Human Relations, 56*(2), 167–185.

Watson, T. J. (2006). *Organising and managing work: Organisational, managerial and strategic behaviour in theory and practice* (2nd edn). Harlow: Financial Times/Prentice Hall.

Weick, K. E. (1995). *Sensemaking in organizations*. Thousand Oaks, CA: Sage.

Williams, R. M. (1979). Change and stability in values and value systems. In M. Rokeach (Ed.), *Understanding human values: Individual and societal* (pp. 15–46). New York: Free Press.

Wordsworth, W. (1798). *Lyrical Ballads*. London: J. & A. Arch.

Wright, T. A., & Quick, J. C. (2011). The role of character in ethical leadership research. *The Leadership Quarterly, 22*(5), 975–978. doi:10.1016/j.leaqua.2011.07.015

Yukl, G. (2010). *Leadership in organizations* (7th edn). Upper Saddle River, NJ: Prentice Hall.

Yukl, G., Mahsud, R., Prussia, G. E., & Hassan, S. (2013). An improved measure of ethical leadership. *Journal of Leadership and Organizational Studies, 20*(1), 38–48. doi:10.1177/1548051811429352.

5 Leadership responsibility and calling

The role of calling in a woman's choice to lead

Susan R. Madsen

A man saw three fellows laying bricks at a new building: He approached the first and asked, 'What are you doing?' Clearly irritated, the first man responded, 'What the heck do you think I'm doing? I'm laying these darn bricks!' He then walked over to the second bricklayer and asked the same question. The second responded, 'Oh, I'm making a living'. He approached the third bricklayer with the same question, 'What are you doing?' The third looked up, smiled, and said, 'I'm building a cathedral'.

(Joan Borysenko, n.d.)

Borysenko's story provides an example of the different views or perspectives employees may have for their work. In fact, researchers (Bellah, Madsen, Sullivan, Swidler, & Tipton, 1985; Wrzesniewski, McCauley, Rozin, & Schwartz, 1997) have identified three perspectives individuals may have regarding the purpose of their work. A *job* is something done primarily to make money with the interest being in the material benefits and no other reward. A *career* can be moderately fulfilling but involves a constant process of trying to get promoted. According to Wrzensniewski *et al.*, 'People who have [c]areers have a deeper personal investment in their work and mark their achievement not only through monetary gain, but through advancement within the occupational structure' (p. 22). The third, *calling*, is valuable as an end in itself and serves the greater good; work is inseparable from overall life because of its meaning and its integration with identity. With calling, financial gain or career advancement are not primary purposes attributed to work; the fulfilment the individual receives from doing the work is most essential (Bellah *et al.*, 1985; Wrzesniewski *et al.*, 1997). Although other scholars may disagree with these definitions, they provide insight into potential differences individuals may have regarding the purpose and value of work – with calling having the deepest meaning. And I would argue that it is within this construct of calling, or service for the greater good, that responsible leadership is both directly and indirectly linked. Further, and drawing from these definitions, calling as responsibility is both a sense of realism (for example, the recognised need to address some pressing aspect) and romanticism linked to ideal notions of a greater good (for example, drawing on imagination of possibilities not yet realised but optimistic for such fulfilment).

Although Dik and Duffy (2009) argued that there has been relatively little empirical research on purpose or meaningfulness in the work domain, the topic of 'meaningful work' has recently become a popular area of research. People typically do want to experience more meaning in their lives as a whole. In fact, a decade ago a *USA Today* poll found that if people could ask God just one question, most would want to know, 'What's my purpose in life?' (quoted in Brennfleck & Brennfleck, 2005, p. 3). Smith (1999) stated, 'We long to find and do work that is meaningful, that makes a difference and needs to be done' (p. 31). According to Steger, Pickering, Shin, and Dik (2010), 'Research is quickly accumulating, suggesting that many people want to experience a sense of calling in their work' (p. 90).

Individuals want to believe there is something special within them and that they have some type of life mission to discover and fulfill (Brennfleck & Brennfleck, 2005). Although many are unsure about what that might look like, they still feel driven to prepare for and accomplish this work or mission. A strong sense of calling lies at the core of meaningful work for many people, and researchers (e.g. Dik & Duffy, 2009; Hall & Chandler, 2005; Steger *et al.*, 2010) have stated that more individuals now are seeking deep meaning in their work. Why is this so? Parker Palmer (2000, p. 16) once said,

> Our deepest calling is to grow into our own authentic selfhood, whether or not it conforms to some image of who we ought to be. As we do so, we will not only find the joy that every human being seeks – we will also find our path of authentic service in the world.

And, as Frederick Buechner (1973) asserts, true vocation joins self and service in 'the place where your deep gladness meets the world's deep need' (p. 119).

The concept of calling as a research construct has been explored for the past few decades, most often using mixed-gender samples. However, my interests focus on the ways that calling plays out in women's lives, especially those who aspire to, seek out, then acquire and maintain leadership roles in workplaces (e.g. business, non-profit, government, and political). The emphasis on women is particularly important because low numbers of women continue to hold top leadership positions in nearly all countries and industries (Adler, 2015; Madsen, Ngunjiri, Longman, & Cherrey, 2015). Although progress has been made, there remain many barriers that arise from within the complex team and organisational environments (external) and also within women themselves (internal) (Longman & Madsen, 2014; Ngunjiri & Madsen, 2014). External barriers, among a host of others, include the glass ceiling, pay inequity, organisational practices (e.g. biased recruiting, hiring, career development, training, promotion), others' perceptions (e.g. likeability, attractiveness, discrimination), and a lack of opportunities related to things like role models, networking, and socialising. Internal barriers may include such elements as confidence, leaning in, negative messages, negotiation skills, aspirations, and feedback.

Along with addressing and assisting women with these internal and external barriers, I would argue that recruiting, hiring, promoting, mentoring, and sponsoring women into formal and informal positions of influence is an important imperative in responsible leadership today. Efforts toward diversity and inclusion have been shown to benefit organisations and entities (e.g. corporate, non-profit, political, government, community) through improving financial performance, strengthening organisational climate, increasing corporate social responsibility and reputation, leveraging talent, and enhancing innovation and collective intelligence (Madsen, 2015). The various dimensions of responsible leadership (e.g. ethics, duty of care, sustainability over the long term, aligned purposes, and relational and shared), as outlined by Kempster and Watton (2014), clearly align with the benefits of workplace diversity. The bottom line is that workplace diversity and inclusion initiatives are now foundational to responsible leadership in today's global economy today.

In finding ways to better encourage women toward and to prepare them for leadership, one of the most important and foundational areas of emerging research focuses on understanding women's aspirations and motivations to lead (Madsen, 2008, 2009). In many cases, the aspirations and motivations appear to be different for women than for men. In fact, some initial studies (Longman, Dahlvig, Wikkerink, Cunningham, & O'Connor, 2011; Tunheim & Goldschmidt, 2013) have found that a powerful motivator for many women who have stepped forward to lead is that they believe they have been 'called' to do so. After becoming aware of their own giftedness and then understanding their call to lead, it appears that, among other things, their self-efficacy, self-awareness, and ability to become more resilient – key characteristics women need in order to assume leadership roles – seem to increase.

Although scarce, research is emerging regarding the intersection of women, leadership, and calling, and recent research has inspired me to write this piece. Hence, this chapter explores the multifaceted phenomena of women, calling, and leadership by first providing literature and insight on the history, definition, related constructs, and benefits of the term 'calling'. I then discuss the existing literature on the intersections arising among the constructs of women, work, leadership, and calling. The chapter concludes with a discussion of the applications to the leadership research, theory, and practice. My hope is that this chapter will encourage others to include the calling construct in future studies, as understanding women's aspirations and motivations more deeply can, in my opinion, lead to more women leading – something that can ultimately change the world.

Background and characteristics of calling

History

According to Tunheim and Goldschmidt (2013), the term 'calling' was coined in 1522 by the German theologian, Martin Luther, from the University of Wittenburg. His view, which was different from that of the Catholic Church at the time, was that everyone – not just religious leaders – has a calling from God. Hence, he believed that both religious and common occupational work could hold spiritual significance (Oates, Hall, Anderson, & Willingham, 2008). Luther believed that this sense of being called could motivate people to serve their neighbours and communities more effectively. Calvinism, which also has its origins in the Protestant Reformation, also conveys a sense of calling that looks at the question of the control that God exercises over the world and teaches that people must be predestined and then called to be among the elect. Hence, people sought for evidence that they were among the elect (Swezey, 2009).

Calling for women was also addressed during the Protestant Reformation, but it focused primarily on motherhood (Oates *et al.*, 2008). Calling in this context took on a special meaning particularly for women because the role of motherhood held spiritual connotations. As Oates *et al.* explained, 'Luther gave wives and mothers a sense that they were fulfilling the Lord's work, too' (p. 230). Luther also taught, however, that one need not go in search of a vocation, but should stay in his or her 'place' (home) to fulfill God's purpose. Of course this had less positive implications for women who had aspirations beyond raising children. However, this reformation provided at least some initial space for emotion, inspiration, subjectivity, imagination, and beauty, which was part of the romanticism movement of the late eighteenth century. It pushed back at the notions of objectivity, control, restraint, logic, and rational behaviour being valued as the sole framework for finding truth and purpose.

Definitions

Calling has often been used interchangeably with the concept of 'vocation', which involves living a life of meaning and purpose. In fact, the translation of the Latin word *vocare* (hence 'vocation') is 'to call' (Brennfleck & Brennfleck, 2005). Some believe that the vocational call is 'a summons from God' to use one's gifts in the world, 'whether it be within paid employment, the home, or volunteer activities' (p. 7). According to Dik and Duffy (2009, p. 427), these terms are used to

> refer to a sense of purpose or direction that leads an individual toward some kind of personally fulfilling and/or socially significant engagement within the work role, sometimes with reference to God or the divine, sometimes with reference to a sense of passion or giftedness.

Dik and Duffy (2009) also stated that 'a vocation is an approach to a particular life role that is oriented toward demonstrating or deriving a sense of purpose or meaningfulness and that holds other-oriented values and goals as primary sources of motivation' (p. 428). The authors acknowledged the considerable overlap between calling and vocation, but noted significant distinctions. Both terms link 'work to an overall sense of purpose and meaningfulness toward other-oriented ends, but only individuals with callings perceive the impetus to approach work in this manner as originating from a source external to the self' (p. 428).

Now, the term 'calling' has also been defined in a variety of ways. Hall and Chandler (2005) simply referred to it as 'work that a person perceives as his purpose in life' (p. 161). Dik and Duffy (2009, p. 427) defined it as

> a transcendent summons, experienced as originating beyond the self, to approach a particular life role in a manner oriented toward demonstrating or deriving a sense of purpose or meaningfulness and that holds other-oriented values and goals as primary sources of motivation.

In their research instrument, Davidson and Caddell (1994) described calling as follows: 'My work has special meaning because I have been called to do what I'm doing regardless of how much time it takes or how little money I earn; I was put on this earth to do what I am doing' (p. 138). Common themes in a number of definitions include that calling 'arises from some force outside the person and is thought to pertain to careers that an individual sees as meaningful and that promote the greater good in some way' (Duffy & Sedlacek, 2007, p. 591). Longman *et al.* (2011) clarified, identifying two influences inherent in definitions of calling: first, the *external* recognition of a divine call to serve God, a transcendent summons, or some guiding force, and, second, the *internal* search for purpose and meaning that is sought through self-reflection, prayer, and meditation. They found that it is the 'recognition and embracing of personal gifts, talents, and strengths that enables individuals to contribute to the good of humanity' (p. 258).

Religious vs. secular

Historically, the term 'calling' carries a religious connotation. The early notion of a calling was described as 'a divine inspiration to do morally responsible work' (Hall & Chandler, 2005, p. 160). However, modern researchers have adopted a 'more expansive and secular conceptualisation of calling, emphasising meaning and personal fulfillment in work' (Steger *et al.*, 2010, p. 82). The secular view includes the characterisation that an individual does work because of a strong sense of inner direction, with the calling coming from an internal motivation that is not specifically driven by instrumental goal-seeking – a form of psychological engagement with the meaning of work (Hall & Chandler, 2005). The term 'calling' now applies to individuals with either religious or secular views. A few studies have explored specifically whether both religious and non-religious people experience a sense of calling. For example, Steger *et al.* (2010) found that both highly religiously committed people and those who were less religiously committed felt 'called'. They concluded that self-efficacy, meaningfulness, and a value of serving a greater good were common for both highly religious and non-religious individuals. I would argue that whether one uses calling within either the religious or secular framework, 'morally responsible work' (Hall & Chandler, 2005, p. 160) and responsible leadership is still at its foundation.

Hall and Chandler (2005) compared the two views, and in terms of the source of the call, they said that the religious view includes a belief that the call comes from God or a higher power, while individuals with the secular view believe it comes from within. Both religious and non-religious individuals believe that their callings serve the community, but, according to Hall and Chandler, the latter may also view their callings as serving him/herself. The means of identifying a call differ as well: the religious view the call through discernment (e.g. prayer, listening), while those with secular views perceive the call by means of introspection, reflection, meditation and other relational activities. According to Brennfleck and Brennfleck (2005), non-religious people believed their calls were directed by duties and roles in society instead of by God or some higher power.

The literature agrees that each person's calling is unique. Having a sense of calling, according to Hall and Chandler (2005), is a highly individual and subjective experience. These authors and others (e.g. Novak, 1996) argued that a calling also involves preconditions. For example, an individual must have strengths or talents (a 'fit') in a specific area, openness to exploring and discovering one's call, and a love for the kind of work that will be involved. The Quaker tradition asserts that an individual's call emerges from personal inspiration. Palmer (2000, p. 2), in *Let Your Life Speak*, stated:

> They remind me of moments when it is clear – if I have eyes to see – that the life I am living is not the same as the life that wants to live in me. In those moments I sometimes catch a glimpse of my true life, a life hidden like the river beneath the ice … before you tell your life what you intend to do with it, listen for what it intends to do with you … let your life tell you what truths you embody, what values you represent.

Finally, Weiss, Skelley, Haughey, and Hall (2003) argued that an individual must have a personal awareness that he or she has been called and then eventually discover the unique path for him or her to take in accomplishing that calling. The literature also highlights the fact that finding one's unique call is not easy, and it often requires a great deal of discussion, reflection, trial and error, and persistence (Hall & Chandler, 2005).

Other characteristics and benefits

Dik and Duffy (2009) clarified that the identification and applications of calling is a lifelong process, not something an individual discovers one time. Rather, it includes an 'ongoing process of evaluating the purpose and meaningfulness of activities within a job and their contribution to the common good or welfare of others' (p. 429). They also posited that everyone potentially has a calling and that it can be in the context of any legitimate area of work, not just religious, teaching, or social service careers. Indeed, callings can be pursued within all occupations, and Dik and Duffy argued that this includes occupations that may not appear to work toward the wellbeing of society in an obvious way.

It is also important to note that a calling is a dynamic phenomenon and has the ability to change depending on life circumstances (Tunheim & Goldschmidt, 2013). For example, a call may be slightly different when a woman has young children living at home, and it may change as the children grow and move out of the home. Also, a call may change based on a woman's preparedness. For example, she may not take on a leadership role until she has completed her education, or she may move into more influential positions as she gains more confidence and experience with learning and leading.

A few studies explored other facets of callings. For example, Hall and Chandler (2005) argued that one of the deepest forms of psychological satisfaction can occur when work is perceived as a calling. Their calling model of career success also includes interactions involving calling and self-confidence, effort, objective success, identity change, and external recognition. They emphasised that a clear sense of identity is essential to the processes of self-exploration (secular) and discernment (religious) in discovering calling. Further, profound self-awareness includes and integrates a calling with values, life purpose, and gifts. Literature more generally discusses other closely related or interacting and moderating variables, including one's interests, passions, motivations, talents and strengths, skills and abilities, personality traits, openness to call, commitment, courage, gifts, and love for work.

Scholars have found that those who feel called in their employment can have the following benefits: better job performance; heightened job satisfaction; increased organisational citizenship behaviour (Dik & Duffy, 2009; Duffy & Sedlacek, 2007); greater life satisfaction (Hunter, Dik, & Banning, 2010); better psychological wellbeing (less depression and anxiety, increased happiness) (Steger *et al.*, 2010; Steger, Frazier, Oishi, & Kaler, 2006); heightened sense of identity (French & Domene, 2010); enhanced adaptability; lower absenteeism (Hall & Chandler, 2005); greater meaning in life (Dik & Duffy, 2009); increased social connectedness (Longman *et al.*, 2011); satisfaction of fulfilling God's plan (Oates, Hall, & Anderson, 2005); deeper career engagement; heightened sense of contribution and worth (Steger *et al.*, 2010); self-clarity and firmer career decidedness (Duffy & Sedlacek, 2007); increased positive workplace attitudes (Steger *et al.*, 2010); decreased boredom (Oates *et al.*, 2008); greater energy, enjoyment, and vitality (Hall & Chandler, 2005); stronger capability to manage temporary setbacks or failure; and increased self-awareness, self-efficacy, and resilience (Longman *et al.*, 2011). Steger *et al.* (2010) also found that 'people who approach their work as a calling have a career that engages them at a deep level and provides them with a highly valued sense of contribution and worth in their work lives' (p. 91). Research has also found that effective and responsible leaders do have more engaged employees and that when employees are engaged they often receive many of the benefits outlined as well.

Finally, some scholars have argued that calling has substantial overlap with other constructs. These include, but are not limited to, purpose, meaningfulness, personal engagement, flow, psychological participation, psychological success, and intrinsic motivation. Hall and Chandler (2005) stated that the challenge that researchers are currently exploring is 'how to characterize the key facets of a calling and how to distinguish it from separate, but similar, constructs' (p. 161). Yet, Dik and Duffy (2009) and others have already deemed calling to be a sufficiently distinct variable that warrants attention as a unique construct, stating that calling is a 'valuable, inclusive, and cross-culturally relevant' construct that provides a 'promising template for guiding research and practice that targets individuals' experience of work as meaningful' (p. 425). Kempster, Jackson, and Conroy (2011) also make the argument that there is a responsibility of leadership to enable those they lead to find meaning and purpose in everyday activity. They suggest (and this is amplified by Parry and Jackson in Chapter 8 of this volume) the importance of sense-making/sense-giving as a central leadership activity. And building on Drath, McCauley, Palus, Van Velsor, O'Connor, and McGuire (2008) such sense-making/sense-giving can enable an aligned deeper purpose, fulfilment within the leadership relationship and perhaps across the organisation, even extended to connected stakeholders as a consequence of aligned sense of purpose. Emerging examples such as Unilever give a glimpse of such related and aligned sense-making across extensive internal and external relationships.

Women, calling, and leadership

The previous section discussed the definition of calling as well as its benefits, related constructs, and other characteristics. This section highlights studies that have linked calling with women in the workplace more generally, and then homes in on studies that connect women and leadership with calling. It is important to note that nearly all of the existing literature on women and calling is based on research conducted within a Christian (religious view) setting.

Women and calling

There are few studies published on women and sense of calling in different domains, and although some do not focus specifically on women leaders, they do provide some useful insight. The first is French and Domene's (2010) qualitative study of female Christian university students who agreed beforehand that they felt a sense of calling (religious view). The students had examined the experience of 'life calling', which the researchers concluded appears to be deeply intertwined with one's worldviews and life values. They found that life calling, which included occupation, definitely informed these students' choices, career paths, identities, and world lens with a sense of being called to something greater than themselves. The authors (French & Domene, 2010, p. 9) concluded:

> Perhaps people with a strong sense of calling at an early age view their whole life through this lens because they have a strong sense of that calling. Perhaps their adoption of a lens of calling to interpret all aspects of their life is what has allowed them to develop such a strong sense of calling. Perhaps these students' dispositions are prone to becoming absorbed in whatever they do and they have come to interpret such an approach as a 'calling'. In any case, it is evident that calling pervades every area of these people's lives and, as such, may be beneficial to address when counselling such students.

These women felt that life calling was both an inward and an outward experience and that this strong sense of life calling was linked to their skills, personhood, passions, and the desire to help others. The participants admitted, however, that pursuing a calling comes at a cost (e.g. putting aside other areas of interest, relationships, and recreation; expending a lot of effort and dedication; unexpected trials, hurdles, and sacrifices). These women also believed that the support of others through significant relationships (e.g. parent, career counsellor, educator, and friend) was crucial in their development of life calling. Also, during the formative years, exposure to a particular area of interest was an important factor in the discovery of a life calling. These authors also provided a connection between calling and self-efficacy, initiative, engagement in related experiences, challenges and obstacles, resiliency, determination, active versus passive, conscious effort to find calling, and sense of identity.

Next, work-life conflict and integration literature abounds in terms of documenting the high level of stress, concern, and challenge that women, in particular, feel when they attempt to integrate family, career, and community responsibilities. Oates et al. (2005) investigated the role of calling in the lives of working Christian mothers struggling with interrole conflict. Their qualitative study focused on interviews with 32 mothers working in Christian academia. The researchers studied calling attributes, factors that shaped their experience with calling, and related implications. They found that mothers who experienced their profession as a spiritual calling often felt able to adapt and manage the career-smothering tensions more effectively. Further, they found that greater levels of calling conviction, higher sense of meaningful

work, broader comprehensiveness in calling, and perceived collective responsibility were also linked to increased ability to cope with interrole tension.

The grounded theory that emerged from the Oates *et al.* (2005) study was
titled 'The Sanctification Framework', which posits that the sense of calling
was manifest in three areas:

1   Certitude and commitment: The conviction and commitment to calling
    was critical in helping women manage the internal tension inherent in
    multiple roles.
2   Collaboration: The belief that there were adequate interpersonal
    resources assisted women in managing the demands of both parenting
    and career.
3   Context of purpose: The belief that one's work was part of a God's larger
    plan seemed to place their interrole challenges within a transcendent
    perspective.

For many, embracing their calls also led to a decrease in guilt. In sum, the
sanctification of work – through experiencing a sense of calling – assisted
women in coping more effectively with work-family conflicts and other
interrole tension.

A few researchers with mixed-gender studies have noted gender differences
in understanding calling. First, Duffy and Sedlacek (2007) concluded from their
qualitative study that men were more likely to consider their job as a calling
than women were. Second, French and Domene (2010) reported in their literature review that women relied more on relationships and staying connected,
and they cared about and for others because of their perceived calls. Oates *et al.*
(2008) discussed the various benefits for pursuing multiple roles (i.e. career,
motherhood), particularly when the roles are viewed as spiritual callings and
when adequate support systems are available. Another study found that women
who worked with people (as opposed to things) were twice as likely to view
their job as a calling, and, interestingly, as educational level increased, so did a
sense of calling (Duffy & Sedlacek, 2007). Finally, Phillips (2009) found in her
study of college students that both men and women perceived vocational callings from a purposeful and spiritual perceptive; however, they conceptualised
calling in different ways: women interpreted call from a relational (affective)
perspective that was connected to sense of self, while men discerned calling
cognitively and pragmatically. A female student's path to a sense of calling
focused on what they felt good about doing and what makes them feel they
matter, while the male students' sense of calling centred on their paid work and
the belief that they can perform well enough to support their future families.

The call to lead

Because of the 'leader is male' assumption that still exists in most contexts,
there is a misguided perception by many women that being a leader is a

prideful and arrogant role. Since many women's styles are more collaborative, team-focused, nurturing, and developmental, leading is often not something they want to consider, seek, or pursue. Yet, one of my favourite leadership quotations is as follows:

> Leadership is a concept we often resist. It seems immodest, even self-aggrandising, to think of ourselves as leaders. But if it is true that we are made for community, then leadership is everyone's vocation, and it can be an evasion to insist that it is not. When we live in the close-knit eco-system called community, everyone follows and everyone leads.
>
> (Palmer, 2000, p. 74)

Hence, Palmer (2000) argues that leadership is a vocation or calling that all men and women who care about community and society should seek and accept. This section summarises four key studies that combine women, calling, and leadership. There are hints in the literature that, even if women may have the perception just described, if they feel called to lead, they will step forward to make it happen. This, of course, is a powerful insight in motivating and preparing more women for leadership.

First, Dahlvig and Longman (2014) recently published a model that introduced three key contributors to women's leadership development, specifically in Christian higher education: motivators that lead to leadership self-efficacy, leadership experience, and finally leadership competence. They argued that a woman's awareness of calling and giftedness is one of three critical motivators for her to move into more significant leadership roles within higher education. These researchers found that female participants were not motivated by the attractiveness of the career ladder, but rather the (1) awareness of calling, along with (2) relational responsibility, and (3) mentoring/external encouragement. This relational responsibility concept is also captured within the Kempster and Watton (2014) model of responsible leadership. It emerges in Dahlvig and Longman's (2014) research as a 'dedication to personal connections with individuals above, alongside, or beneath – in support of the institutional mission' (p. 12). This relational responsibility dedication was a motivation to engage in higher levels of leadership through the overlapping influences of calling and mentoring.

Second, Tunheim and Goldschmidt (2013) conducted a phenomenological study of the lived experiences of calling in 15 women university and college presidents in the United States, six of whom came from religious institutions. The majority of participants did believe they had been called in some way into the presidency. Researchers described three stages of calling for women:

1   Identifying the call: This was described as a spiritual call, a calling through a match of the institution's needs and the women's own gifts and skills, and/or the process of obtaining more knowledge and information.
2   Interpreting the call: Exploring and interpreting the call was a next step for most participants. Many continued the process of obtaining more

information, continuing an examination of their gifts, while others sought guidance from others, attended workshops or seminars that provided clarity, and continued deep reflection and/or prayer.

3   Pursuing the call: Once an internal call to the presidency was accepted by the women, they then opened themselves to opportunities and, in some cases, actively sought out positions. They moved from understanding their call to making it happen.

As these researchers stated, 'according to Luther in 1521, regardless of how much preparation one has, there comes a time when one just has to take a leap of faith – if the calling is true, the role will be there' (p. 38). Tunheim and Goldschmidt found this to be true, particularly with presidents who felt called to lead.

Third, I have personally collected data for years on the leadership development journeys of female U.S. university presidents and governors, as well as educational, government, and business leaders in the United Arab Emirates, China, and Slovenia. An important component of this research focused on the leadership motivations of these women. Although I have not specifically collected data using the term 'calling', I have re-analysed data from two U.S.-based studies (Madsen, 2008, 2009) to explore whether the women felt called in some way to lead. Although these prominent women leaders did not use the term 'calling', after reviewing transcriptions, it is clear that each of them felt called in either a religious or secular way. The data reflect the following 12 primary leadership motivations (rank order):

1   To make a difference
2   To influence positively
3   To serve the community and help others
4   To make things happen
5   To fulfill accomplishment and achievement needs
6   To fulfill drives and ambition
7   To do what I am meant to do in life
8   To have power
9   To do interesting, exciting, and meaningful work
10   To learn, develop, and grow (liked change)
11   To get great satisfaction from my work
12   To have challenges and important responsibilities.

The motivations listed that most closely align with calling include: to make a difference, to positively influence, to serve the community and help others, and to do what I am meant to do in life. For example, one university president with a religious view stated:

I have always wanted desperately to make a difference. I believe we're put on this earth for some reason, and I believe that very strongly. We must not squander that. There are so many people who can't speak for themselves, and they must have a voice. When we can be that voice, then our lives are really worth living.

(Madsen, 2008, p. 243)

Another woman leader with a more secular view said:

I thrive on challenge. I thrive on doing different things all of the time. I like variety. I like trying to work through and finding solutions to things ... figuring out your way through issues. I like to help make things happen.

(Ibid., p. 244)

She believed that her talents, gifts, and passions were aligned with the position and that she was 'made to do this work'. After completing this data analysis, it became clear that calling – for women with religious and secular views – was an important leadership motivator for the participants in these studies.

Finally, the most comprehensive calling model to date that brings together the constructions of leadership and calling for women has emerged from the work of Longman and colleagues (2011). They explored this phenomenon in a grounded theory analysis based on 16 interviews with women leaders with the Council of Christian Colleges and Universities (CCCU). These researchers discovered that calling is actually centred in leaders' knowing and using their unique talents and strengths, which are 'often recognised as gifts from God that were clues to God's plan for their lives' (Longman *et al.*, 2011, p. 264) (see Figure 5.1). According to Longman *et al.* (ibid., p. 264), the model

conceptualised calling along two continuums: *internal-external* and *specific-general*. *Internal-external* refers to sources of validation from which women experienced confirmation for their giftedness. *Specific-general* identifies a spectrum regarding the nature of calling being a well-defined task or a generalised sense of purpose or direction.

The model also includes four conceptual factors or forces that influenced their sense of calling:

1   Theological influences: principles or beliefs engrained in the historic Christian faith;
2   Family realities: relationships with immediate family, relatives, and friends that contribute to one's sense of self and possibilities;
3   Life circumstances: environmental aspects of life, such as geographical location, socio-economic status, work environment, local community, church, and peers; and
4   Cultural expectations: shared beliefs and practices that influence and impact all life domains.

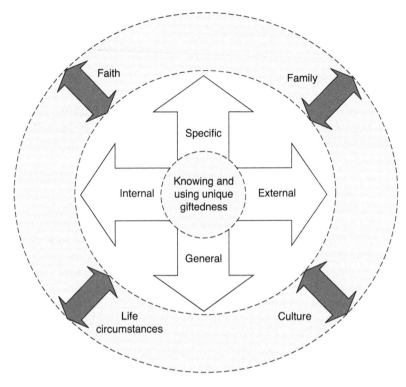

Figure 5.1 A conceptual model of women's calling.

The researchers argued that these four forces or contextual factors could either limit or help expand the women's use of their gifts and talents and also influence (directly or indirectly) the ways women discern and act on their calls.

The larger, shaded concentric circles of the Longman *et al.* (2011) model represent 'the potential for movement or development inherent in a woman's sense of calling' (p. 264). Longman *et al.* observed that the model most likely would not be circular; instead it would depend upon where a woman places herself both on the specific-general or internal-external continuum and with the four factors that may limit or propel the calling embracement. For example,

> If a woman has both a strong sense of self-awareness and self-efficacy (internal) regarding a well-defined task or calling (specific) and is being externally affirmed in her giftedness (external), the woman's self-efficacy through recognition of gifts and talents expand in three directions to depict a strengthened sense of calling. If this same woman has a support-ive family and comes from a supportive theological tradition, and is at a

point in life to be mobile (an aspect of context) to pursue her sense of calling, there would be few environmental limits in fulfilling her call.

(pp. 264–265)

Longman *et al.* summarised that the awareness of giftedness and the act of identifying their calling are important in propelling women to engage in leadership opportunities.

Although two of the four studies were conducted in Christian settings and many of the participants in the other two have the religious view of calling, these studies provide at least a start for understanding the power and potential of the calling construct in the secular or religious view to help women aspire to and become leaders. Clearly, a majority of women in these studies stepped forward, in part, because they felt called to lead.

Implications for research and practice

A number of key findings from this chapter may be useful as implications for research and practice, particularly for those building theory, conducting studies, or designing and facilitating women's leadership development programmes. First, discovering calling can be linked to using talents, gifts, abilities, knowledge, and passions in a way that helps other people and society at large. For some, understanding life and vocational calling can inform their choices, career paths, identities, and world lens with a sense of being called to something greater than themselves. In addition, awareness of calling for women is a critical motivator that can lead to leadership self-efficacy, leadership experience, and, finally, leadership competence. If women discover this call to lead, aspirations and motivations to lead in informal and formal positions of influence may improve. Studying these relationships in more depth will also provide additional insight into helping women see how their unique gifts and talents are connected to the calling to lead. Also, using these constructs in discussions and programmes will assist women in understanding their callings.

It is also important to consider cautiously the advantages and disadvantages for individuals in understanding their calls. Although answering one's call comes with a host of benefits, it may also result in sacrifices. For example, if a mother with small children feels called to take a leadership position within higher education, she will most likely experience heavy work-family conflict, even with a good support system in place. Yet, mothers who feel called in their careers or in other community work may also be able to adapt and deal with the work-family tensions more effectively, and do this with less guilt. Since these are very personal decisions, developmental opportunities should be thoughtfully crafted to help women explore both the pros and cons of career and life choices, including the ways that they relate to calling. Critical reflective activities can be included in programme components geared toward self-awareness. Additional theory and research on these life complexities is also recommended.

Another implication for research and practice relates to understanding the connections among the overarching framework of responsible leadership and the constructs discussed in this chapter (i.e. gender, leadership, and calling). This is important to strengthen organisational efforts and initiatives that focus on getting more women into leadership roles more generally. In addition to work in addressing and assisting women with internal and external barriers, greater understanding and work in refining processes and systems of recruiting, hiring, promoting, mentoring, and sponsoring women is an important imperative for responsible leadership today. Continued research and the evaluation of best practices are strongly encouraged. As previously stated, the bottom line is that workplace diversity and inclusion initiatives are now foundational to responsible leadership in today's global economy.

Finally, the emerging models outlined in this chapter can provide a starting point for more rigorously tested constructs and new theory building (qualitative and quantitative methodologies). For example, constructs of calling for women – i.e. faith, family, life circumstances, culture, validation (internal-external), nature of calling (specific-general), and knowing and using giftedness – can be tested and replicated in additional theory-building processes and research studies. In addition, the calling stages model (i.e. identifying, interpreting, and pursuing calling) may benefit from more extensive studies that elucidate the intricacies of each stage for women. The same is also true for the Dahlvig and Longman (2014) model of key contributors to women's leadership development. Although these models already provide a useful framework for researchers to further explore these phenomena and for practitioners to carefully design development experiences, effective practices – developmental relationships and activities – can be continuously discovered and designed to improve programmes. Carefully designed research and evaluation of these programmes and practices can then help in redesigning or confirming their effectiveness in women's leadership development settings as well.

Conclusion

The existing literature provides initial evidence that, for at least some women, a sense of calling can influence their aspirations and motivations to lead, strengthen their commitment to their work (paid or unpaid), provide a source of personal and professional strength, help manage role conflicts, enhance their ability to prioritise more effectively, provide a difference perspective on challenges and failure, decrease guilt for these failures (in God's hands), and provide the courage to lean in. As Smith (1999, p. 123) stated,

> It takes courage to pursue our vocation, the courage to be – the courage to be true to who we are, even if it means living on the edge, living with risk, living with less security and less influence and less power – because to pursue our vocation means that we have chosen the way that is true to who we are, true to ourselves, true to our call.

The foundation of developing courage – and the identification, interpretation, and pursuit of calling – is critical reflection. And without it, calling may not even be discovered let alone pursued. Warren Bennis (2009, p. 92), one of the best-known leadership writers, once said,

> There are lessons in everything, and if you are fully deployed, you will learn most of them. Experiences aren't truly yours until you think about them, analyse them, examine them, question them, reflect on them, and finally understand them. The point, once again, is to use your experiences rather than being used by them, to be the designer, not the design, so that experiences empower rather than imprison.

By understanding the influence that calling may have for both religious and non-religious women, scholars and practitioners can assist women in facilitating new leadership aspirations and motivations. This could influence more women to seek out opportunities to become leaders in various settings (e.g. business, government, political, non-profit). In addition, by understanding a sense of responsibility for helping others realise meaning and aspirations within their everyday endeavours, calling can be most beneficial for many individuals and organisations. Yet for many, calling in work and life may bring peace to the soul, particularly as it relates to ensuring the time they spend on earth is meaningful, and this is what I believe is truly important.

References

Adler, N. J. (2015). Women leaders: Shaping history in the 21st century. In F. W. Ngunjiri & S. R. Madsen, *Women as global leaders* (pp. 21–50). Charlotte, NC: Information Age Publishing.

Bellah, R. N., Madsen, R., Sullivan, W. M., Swidler, A., & Tipton, S. M. (1985). *Habits of the heart: Individualism and commitment in American life*. New York: Harper & Row.

Bennis, W. G. (2009). *On becoming a leader*. Reading, MA: Addison-Wesley.

Borysenko, J. (n.d.). The story of a man who saw three fellows laying bricks. Retrieved from www.43things.com/entries/view/2534015www.43things.com/entries/view/2534015.

Brennfleck, K., & Brennfleck, K. M. (2005). *Live your calling: A practical guide to finding and fulfilling your mission in life*. San Francisco, CA: Jossey-Bass.

Buechner, F. (1973). *Wishful thinking: A seeker's ABC*. New York: Harper & Row.

Dahlvig, J., & Longman, K. A. (2014). Contributors to women's leadership development in Christian higher education: A model and emerging theory. *Journal of Research on Christian Education, 23*(1), 5–28.

Davidson, J. C., & Caddell, D. P. (1994). Religion and the meaning of work. *Journal for the Scientific Study of Religion, 33*(2), 135–147.

Dik, B. J., & Duffy, R. D. (2009). Calling and vocation at work: Definitions and prospects for research and practice. *The Counseling Psychologist, 37*(3), 424–450.

Drath, W. H., McCauley, C. D., Palus, C. J., Van Velsor, E., O'Connor, P. M. G., & McGuire, J. B. (2008). Direction, alignment, commitment: Toward a more integrative ontology of leadership. *Leadership Quarterly, 19*, 635–653.

Duffy, R. D., & Sedlacek, W. E. (2007). The presence of and search for a calling: Connections to career development. *Journal of Vocational Behavior, 70*(3), 590–601.

French, J. R., & Domene, J. F. (2010). Sense of 'calling': An organizing principle for the lives and values of young women in university. *Canadian Journal of Counselling, 44*(1), 1–14.

Hall, D. T., & Chandler, D. E. (2005). Psychological success: When the career is a calling. *Journal of Organizational Behavior, 26*(2), 155–176.

Hunter, I., Dik, B. J., & Banning, J. H. (2010). College students' perceptions of calling in work and life: A qualitative analysis. *Journal of Vocational Behavior, 76*(2), 178–186.

Kempster, S., Jackson, B., & Conroy, M. (2011). Leadership as purpose: Exploring the role of purpose in leadership practice. *Leadership, 7*(3), 317–334.

Kempster, S., & Watton, E. (2014). How you can explore the case for responsible management with colleagues and senior managers. Paper presented at PRME (Principles for Responsible Management Education), Winchester, United Kingdom.

Longman, K., Dahlvig, J., Wikkerink, R., Cunningham, D., & O'Connor, C. M. (2011). Conceptualization of calling: A grounded theory exploration of CCCU women leaders. *Christian Higher Education, 10*(3–4), 254–275.

Longman, K., & Madsen, S. R. (Eds.) (2014). *Women and leadership in higher education.* Charlotte, NC: Information Age Publishing.

Madsen, S. R. (2008). *On becoming a woman leader: Learning from the experiences of university presidents.* San Francisco, CA: Jossey-Bass.

Madsen, S. R. (2009). *Developing leadership: Learning from the experiences of women governors.* Lanham, MD: University Press of America.

Madsen, S. R. (2015). Why do we need more women leaders in Utah? Retrieved from www.uvu.edu/uwlp/docs/uwlpbrief2015no5.pdf.

Madsen, S. R., Ngunjiri, F. W., Longman, K. A., & Cherrey, C. (Eds.) (2015). *Women and leadership around the world.* Charlotte, NC: Information Age Publishing.

Ngunjiri, F. W., & Madsen, S. R. (2014). *Women as global leaders.* Charlotte, NC: Information Age Publishing.

Novak, M. (1996). *Business as a calling: Work and the examined life.* New York: The Free Press.

Oates, K. M. L., Hall, E. L., & Anderson, T. L. (2005). Calling and conflict: A qualitative exploration of interrole conflict and the sanctification of work in Christian mothers in academia. *Journal of Psychology and Theology, 33*(3), 210–223.

Oates, K. L. M., Hall, M. E. L., Anderson, T. L., & Willingham, M. M. (2008). Pursuing multiple callings: The implications of balancing career and motherhood for women and the Church. *Journal of Psychology and Christianity, 27*(3), 227–257.

Palmer, P. J. (2000). *Let your life speak: Listening for the voice of vocation.* San Francisco, CA: Jossey-Bass.

Phillips, S. (2009). *Predictors of vocational calling in students: A structural equation model.* Unpublished doctoral dissertation, Azusa Pacific University, Azusa, California.

Smith, G. T. (1999). *Courage and calling: Embracing your God-given potential.* Downers Grove, IL: IVP.

Steger, M. F., Frazier, P., Oishi, S., & Kaler, M. (2006). The meaning in life questionnaire: Assessing the presence of and search for meaning in life. *Journal of Counseling Psychology, 53*(1), 80–93.

Steger, M. F., Pickering, N. K., Shin, J. Y., & Dik, B. J. (2010). Calling in work: Secular or sacred? *Journal of Career Assessment, 18*(1), 82–96.

Swezey, J. A. (2009). Faculty sense of religious calling at a Christian university. *Journal of Research on Christian Education, 18*(3), 316–332.

Tunheim, K. A., & Goldschmidt, A. N. (2013). Exploring the role of calling in the professional journeys of college presidents. *Journal of Leadership, Accountability and Ethics, 10*(4), 30–40.

Weiss, J. W., Skelley, M. F., Haughey, J. C., & Hall, D. T. (2003). Calling, new careers and spirituality: A reflective perspective for organizational leaders and professionals. In *Spiritual intelligence at work: Meaning, metaphor, and morals. Research in Ethical Issues in Organizations*, Volume 5 (pp. 175–201). Amsterdam: Elsevier.

Wrzesniewski, A., McCauley, C., Rozin, P., & Schwartz, B. (1997). Jobs, careers, and callings: People's relation to their work. *Journal of Research in Personality, 31*, 21–33.

6 Responsible leadership

A radical view

Karen Blakeley

Leadership theories emerge and flourish in contexts that give them meaning. Responsible leadership is no exception. We are living in a complex world which is increasingly viewed as lacking effective, ethical, and courageous leadership (Ashforth, Gioia, Robinson, & Treviño, 2008; Cowell, 2012; Iszatt-White & Saunders, 2014, p. 215). Of the top ten trends identified by respondents to the World Economic Forum global survey of 2015, a lack of leadership was number three on the list, with 86 per cent strongly agreeing that the world is facing a leadership crisis (World Economic Forum, 2015b). In summarising the survey, Professor David Gergen, Co-director of the Center for Public Leadership, Harvard Kennedy School of Government, claims '[w]e need moral, effective leadership to step up across our society – business, non-profit, and political leaders all have a role to play (World Economic Forum, 2015a). Gergen also points out that we get the leaders we deserve, suggesting that all citizens need to engage in responsible leadership, for the crisis of leadership implicates us all.

The increasing recognition that we face a crisis in both the effectiveness and legitimacy of leadership has generated an incipient research agenda and growing academic interest in the area of responsible leadership. What follows is an attempt to:

1   make sense of the context that has given rise to this interest;
2   undertake a critique of current responsible leadership theory in the light of this context;
3   provide a more radical view of responsible leadership that may be better placed to meet these contextual challenges.

The context

All school children in the developed world learn about the problems of sustainability – the exponential growth in world population, the concept of peak oil, the growing competition for water and other natural resources, and, of course, climate change. They may be less aware of human rights issues – that their mobile and electronic devices depend upon rare earth minerals gained through the exploitation of some of the poorest in Africa (Global Witness, 2015; European Parliament, 2015); that their throw-away fashion is manufactured by children as young as five in Asia; and that they themselves are being sexualised at younger and younger ages for the purposes of commercial profit (Walter, 2010). It is even more unlikely that they understand crucial issues of power. They probably do not question that their parents are working longer hours for a reducing share of the country's wealth (Bunting, 2005; Harvey, 2007); that the conditions of systematic control experienced by their parents at work (top-down targets, electronic supervision, zero hours contracts) have contributed to growing disempowerment, rising levels of stress, and a con-flict between work and family life (Bunting, 2005). It is highly unlikely that they understand the ways in which business elites influence governments and transnational entities often manifesting greed, selfishness, and sometimes unethi-cal behaviour (Asthana, 2008; Richardson, Kakabadse, & Kakabadse, 2011; Shaxson, 2012; Thomas 2008). These issues – threats to sustainability, abuse of human rights, falling levels of wellbeing, growing centralisation of power, and highly problematic standards of ethics in business – are the context within which responsible leadership theory has flourished.

Responsible leadership

Responsible leadership is rooted in stakeholder theory and founded on the premise that corporate leaders have a responsibility to a broader range of stakeholders than normally included in mainstream leadership theory. These stakeholders comprise non-governmental organisations, employees, and cus-tomers, people throughout the supply chain, governments, societies, and future generations, all of whom are affected by the organisation's activities. Thomas Maak and Nicola Pless are two of the most prolific writers in this area and have defined responsible leadership as

> [a] values-based and principle-driven relationship between leaders and stakeholders who are connected through a shared sense of meaning and purpose through which they raise to higher levels of motivation and com-mitment for achieving sustainable value creation and responsible change.
>
> (Maak & Pless, 2009, p. 539)

At the global level, responsible leaders act as 'agents of world benefit' (Pless & Maak, 2009, p. 60), leveraging stakeholder relationships, and organisational resources to bring about improvements in social justice, environmental sus-tainability, and governance and ethical behaviour on a worldwide scale.

What is unusual about responsible leadership theory is that it is content-led. Unlike previous well-known leadership theories (transformational leader-ship, authentic leadership, situational leadership), this is not a theory outlining 'how' best to motivate, inspire, and develop outstanding performance in fol-lowers; rather it focuses on a set of specific desired outcomes loosely brought together under the heading of 'corporate social responsibility' (CSR). This implies that those who are not committed in some way to bringing about improvements in social justice, human rights, sustainability, integrity, and the re-distribution of power (however you define and construe these goals) would not normally come under the rubric of responsible leadership theory. That is not to say that those who are uncommitted to these goals are necessarily 'irresponsible' leaders but just that responsible leadership theory has emerged from and become inextricably entwined in the debate around corporate responsibility.

This might explain, at least in part, another interesting aspect of responsible leadership theory, that it appears to have been embraced as much by practitioners as by academics (Moody-Stuart, 2014; Richardson, 2015). With the theory and practice of corporate responsibility thoroughly endorsed by the UN and other influential bodies, there are now a plethora of initiatives such as the UN Global Compact, the Global Reporting Initiative, FTSE4Good, the Dow Jones Sustainability Index and the World Business Council for Sustainable Development, all available for companies to sign up to and gain a reputational boost to their brand.

Perhaps the leader currently seen as most representing the ideal of responsible leadership is Paul Polman, CEO of Unilever. Termed 'Captain Planet' by the Harvard Business Review (Ignatius, 2012), he symbolises the archetypal responsible leader, addressing and going beyond the challenges of the UN Global Compact, unilaterally deciding to terminate quarterly reporting due to the short-termism it encourages and representing alternative values to those of materialism and greed. However, whilst there are many responsible leaders, past and present, doing great jobs in a variety of contexts, the number of members of the responsible leadership club is relatively small. This is problematic, particularly with regards to large corporations, partly because of the overwhelming power that these transnational entities exercise and partly because, after a 30-year history of increasing awareness of CSR, CSR itself stands accused of having failed, one of the reasons being a lack of committed and substantive responsible leadership within global corporations (Milne & Gray, 2013; Visser, 2011).

The rest of this chapter is dedicated to exploring the reasons for this in more detail and will end by suggesting a more radical approach to responsible leadership that better meets the challenges outlined above.

Corporate responsibility, responsible leadership, and the case for reform

In order to understand the limitations of CSR and its links to some of the failures of responsible leadership I present three important arguments:

1   Corporates have contributed to many of the problems around sustainability, human rights violations, lack of integrity, and increasing imbalances of power.

2   The leaders of multinational corporations have the power and influence to address many of these issues.
3   Despite claiming to address the issues, they are failing to do so.

1 Corporates have contributed to many of the problems around sustainability, human rights violations, lack of integrity, and increasing imbalances of power

When looking at the complex problems facing our world today, multinational corporations play an important role in their causation, continuation, and exacerbation. The most obvious example is the role of the banks in the global financial crisis of 2008. This can be viewed systemically as an outworking of the banks' role in driving capital accumulation; culturally as a particular characteristic of Anglo-American capitalism; legally as a failure of corporate governance; or individually as a function of personal greed fuelled by inappropriate reward structures and recruitment. All explanations contain a degree of merit but, as a number of leading thinkers have clearly demonstrated, *unregulated* capitalism encourages corporate entities to maximise profit regardless of externalities and the needs of weaker stakeholders, benefiting a minority of wealthy elites who, by dint of their roles in the system, have unlimited access to increasingly concentrated sources of wealth and power (Cronin, 2013; Harvey, 2007; Kaletsky, 2010; Wilks, 2013).

Multinationals are often alleged to be inextricably linked to the problems of exploitation in developing countries. Mining companies, for example, are implicated in the exploitation of miners and their communities, particularly in parts of Africa and South America (FT.com, 2014; Siegel, 2013). Klein (2000) demonstrated how clothing companies consciously outsourced their manufacturing to developing countries in order to save money, undermine unions, and rid themselves of costly labour regulations. She describes how this led directly to sweat shops in Asia and China. This strategic move was promoted by the advertising industry which introduced the revolutionary notion of companies no longer being producers of 'goods' but rather embodiments of 'brands'. As brands became important means of identity formation, young people became targets, leading to unethical advertising strategies, the sexualisation of children, and the use of neuroscience to promote soaring levels of consumerism and debt (Lindstrom, 2012; Walter, 2010).

There have been allegations of negligence and cost-cutting in BP leading to the worst oil spill in history (Kurtz, 2013) and the extensive brutality perpetrated by dictators sponsored by an oil company in alliance with the French government (Shaxson, 2012, pp. 2–3). More recently, ordinary people's pensions and livings have been destroyed by corrupt company failures such as Enron and WorldCom. Innocent people lost their lives in cars that were known by senior management to have life-threatening faults (Kaufman, 2014; Taylor, 2010). This is to say nothing of armament corporations implicated in corruption, large corporations avoiding tax, one of the largest corporations in the world accused of union busting, low wages, sexual discrimination, and unsafe factories in Bangladesh (Greenhouse, 2015); poor treatment of workers in developed countries (Young, 2013); and a group of multinationals and government elites secretly agreeing new laws enabling corporations to pro-secute governments that inhibit their ability to make profit (Corporate Europe Observatory, 2015; Williams, 2014).

Multinational corporations touch every facet of our lives – from the health systems within which we are born, to identity formation during our teens, to the wellbeing we experience during our working lives, to our wages, pensions, and debt, to our genes, and the health systems that care for us as we die.

This is not to say that multinational corporates are rapacious super-organisms that contribute nothing to society. Without global corporations, their drive, inventiveness, risk-management, operational efficiency and vision, our lives would be immeasurably shorter and poorer. It is simply to point out that these corporate entities are immensely powerful and, particularly in the last 30 years, they have been led by many who have abused the power invested in them to the detriment of many of the corporation's stakeholders – which means all of us. This leads on to the next argument.

2 The leaders of multinational corporations have the power to address many of these issues

Of the largest economic entities in 2012, 40 per cent were corporations (Global Trends, 2015). There is a growing consensus that the power of cor-porations is expanding and is growing beyond the regulative capacity of indi-vidual states (Fuchs, 2005; Scherer & Palazzo, 2011). Perhaps nowhere is this more dramatically seen than in gatherings such as Davos and, more interest-ingly, in Bilderberg.

Bilderberg is an annual gathering of the world's most powerful political, financial, and business leaders. The intention of the meetings is to establish a climate where powerful and influential people can discuss world economic and political affairs without being reported outside the confines of the meeting – the aim being to reach consensus on some of the world's most intractable problems. There is not the space to cover the problematic moral, social, and political issues raised by this kind of institutional gathering; readers are referred to the work of Richardson *et al.* (2011) in this area. What is notable, however, is that of the more than 135 members attending the meeting in 2014, approximately 63 were from recognisable business back-grounds (mostly banks, oil, and technology companies). In addition, some members represented various neutral-sounding institutes which in fact turn out to be business interests presenting as independent, quasi-academic think tanks, such as the KKR 'Institute', representing one of the world's most powerful venture capital firms, and the Lundbeck Foundation, which aims to 'maintain and expand the activities of the Lundbeck Group', a pharmaceutical company.

In Bilderberg, business interests mix with the world's political, military, and intelligence leaders to come to a consensus about world affairs, a consensus that is then acted out on the world stage (Richardson *et al.*, 2011). Moreover, business leaders form the largest single stakeholder group, outnumbering the individual groups of politicians, academics, military, and intelligence leaders by far. This is not a global stakeholder group – clearly missing from Bilderberg are representatives of working people in the developed countries, environmentalists, third sector NGOs and direct representatives of the world's poor, misgoverned, and exploited in developing countries.

In addition to their political influence, CEOs, their teams and representatives have control over financial resources the size of national economies and access to leading-edge expertise in information technology, bio-technology, disease-control, financial systems, logistics, and opinion-formation. They also influence policy indirectly through highly intensive lobbying activities.

Additionally, the process of globalisation has enabled multinational corporations to escape protective laws, norms, and practices instituted by people and their governments throughout history, retreating to territories where such laws are minimal. They play governments off against each other and, in turn, governments lure businesses with financial and legal enticements which may function to the detriment of many working people in developed countries around the world. This leads Scherer and Palazzo (2011) to propose a new theory of the firm, one in which the corporation is now a global 'political' actor, with powers to affect the behavioural norms and practices of the states in which they function.

Alongside their growing power, the corporate elite have awarded themselves increasing proportions of their company's profits, giving them high levels of *personal* influence. Between 1945 and 1975, the top 1 per cent of earners in the US took 8 per cent of the national income. By the end of the twentieth century, this had soared to 15 per cent, with the top 0.1 per cent of the population increasing their share of the national income from 2 to 6 per cent (Harvey, 2007, pp. 15–16). Many of these top earners were senior corporate executives. Standard and Poors, for example, reported that in 2002, 20 per cent of reported corporate profits was set aside to reward top executives (Mount, 2012, p. 59). Between 2000 and 2008, whilst the FTSE All-Share Index fell by 30 per cent, payments to executives increased by 80 per cent (Mount, 2012, p. 61).

It is clear that key issues such as environmental degradation and climate change, human rights, corporate ethics, and the distribution of wealth will never be addressed without the active involvement of these global corporates. No longer should they be viewed as privately owned entities, legitimately dedicated to profit maximisation. I suggest that it would be better to view them as 'corporate microstates', protected by powerful governments, but with powers greater than many national governments, their shares owned by savers all over the world who have no power to control or regulate them. These corporate microstates have no democratic processes and look more like oligarchies (think Russia) than social democracies (think Western Europe). Now, more than ever, we need responsible leaders in these positions of power. This will not come about until we change our social construction of companies.

3 They are failing to address the issues

Many business leaders, responding to an array of influences including stake-holder lobbying, NGO campaigns, peer pressure (e.g. the UN Global Compact and the Global Reporting Initiative) and an increasing recognition of their own power, influence, and responsibility, have seriously engaged with corporate responsibility. However, there is increasing consensus that relying on responsible leaders will not sufficiently address the problems we face (Visser, 2011; Wilks, 2013). There are a number of reasons for this.

First, there is the problem of conflicts of interest. Current responsible leaders have over time advocated only incremental and marginal improvements that do not match the scale of the problems we face (Scherer & Palazzo, 2011). In part, this simply reflects the obvious fact that those in charge of our organisations have most benefited from their profitability and increasing influence. Hence, whilst companies may respond to tragedies such as the Bangladesh factory fire by insisting on a stronger system for auditing health and safety compliance, they are highly unlikely to increase wages or reduce working hours in order to give their workers a degree of economic freedom and psychological wellbeing. To illustrate this point, Foxconn responded to the 13 suicides by young people at their factory in China by constructing suicide nets rather than by addressing the issue of excessive working hours, lack of holidays, overcrowding, and poor working conditions. Currently, as far as I am aware, few leaders have ever instigated reductions in their pay or a significant redistribution of profit in favour of employees, people in the supply chain, or even shareholders (the past 30 years has demonstrated the opposite). Nor are they likely to vote for a diminution of their powers to govern. Whilst CSR theorists talk about the need to incorporate stakeholders into corporate dialogue this is only likely to go so far. Corporations and their leaders only talk to the stakeholders that they choose and only respond in ways that they decide.

Second, there is the significant problem of how we have socially constructed the corporation. Companies are economic entities, tasked with making money, and as long as they remain within the law, they are regulated only by market forces. By construing the corporation solely as a profit-making entity, the discourse around CSR is often strongly functionalist, focusing on the business case and suggesting that only policies that make economic sense can be legitimised. This focus on the bottom line is often legitimised by reference to 'shareholder interests'. However, evidence suggests that corporations have been hijacked by a small oligarchy who have milked these money-making entities for personal gain, awarding themselves excessively high levels of remuneration regardless of performance and at the expense of other stakeholders (Mount, 2012). The discourse that legitimises these actions (we need to pay the highest rates to attract the best talent; frequent references to shareholders' interests) is simply a narrative that disguises the fact that CEO pay has risen much faster than the increase in the FTSE100 index. According to the UK Government's Department for Business Innovation and Skills, CEOs of FTSE100 companies received average increases of 13.6 per cent per annum between 1999 and 2010. This compares with just 1.7 per cent annual increase in the FTSE index during the same period. They conclude that the FTSE index appears 'to have had no impact on the level of remuneration awarded' (Department of Business Innovation and Skills, 2011, p. 11). Even critical voices in the media repeat the 'talent' and 'shareholder value' arguments as if they were inviolable truths and yet, those in positions of power know otherwise. In a BBC interview, David Ellis, Head of Remuneration at KPMG opined on the high levels of executive pay:

> Pay is also a function of the capacity of the entity concerned to make profit and there is no doubt that there is a link between that capacity and the amount people earn. It is not about, 'do you agree with that or not', I think it is more about saying they have got that capacity and there is that profit there. What is the appropriate sharing of the spoils that that business has created between its shareholders, between its broader employee base, between its senior people and in fairness between its customers too. So that concept of sharing of the spoils is absolutely critical in the context of balancing what the right answer is.
>
> (Today Programme, BBC Radio 4, 2014)

Here, Ellis points out that companies are simply money-making entities with different capacities to generate profit. Different companies generate different levels of 'spoils'. The problem of excessive pay arises when those who are at the helm of these money-making entities simply help themselves to the spoils, much as pirates help themselves to the spoils of ships, without any regard to who actually 'owns' the spoils (e.g. individual pension-fund holders) or who may have a legitimate interest or stake in them (Freeman, 1994).

Third, there is the issue of power. Companies are not formally accountable to anyone for their actions in the field of CSR. Whilst countries may issue codes of conduct, in many cases these are not binding and compliance is purely voluntary. Hence companies which respond in a minimal or tokenistic way to ethical challenges do not face any repercussions. This lack of accountability is most apparent in corporate sustainability reporting which, according to Milne and Gray, has boomed over the past ten years. However, these reports fail to define sustainability in any meaningful sense and tend to 'cover few stakeholders, cherry pick elements of news and generally ignore the major social issues that arise from corporate activity such as lobbying, advertising, increased consumption, distributions of wealth and so on' (Milne & Gray, 2013, p. 17).

Fourth, there is the issue of human nature. There is now significant evidence to suggest that there is a relationship between attraction to power (as measured by social dominance orientation) and reduced empathy, compassion, and concern for others (Anderson & Brown, 2010). People with high social dominance orientation display a preference for hierarchical systems within which their in-group is perceived as superior to out-groups and where power inequalities are both valued and legitimised. Those with high levels of social dominance orientation tend to view life as a zero-sum competition with clear winners and losers and perceive ruthlessness as a necessary and valued trait (Aiello, Pratto, & Pierro, 2013).

It is suggested that business people have higher levels of social dominance than professions such as teaching, social work, or nursing (Sidanius, Van Laar, Levin, & Sinclair, 2003), implying that business leaders will be more power-oriented, less compassionate, and less concerned for others than leaders from other sectors. According to Anderson and Brown (2010) research has demonstrated that the personality trait of 'agreeableness' is negatively associated with leader emergence but positively associated with leader effectiveness. On the other hand the simple desire for promotion to senior posts (a facet of social dominance orientation) is associated both with the achievement of power and with high levels of selfishness. Moreover, psychopaths are found in disproportionate numbers in business, particularly in more senior positions, giving rise to the assertion that the presence of psychopathic leadership was a significant contribution to the 2007/08 financial crisis and continues to underpin lack of support for ethical change in business (Boddy, 2013).

In addition to this, business theories and cultures tend to reinforce competition, the pursuit of self-interest and the delegitimation of prosocial behaviour unless it can be definitively linked to increased levels of efficiency and profitability. Spending time in a business environment, therefore, socialises executives into a world where materialism, competitiveness, and success are the only values that are pertinent. Even those with less materialistic values can lose their bearings when prosocial and ethical behaviours are neither recognised nor rewarded.

Moreover, recent research into the effects of power on the brain shows that levels of testosterone rise (responsible for aggression and competition) and levels of oxytocin decline (responsible for empathy and prosocial behaviour) (Daedalus Trust, 2015; Hogeveen, Inzlicht, & Obhi, 2014; Israel *et al.*, 2009; Robertson, 2012). In other words, power impacts the brain in such a way as to generate the hubris syndrome – an over-inflated self-opinion and derision for the opinions of others, a tendency to conflate self-interest with the interests of super-ordinate constructs such as the company, the nation or even God, recklessness, a tendency to treat others as objects and a loss of contact with reality (Owen, 2012).

In summary, multinational corporations attract and select those who are more competitive, selfish, and less prosocial; they reward and promote the selfish and competitive over the prosocial and, as these executives rise into the most powerful positions, their brains generate higher levels of testosterone making them even less prosocial.

The implications of all this are that, due to a number of human and systemic drivers, it is more likely than not that the more ruthless will gain access to power in these companies minimising their capacity for responsible leadership.

Again, this is not to decry the tremendous efforts that some companies and executives have made with regards to corporate social responsibility (Aguinis & Glavas, 2013; Bader, 2014; Blowfield & Murray, 2011; Chouinard & Stanley, 2012). There is no doubt that many executives are sincerely dedicated to doing good through the means at their disposal – it is rather that companies socialise, rationalise and reward performativity so effectively that there are simply not enough of these responsible leaders, they often find themselves isolated and exhausted, and they are constrained by the systems within which they operate.

In sum, I hope to have shown that corporations and their leaders play an important role in both causing and addressing the problems of sustainability, human rights, and power inequalities. After at least two decades of claiming to address them, there has been a failure to grapple with the challenging root causes which, in part at least, is due to a lack of responsible leaders able and willing to ask radical, challenging questions.

A more radical view of responsible leadership

In response to the issues above, a number of thinkers are redefining corporate responsibility. Visser (2011) has suggested that we need a new model of CSR, CSR 2.0, involving a more inclusive, decentralised approach where problems and solutions are identified and addressed by means of diverse stakeholder panels, innovative partnerships, real-time reporting, and genuine collaboration with currently marginalised stakeholders.

Milne and Gray suggest the use of better tools that truly measure the ecological footprint of commercial activities recognising that, as cited in the UNEP Sustainability Report of 1994 'some products, processes and even entire industries may prove to be unsustainable – even when run efficiently' (Milne & Gray, 2013, p. 25).

Wilks (2013) has called for fundamental changes in corporate governance, drawing on models common in Europe and Asia, where companies are governed by bodies that consider the joint interests of shareholders, workers, communities, and government.

It follows that responsible leadership theory itself needs redefining to incorporate this growing recognition that genuine accountability, a commitment to personal ethics, and a significant questioning of the structure, role, and governance of commercial bodies are central to CSR.

We need new kinds of responsible leaders who are more radical in the changes they seek and who are prepared to reframe their self-interest in the context of the wider good. These more radical responsible leaders facilitate efforts and influence others to bring about a more equitable, just, democratic, and sustainable world, in part by working towards significant changes in institutional power structures and in part by means of their own personal transformation and ongoing development of character. Whilst recognising the diversity of the values and beliefs that comprise normative systems, responsible leaders commit to an explicit, ethically driven agenda and strive to develop universally admired virtues such as wisdom, courage, compassion, humility, integrity, and self-control. They empower others, embed robust systems of accountability, and help create and sustain powerful social movements dedicated to the beneficial flourishing of people and society.

Whilst this description may have echoes of transformational leadership there are important distinctions between these two theories. First, responsible leaders can come from any part of the system and will influence a wide range of people rather than focusing their attention only on those in some form of reporting relationship to them. Second, responsible leaders recognise the complexity of the systems that they work in and do not articulate a vision that claims to have all the answers; rather they engage with a range of stakeholders so that progress emerges from dialogue. Third, responsible leaders do not need to be charismatic individuals but rather see themselves as partners in the process of addressing highly complex problems. They recognise that they themselves will engage in behaviours likely to be problematic, probably benefiting from systems that are unjust or unsustainable. In fact, a helpful leadership paradigm to underpin responsible leadership is 'shared leadership' whereby 'the social actors in an organization or group are involved in the process of leading one another toward productive ends' (Pearce, Waasenaar, & Manz, 2014, p. 277).

There are a number of elements in this notion of responsible leadership that would benefit from further explanation. I outline in what follows five important propositions.

Proposition 1 Responsible leaders are committed to an explicit, ethically driven agenda

As mentioned before, responsible leadership is unlike previous leadership theories in that it is committed to a specific agenda of bringing about a more equitable, just, and sustainable world. It is also dedicated to a set of specific values, however they may be interpreted – those of human rights, sustainability, the redistribution of power, human flourishing, and personal transformation. Responsible leadership in a business context is a commitment to a particular view of the company and its role in society. This has important implications. Responsible leaders believe *in* something. That is not to revisit the now unfashionable 'vision' word but rather to assert that certain core beliefs and values need articulating and promoting. Once a leader has committed to a set of beliefs, values, and actions, it is incumbent on that leader to promote understanding and receptivity towards that agenda.

The resilience of neoliberalism, despite the recession, the growth of inequality, and declining levels of trust in corporate elites, has left many angry and disempowered, with no recourse to an alternative narrative or sense-making paradigm. Responsible leaders spend time understanding, constructing, and articulating their own beliefs and share those with others in order to help people make sense of their lives and articulate their own hopes for the future. Responsible leaders help to build communities and movements committed to joint action around a shared agenda empowering both themselves and others.

Proposition 2   Responsible leaders believe that there are some universal human values

It is very unfashionable in postmodern times to claim that there are universal values. However, postmodernism has increasingly come under attack by those who construe that its relevance has passed (Kirby, 2010). For over five decades postmodern irony, incredulity, deconstruction, scepticism, and moral detachment strongly influenced thought, so much so that it is now commonplace to hear people state (without understanding the philosophical influences on their statements) that everything is relative and that there is no such thing as truth.

Despite popular acceptance of the most basic of its tenets, postmodernism is being superseded by an array of post-postmodernist theories, approaches, and practices. These offer a baffling range of alternatives from digimodernism, metamodernism, altermodernism, hypermodernity, and automodernity. Nevertheless, one interesting thread runs through many of them – that is a rediscovery of a new authenticity, a new compassion, and a new commitment to values.

The horror of the attack on the World Trade Centre and the subsequent wars in the Middle East and Afghanistan, the rise of religious fanaticism, the global financial crisis and ongoing corporate scandals have all contributed to a state of consciousness inimical to postmodern play and irony. There is a desire for 'hope', 'faith', 'love', 'compassion', and 'authenticity', the pillars of any morality, but all these words must carry a sense of awareness of the postmodern critique – we want faith, but not 'Faith in a New World Order' but rather 'faith' in our friends, neighbours, and co-workers – a faith that is limited in time, space, and context. This is a relational kind of faith, a recognition and understanding of the fact that our world comprises a range of highly complex systems in which our fates are closely linked to one another.

There has also been increasing interest in leaders who demonstrate 'character', a notion that is rooted in the idea of universally admired values such as courage, humanity, and honesty, and there is a growing movement of academics and practitioners exploring what this might look like in the twenty-first century business context (Covey, 2004; Crossan, Mazutis, Seijts, & Gandz, 2013; Seijts, Gandz, Crossan, & Reno, 2015). There are in fact two possible sources for the claim that there might be some universal values that we should strive to protect and promote.

The first comes from moral psychology. Haidt (2012) shows how even infants as young as six months are attracted to puppets that 'help' other puppets rather than those who are aggressive and unhelpful. Haidt suggests in fact that human beings are 'pre-wired' for five core moral sentiments – care, fairness, authority, loyalty, and sacredness/cleanliness.

The second comes from positive psychology. Christopher Peterson and Martin Seligman completed an extensive piece of research that involved them identifying and cross-matching lists of virtues that seem to have been revered across all times, places, and cultures (Peterson & Seligman, 2006). They analysed the world's great religions and great intellectual and philosophical traditions to identify six universal virtues: wisdom, courage, humanity, justice, temperance, and transcendence.[1] These six virtues are admired across time and place and are not culturally relative.

Both lists share 'care for others', 'fairness/justice', and 'transcendence' (feelings of interconnectedness, human flourishing, awe and wonder, meaning and purpose). One way of summarising this is by claiming that responsible leaders must at the very least be committed to human rights (compassion, fairness, and justice) and human flourishing (transcendence). Other values core to responsible leadership include 'sustainability' and 'empowerment', particularly stakeholder empowerment – both of which are central to responsible leadership theory.

When discussing values and ethics, extreme relativism can lead to the adoption of absurd and immoral positions, potentially justifying genocide, and hence for most people it is completely untenable (Beauchamp, 2010). Responsible leaders challenge postmodernist assertions that everything is relative – that corruption is fine if it takes place in India or that paying less than a subsistence wage is acceptable in the Democratic Republic of Congo. Even paying just a subsistence wage is unacceptable to a responsible leader who, by dint of their commitment to human rights and human flourishing, will believe, even if they are not in a position to facilitate this, that any human being should have enough resources to raise and educate a family.

This is not to ignore the problems and complexity inherent in the vast differences between cultures in terms of norms, mores, and what is considered right and wrong. It is simply to give responsible leaders the confidence to claim that there are some universal values that are worth standing for.

Proposition 3 Responsible leaders commit to the democratisation of institutions

David Ellis' notion of companies as simply the neutral generators of spoils is a useful one (Today Programme, BBC Radio 4, 2014). By viewing multinational corporations as powerful money-making machines, capable of being wielded for good or bad, but susceptible to control by executives seeking to maximise their own share of the spoils, it is then clear that *how* we have constructed the ownership, control, and governance of companies is the cause of many of the issues discussed here. The problem with construing corporates as private concerns, belonging to shareholders, controlled by executives and imbued with rights to pursue their 'self-interest', is that these institutions become very attractive to what Boddy (2013) terms corporate psychopaths who are disproportionately represented at senior levels of management. These are skilled operators in political dynamics and are attracted to positions of seniority in multinational corporations by the access to wealth and power. If legitimate societal institutions do not exercise some form of control over these corporates, they will increasingly be dominated by people psychologically incapable of exercising compassion, respect for others, or personal restraint.

As far as ownership is concerned, responsible leaders recognise that companies should belong to us – all of us. The status quo deeply challenges this. In Anglo-American law companies do not belong to anyone but are self-constituted entities that operate as 'individuals' but with a fiduciary duty to look after the long-term interests of shareholders. They do not belong to the senior executives who reward themselves from them, nor to the institutional shareholders who *represent* the interests of pensioners and savers (who together own around 47 per cent of corporates shares in the USA). Corporations do not belong to anyone; they simply have to look after the long-term interests of the shareholders (Tudway, 2014). As owners of shares, as workers who add value, as consumers who pay for their services, as stakeholders in their activities, companies should be accountable to us and we need governance structures that properly represent this position.

Responsible leaders will be in the forefront of debate around corporate governance. They will be considering bold new options such as the possibility of electing CEOs or of ensuring non-executive boards are comprised of representatives from labour, NGOs, local communities, and other stakeholder groups. They will be exploring how senior executives can be held accountable to independent non-executive boards who will be responsible for their pay and remuneration. They will be investigating methods for 'screening out' the irresponsible, hubristic individuals who are most attracted to power but least worthy of it.

That is not to take away the rights of senior executives to manage or lead, and there is a danger of over-democratisation. Moreover, democratisation in mutual institutions such as The Co-op in the UK did not prevent corruption and greed at the top. However, greater accountability and the more equitable distribution of power in these money-making entities is crucial for any effective addressing of the issues discussed here. Responsible leaders understand this and work towards novel mechanisms for greater democratisation of our organisations.

Proposition 4 Responsible leaders are committed to an ongoing personal transformation of character

I have already argued that business tends to attract those who are more self-oriented and less prosocial; it is precisely these individuals who run and control some of the most powerful institutions in the world.

It would be easy to despair in the face of this kind of argument which is reminiscent of the well-known aphorism by Lord Acton: 'Power tends to corrupt, and absolute power corrupts absolutely. Great men are almost always bad men.' However, there are signs for optimism.

First, it has been argued that whilst those in business are less prosocial and more self-interested, this is partly explained by the fact that the world of business is highly focused on competition and success and hence moral concerns are simply not given attention (Segal, Gideon, & Haberfeld, 2011). This is not a conspiracy of the wicked but rather a blind spot that can be addressed (Blakeley, 2007), and in fact is partly being addressed by the increasing focus on CSR and responsible leadership.

Second, the most recent research in positive psychology and neuroplasticity suggests that certain kinds of training cultivate a greater tendency to demonstrate prosocial behaviour (Jazaieri, McGonigal, Jinpa, Doty, Gross, & Goldin, 2014). For example, one scientific study showed how compassion training generated stronger activations in neural networks associated with positive valuation, love, and affiliation (Klimecki, Leiberg, Lamm, & Singer, 2013). Numerous studies from positive psychology have demonstrated that it is possible to cultivate gratitude, empathy, and compassion simply through the process of regular practice and by paying more focused attention to relevant stimuli (Stanford School of Medicine, 2014).

Third, emerging evidence from leadership development demonstrates that *some* people do profoundly change when they experience situations involving the suffering and deprivation of others (Pless, Maak, & Stahl, 2011). This kind of exposure to 'crucible experiences' can lead to a shift in perspective, a kind of transformational learning often cultivated in programmes using service learning agreements. This transformational learning includes the development of compassion, altruism, the desire to pay back, and the gaining of a sense of meaning in one's life.

The argument so far suggests that not only can we do something to combat self-interested tendencies in those who control our corporations but that it is vital that we do so.

Of course, cultivating the virtues (e.g. of wisdom, courage, humanity, justice, temperance, and transcendence) is a struggle, particularly in positions of seniority and responsibility. Nevertheless, responsible leaders recognise the importance, challenge, and benefits inherent in developing character. They actively seek feedback and they ensure that they are held accountable for their actions and decisions to others.

At the same time, the system has to develop its own virtues. Research shows that whilst prosocial leaders are more effective in leading organisations, organisational systems and selection processes are poor at promoting such leaders to positions of power (Anderson & Brown, 2010). Hence, I suggest that we build organisations with systems and processes that cultivate virtue. These include assessing leaders' psychological fitness for power through robust selection processes; developing prosocial leaders by means of evidence-led interventions such as those emanating from the positive psychology movement; coaching by highly qualified coaches specialising in the virtues and character development; regular psychological assessment of leaders in terms of their 'fitness to lead' (see Wiscarson, 2015 for a discussion of how annual CEO checks can be implemented to spot and deal with hubris before it becomes a problem); allocating responsibility for appointing leaders to independent boards which represent a range of stakeholders including employees and shareholders. These are just a few ideas that would help build more virtuous organisations.

Proposition 5 Responsible leaders are committed to co-creating an organisational, social, and political movement dedicated to serving society

You do not need to belong to a multinational corporation to become a responsible leader nor have to attend a corporate programme to develop responsible leadership skills. Anyone who facilitates efforts and influences others to bring about a significantly more equitable, just, and sustainable world, in part by working towards transformational changes in organisational power structures and in part by means of their own ongoing development of character, is a responsible leader. This means that the young graduate who garners support for a new initiative to support a local charity in her company is a responsible leader; a middle manager who incorporates the voices of community leaders into a project management process is a responsible leader; a member of the Occupy movement who lobbies for changes in corporate governance is also a responsible leader.

In this sense anyone can be a responsible leader – it is not a position but a movement. Some responsible leaders will be located outside the organisation and devote their energies to lobbying and campaigning for change. However, others will adopt the mantle of 'tempered radical' (Meyerson, 2001) and work inside the system to change it. Tempered radicals, according to Meyerson, are:

> People who want to succeed in their organizations yet want to live by their values or identities, even if they are somehow at odds with the dominant culture of their organizations. Tempered radicals want to fit in *and* they want to retain what makes them different. They want to rock the boat, and they want to stay in it.
>
> (Meyerson, 2001, p. xi, italics in original)

Meyerson's (2001) research shows that change can be effected from within by people willing to take risks and challenge the system (see also Bader's personal account of being a tempered radical inside BP: Bader, 2014). However, this is a tough choice and it may be that significant change will not be achieved without a powerful social movement, consisting of people both inside and outside of organisations, to support and lobby for change.[2]

So what next?

Taking the definition of responsible leadership identified above, it would appear that within it are some very clear principles and actions which can be illustrated in the following model. This can help give a focus for action and embodiment.

Responsible leaders are aware of the debates surrounding business activities in areas such as sustainability, social justice, individual and societal wellbeing, and the democratisation of power and governance structures (the darker outer circles). In order to work in these areas they realise that they need to develop a clear sense of purpose capable of generating an explicit, ethically driven agenda. They also need to be able to deal with power – both giving it away (if they are in a position to do so, for example by involving stakeholders in decisions that affect them) and, equally important, taking it back. As part of this agenda, responsible leaders also realise that change comes about through mobilisation. Whilst individual members of society in isolation wield little power, history has shown that when people organise themselves into groups and communities, they can change laws, systems, governments, and whole societies. Hence, responsible leaders are dedicated to leading change by building a responsible leadership movement. Clarifying purpose, giving, and taking power and leading change are shown in the lighter outer circles. Finally, these principles and actions are all founded on the premise that, like Ghandi, Martin Luther King, Nelson Mandela, and Mother Teresa, we have to 'be the change we want to see'. The foundation of responsible leadership is our

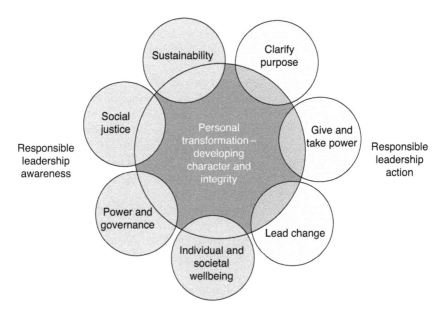

Figure 6.1 Responsible leadership – awareness, action, and personal transformation.

own personal transformation of character and the ongoing development of the virtues.

This approach to responsible leadership theory might easily be accused of being overly 'romantic' (Meindl, Ehrlich, & Dukerich, 1985), even naive. It would appear that this emphasis on the individual, at the expense of structural and cultural factors, glorifies 'leadership as a causal category' and, as a result, elevates the concept of leadership 'to an unwarranted status and significance' (Bligh & Schyns, 2007, p. 343). However, the concept of naivety and the beliefs and commitments so described, are socially constructed according to time, fashion, and culture. Whilst commitment to the overthrow of communism may have appeared naïve to onlookers of Lech Wałesa's Solidarity movement in 1979, in 1989 it would not have appeared as such. In the second decade of the twenty-first century, a century that might so far be described as the century of social movements, the idea that individuals committed to certain ideas, relationships, identities, and goals, can instigate global change (for better or worse) does not appear naïve. As previously mentioned, we may be entering a post-postmodern society, one in which due respect may be paid to the constraints of structure, to the phenomenology of the individual, to the emergent dynamics of groups, to the co-creation of identity and culture, and even more to the unpredictability of complex systems. The admixture of these paradigms, the bricolage of ideas, values, and stories they offer, reveal new possibilities for action and suggest that the ideals, beliefs, and behaviours that we embody might actually matter.

Responsible leadership theory, for this reason, is a theory that belongs to the twenty-first century. First, it acknowledges not the salvatory notion of the individual leader as messiah (Western, 2008) but, more interesting and challenging, the idea that as we all embody beliefs and values and exert influence on those around us, we are all leaders, whether we wish to be or not. Responsible leadership theory simply asks what kind of leader we want to be.

Responsible leadership offers the possibility of connecting to our deepest values and to like-minded others in order to enact leadership across, outside, and despite the corporates who have so dominated our ideas of what leadership should look like. To some extent the values of responsible leadership are 'given' too, though the interpretation of these values can be broadly construed. However, responsible leadership is not compulsory; rather it is a personal choice and how each individual chooses to enact that choice can range from putting in place a mindfulness practice, to ensuring the organisation they work for reduces water usage or, more radically, incorporates marginalised stakeholders into policy-making bodies.

This leads to my next point that in challenging companies to allocate resources to complex global issues of sustainability and human rights, responsible leadership feeds into contemporaneous and emergent perspectives of the idea of leadership as resistance to the dominant organisational norms and practices (Blakeley & Higgs, 2014; Carroll & Nicholson, 2014; Collinson, 2005). Carroll and Nicholson (2014, p. 1414), for example, suggest that leadership development spaces are 'steeped in power, resistance and struggle that entangle facilitators and participants alike; yet … few … know how to work with its energies and insights'. Responsible leadership is intended to create dissonance and reframe the leadership role to incorporate broader stakeholder interests. This implies a new agenda for leadership development, with new skills focused on the exercise of power and politics and new understandings of the leadership context with concepts such as 'framing' and 'mobilization' borrowed from social movement theory and transplanted into the workplace.

This then brings me to the last point where responsible leadership might best be construed, not as a theory supporting organisational performativity, but rather as a theory in some way connected to social movements and the theories associated with them such as social movement theory (Edwards, 2014; Jasper, 2010), collective identity theory (Hunt & Benford, 2007) and resource mobilization theory (McCarthy & Zald, 1977). Responsible leadership already has links to social movements such as environmentalism (Chouinard & Stanley, 2012), human rights movements (Ignatius, 2012; Roddick & Miller, 1991), and more recently shareholder activism such as the UK Shareholders Alliance. Responsible leadership cannot be mandated and will not be assessed in a performance review or rewarded in the form of bonus or promotion. As a result it has to inspire personal commitment. A social movement is an ideal vehicle through which to embody this commitment. According to James and Van Seter (2014, p. xi) a social movement is an 'association between persons who have at least a minimal sense of themselves as connected to others in common purpose and who come together across an extended period of time to effect social change in the name of that purpose'. Linking responsible leadership to social movement theory could provide the conceptual architecture to conjoin theory and practice, the realistic and romantic without which responsible leadership, with its challenge to the performativity agenda, is in danger of becoming an interesting footnote in history.

Notes

1 However, they did not cover the non-literate traditions such as tribal and communal cultures that do not record their cultural sense-making in written form.
2 Marshall Ganz' work in facilitating social movements to effect change within organisations is of relevance here (Ganz, 2010).

References

Aguinis, H., & Glavas, A. (2013). Embedded versus peripheral corporate social responsibility: Psychological foundations. *Industrial and Organizational Psychology, 6*(4), 314–332.
Aiello, A., Pratto, F., & Pierro, A. (2013). Framing social dominance orientation and power in organizational context. *Basic & Applied Social Psychology, 35*(5), 487–495.

Anderson, C., & Brown, C. E. (2010). The functions and dysfunctions of hierarchy. *Research in Organizational Behavior, 30*, 55–89.

Ashforth, B. E., Gioia, D. A., Robinson, S. L., & Treviño, L. K. (2008). Re-viewing organizational corruption. *Academy of Management Review, 33*(3), 670–684.

Asthana, A. N. (2008). Decentralisation and corruption: Evidence from drinking water sector. *Public Administration and Development, 28*(3), 181–189.

Bader, C. (2014). *The evolution of a corporate idealist: When girl meets oil.* Brookline, MA: Bibliomotion.

Beauchamp, T. L. (2010). Relativism, multiculturalism and universal norms: Their role in business ethics. In G. G. Brenkert & T. L. Beauchamp (Eds.), *The Oxford handbook of business ethics* (pp. 235–266). Oxford: Oxford University Press.

Blakeley, K. (2007). *Leadership blind spots – and what to do about them.* Chichester: Wiley.

Blakeley, K., & Higgs, M. (2014). Responsible leadership development: Crucible experiences and power relationships in a global professional services firm. *Human Resource Development International, 17*(5), 560–576.

Bligh, M. C., & Schyns, B. (2007). The romance lives on: Contemporary issues surrounding the romance of leadership. *Leadership, 3*(3), 343–360.

Blowfield, M., & Murray, A. (2011). *Corporate responsibility* (2nd edn). Oxford: Oxford University Press.

Boddy, C. R. P. (2013). Turning point: Corporate psychopaths – uncaring citizens, irresponsible leaders. *Journal of Corporate Citizenship, 49*, 8–16.

Bunting, M. (2005). *Willing slaves: How the overwork culture is ruling our lives.* London: Harper Perennial.

Carroll, B., & Nicholson, H. (2014). Resistance and struggle in leadership development. *Human Relations, 67*(11), 1413–1436.

Chouinard, Y., & Stanley, V. (2012). *The responsible company: What we've learned from Patagonia's first 40 years.* Ventura, CA: Patagonia Books.

Collinson, D. (2005) Dialectics of leadership. *Human Relations, 58*(11), 1419–1442.

Corporate Europe Observatory. (2015). Regulatory cooperation in TTIP: United in deregulation. Retrieved 11 April 2015, from http://corporateeurope.org/international-trade/2015/04/regulatory-cooperation-ttip-united-deregulation.

Covey, S. R. (2004). *The eighth habit.* London: Simon & Schuster.

Cowell, J. (2012). *White Paper 2012: Is there a crisis in confidence in UK leadership?* Bristol: Edgecumbe Consulting. Retrieved 6 August 2015, from www.primarycoloursconsulting.co.uk/resources/articles/white-paper-2012.

Cronin, D. (2013). *Corporate Europe: How big business sets policies on food, climate and war.* London: Pluto Press.

Crossan, M., Mazutis, D., Seijts, G., & Gandz, J. (2013). Developing leadership character in business programs, *Academy of Management Learning & Education, 12*(2), 285–305.

Daedalus Trust. (2015). *About hubris.* Retrieved 13 April 2015, from www.daedalus-trust.com/about-hubris.

Department of Business Innovation and Skills. (2011). *Executive remuneration: Discussion paper.* Retrieved 23 August 2015, from www.gov.uk/government/uploads/system/uploads/attachment_data/file/31660/11-1287-executive-remuneration-discussion-paper.pdf.

Edwards, J. (2014). *Social movements and protest.* Cambridge: Cambridge University Press.

European Parliament. (2015). *Conflict minerals: Preventing military groups from funding their activities*. Retrieved 15 April 2015, from www.europarl.europa.eu/news/en/news-room/content/20150413STO41613/html/Conflict-minerals-preventing-military-groups-from-funding-their-activities.

Freeman, R. (1994) The politics of stakeholder theory: Some future directions. *Business Ethics Quarterly, 4*(4), 409–421.

FT.com. (2014). *South African mining: Stuck in the past*. Retrieved 15 April 2015, from www.ft.com/cms/s/0/e0b9bee0-b0e4-11e3-bbd4-00144feab7de.html#axzz3XMqrAPLy.

Fuchs, D. (2005). Commanding heights? The strength and fragility of business power in global politics. *Millennium – Journal of International Studies, 33*(3), 771–801.

Ganz, M. (2010). Leading change: Leadership, organization and social movements. In N. Nohria & R. Khurana (Eds.), *Handbook of leadership theory and practice* (pp. 527–568). Boston, MA: Harvard Business Press.

Global Trends. (2015). *Corporate clout 2013: Time for responsible capitalism*. Retrieved 11 April 2015, from www.globaltrends.com/knowledge-center/features/shapers-and-influencers/190-corporate-clout-2013-time-for-responsible-capitalism.

Global Witness. (2015). *Conflict minerals*. Retrieved 15 April 2015, from www.global-witness.org/conflictminerals.

Greenhouse, S. (2015). *Workers and critics greet Walmart pay raise but say much remains to be done*. Retrieved 15 April 2015, from www.theguardian.com/business/2015/feb/23/workers-activists-walmart-pay-raise.

Haidt, J. (2012). *The righteous mind: Why good people are divided by politics and religion*. London: Penguin Books.

Harvey, D. (2007). *A brief history of neo-liberalism*. Oxford: Oxford University Press.

Hogeveen, J., Inzlicht, M., & Obhi, S. S. (2014). Power changes how the brain responds to others. *Journal of Experimental Psychology, 143*(2), 755–762.

Hunt, S. A., & Benford, R. D. (2007). Collective identity, solidarity, and commitment. In D. A. Snow, S. A. Soule, & H. Kriesi (Eds.), *The Blackwell companion to social movements* (pp. 433–457). Malden, MA: Blackwell Publishing.

Ignatius, A. (2012). Captain Planet. *Harvard Business Review, 90*(6), 112–118.

Israel, S., Lerer, E., Shalev, I., Uzefovsky, F., Riebold, M., Laiba, E., *et al.* (2009). The Oxytocin receptor (OXTR) contributes to prosocial fund allocations in the dictator game and the social value orientations task. *PLoS ONE, 4*(5), e5535. doi:10.1371/journal.pone.0005535.

Iszatt-White, M., & Saunders, C. (2014). *Leadership*. Oxford: Oxford University Press.

James, P., & van Seter, P. (2014). *Globalization and politics. Volume 2: Global social movements and global civil society*. London: Sage Publications.

Jasper, J. M. (2010). Social movement theory today: Toward a theory of action? *Sociology Compass, 4*(11), 965–976.

Jazaieri, H., McGonigal, K., Jinpa, T., Doty, J. R., Gross, J. J., & Goldin, P. R. (2014). A randomized controlled trial of compassion cultivation training: Effects on mindfulness, affect, and emotion regulation. *Motivation and Emotion, 38*(1), 23–35.

Kaletsky, A. (2010). *Capitalism 4.0*. London: Bloomsbury Publishing.

Kaufman, A. C. (6 May 2014). GM fires 15 workers as CEO admits 'History of failures'. *The Huffington Post*. Retrieved 21 July 2015, from www.huffingtonpost.com/2014/06/05/gm-ignition-recall_n_5452285.html.

Kirby, A. (2010). *Successor states to an empire in free fall*. Retrieved 23 March 2015, from www.timeshighereducation.co.uk/411731.article.

Klein, N. (2000). *No logo*. London: HarperCollins.

Klimecki, O. M., Leiberg, S., Lamm, C., & Singer, T. (2013). Functional neural plasticity and associated changes in positive affect after compassion training. *Cerebral Cortex, 23*(7), 1552–1561.

Kurtz, R. S. (2013). Oil spill causation and the Deepwater Horizon spill. *Review of Policy Research, 30*(4), 366–380.

Lindstrom, M. (2012). *Brandwashed: Tricks companies use to manipulate our minds and persuade us to buy*. London: Kogan Page Publishers.

Maak, T., & Pless, N. M. (2009). Business leaders as citizens of the world: Advancing humanism on a global scale. *Journal of Business Ethics, 88*(3), 537–550.

McCarthy, J. D., & Zald, M. N. (1977). Resource mobilization and social movements: A partial theory. *American Journal of Sociology, 82*, 1212–1241.

Meindl, J. R., Ehrlich, S. B., & Dukerich, J. M. (1985). The romance of leadership. *Administrative Science Quarterly, 30*, 78–102.

Meyerson, D. E. (2001). *Tempered radicals: How people use difference to inspire change at work*. Boston, MA: Harvard Business School Press.

Milne, M. J., & Gray, R. (2013). W(h)ither ecology? The triple bottom line, the global reporting initiative, and corporate sustainability reporting. *Journal of Business Ethics, 118*(1), 13–29.

Moody-Stuart, M. (2014). *Responsible leadership: Lessons from the front line of sustainability and ethics*. Sheffield: Greenleaf.

Mount, F. (2012). *The new few or a very British oligarchy: Power and inequality in Britain now*. London: Simon & Schuster.

Murray, P. (2011). *The sustainable self: A personal approach to sustainability education*. Abingdon: Earthscan.

Owen, D. (2012). *The hubris syndrome: Bush, Blair and the intoxication of power*. London: Politico's Publishing.

Pearce, C. L., Waasenaar, C. L., & Manz, C. C. (2014). Is shared leadership the key to responsible leadership? *The Academy of Management Perspective, 28*(3), 275–288.

Peterson, C., & Seligman, M. E. P. (2006). *Character strengths and virtues: A handbook and classification*. New York: Oxford University Press.

Pless, N., & Maak, T. (2009). Responsible leaders as agents of world benefit: Learnings from 'Project Ulysses'. *Journal of Business Ethics, 85*, Supplement 1: 14th Annual Vinventian International Conference on Justice for the Poor: A Global Business Ethics, pp. 59–71.

Pless, N. M., Maak, T., & Stahl, G. K. (2011). Developing responsible global leaders through international service-learning programs: The Ulysses Experience. *Academy of Management Learning and Education, 10*(2), 237–260.

Richardson, I. N., Kakabadse, A. P., & Kakabadse, N. K. (2011). *Bilderberg People: Elite power and consensus in world affairs*. Abingdon: Routledge.

Richardson, T. (2015). *The responsible leader: Developing a culture of responsibility in an uncertain world*. London: Kogan Page.

Robertson, I. H. (2012). *The winner effect: How power affects your brain*. London: Bloomsbury.

Roddick, A., & Miller, R. (1991). *Body and soul: How to succeed in business and change the world*. London: Ebury Press.

Scherer, A. G., & Palazzo, G. (2011). The new political role of business in a globalized world: A review of a new perspective on CSR and its implications for the firm, governance, and democracy. *Journal of Management Studies, 48*(4), 899–931.

Segal, L., Gideon, L., & Haberfeld, M. R. (2011). Comparing the ethical attitudes of business and criminal justice students. *Social Science Quarterly, 92*(4), 1021–1043.

Seijts, G., Gandz, J., Crossan, M., & Reno, M. (2015). Character matters: Character dimensions' impact on leader performance and outcomes. *Organizational Dynamics, 44*(1), 65–74.

Shaxson, N. (2012). *Treasure islands: Tax havens and the men who stole the world.* London: Vintage.

Sidanius, J., Van Laar, C., Levin, S., & Sinclair, S. (2003). Social hierarchy maintenance and assortment into social roles: A social dominance perspective. *Group Processes & Intergroup Relations, 6*(4), 333–352.

Siegel, S. (2013). *The missing ethics of mining.* Retrieved 7 July 2015, from www. ethicsandinternationalaffairs.org/2013/the-missing-ethics-of-mining-full-text.

Stanford School of Medicine. (2014). *Stanford Centre for Compassion and Altruism Research and Education.* Retrieved 21 July 2015, from http://ccare.stanford.edu.

Taylor, A. (2010). How Toyota lost its way, *Fortune International, 162*(2), 84–91.

Thomas, M. (2008). *Belching out the devil: Global adventures with Coca-Cola.* London: Random House.

Today Programme. (2014, 30 July). Interview with KPMG's David Ellis on Executive Pay. *BBC Radio 4.*

Tudway, R. (2014). *The looming corporate calamity.* London: Heterodox.

Visser, W. (2011). *The age of responsibility: CSR 2.0 and the new DNA of business.* Chichester: John Wiley & Sons.

Walter, N. (2010). *Living dolls: The return of sexism.* London: Virago.

Western, S. (2008). *Leadership: A critical text.* London: Sage.

Wilks, S. (2013). *The political power of the business corporation.* Cheltenham: Edward Elgar Publishing.

Williams, L. (2014, October 7). What is TTIP? And six reasons why the answer should scare you. *Independent.* Retrieved 21 July 2015, from www.independent. co.uk/voices/comment/what-is-ttip-and-six-reasons-why-the-answer-should-scare-you-9779688.html.

Wiscarson, C. (2015). *Chief executives need an annual hubris MOT.* Retrieved 13 April 2015, from www.daedalustrust.com/chief-executives-need-annual-hubris-mot-2015.

World Economic Forum. (2015a). *A call to lead: The essential qualities for stronger leadership.* Retrieved 8 April 2015, from http://reports.weforum.org/outlook-global-agenda-2015/global-leadership-and-governance/the-call-to-lead.

World Economic Forum. (2015b). *Outlook on the global agenda 2015.* Retrieved 8 April 2015, from http://reports.weforum.org/outlook-global-agenda-2015/top-10-trends-of-2015/3-lack-of-leadership.

Young, A. (2013, December 19). Amazon.com's workers are low-paid, overworked and unhappy: Is this the new employee model for the internet age? *International Business Times.* Retrieved 18 August 2015, from www.ibtimes.com/amazoncoms-workers-are-low-paid-overworked-unhappy-new-employee-model-internet-age-1514780.

Part III

Developing responsible leadership

7 Responsible leadership, trust, and the role of Human Resource Management

Stefanie Gustafsson and Veronica Hope Hailey

Introduction

Although there are suggestions that trust in business has improved since the financial crisis, it remains a concern for institutions, organisations, and leaders alike. For example, recently, the *2014 Edelman Trust Barometer*, a survey of trust levels involving more than 33,000 respondents across 27 countries, found that people in Britain trusted their government representatives less than the year before. The reasons that are frequently cited for a lack of trust in senior leaders in the public sector as well as the private include leaders engaging in business activities where any motive beyond making profit appears illusive, ambitious change programmes causing redundancies in the thousands that apparently lack any kind of care or concern for those affected, and instances which evidence a total disrespect for nature, the environment, and the wider world in which we live.

Evidently these are things that one would usually not associate with responsible leadership (Maak & Pless, 2006). On the contrary, responsible leadership as the 'relational and ethical phenomenon, which occurs in social processes of interaction with those who affect or are affected by leadership and have a stake in the purpose and vision of the leadership relationship' (Maak & Pless, 2006, p. 103), requires integrity, compassion, consistency, and morality. It necessitates leadership that is considered just, fair, and humane, as well as leaders who act as 'citizens of the world' (Maak & Pless, 2009, p. 537). Importantly, the question of responsible leadership is not purely a deontological one. Rather, organisations such as the Co-operative Bank had to learn the hard way what it means to be put under scrutiny when one of its senior leaders was accused of irresponsible behaviour. In addition, many modern-day businesses such as Unilever have recognised the business case for responsibility, as their 'Sustainable Living Plan' has helped them to achieve healthy profits and an increase in share price (Balogun, Hope Hailey, & Gustafsson, 2015).

Thus, behaving responsibly seems to make business sense and hence may be something that organisations may want to encourage, cultivate, or develop in their leaders. From an organisational perspective, leadership development is often considered to be the responsibility of the HR (Human Resources) function. Under this umbrella it includes practices aimed at the development of particular skills of individual leaders, as well as the social processes of leadership such as 360-degree feedback, training, mentoring, and coaching schemes (Day, 2000, 2011). Yet, although HR is attributed an important role in leadership development, to date the extant literature does not address its role in relation to responsible leadership. However, given the events leading up to the financial crisis, we may argue that the association between the two is at least a contested one as, particularly in the financial services sector, HR practices around leadership remuneration and reward have been under public scrutiny, leading to the demonisation of an entire profession.

In this chapter we therefore seek to develop existing understanding of the role of HR in responsible leadership. To do so we adopt a trust lens, building on previous research which perceives responsibility and trust as interwoven and mutually constitutive (Maak & Pless, 2006, 2009; Pless & Maak, 2011; Stahl & DeLuque, 2014; Voegtlin, Patzer, & Scherer, 2012). We complement our review of the literature with empirical material that we have collected in two organisations in the UK – BAE Systems and BBC Worldwide. The cases we present here form part of a wider research project involving a total of 22 organisations. The findings suggest that in these organisations the role of HR is one in creating a story of realism rather than romanticism, as those leaders who take their responsibility to perform and evidence competence seriously tend to be seen as more trustworthy.

Leadership, responsibility, and trust

Studies on responsible leadership tend to conceptualise the relationship between trust and responsibility as mutually constitutive (Maak & Pless, 2006, 2009; Pless & Maak, 2011; Stahl & DeLuque, 2014; Voegtlin *et al.*, 2012). On the one hand, behaving responsibly is seen as a prerequisite of building trust while on the other, responsible leaders through their actions create relationships where others can trust them (Maak & Pless, 2006). In proposing that 'responsible leadership is about building trust and cultivating sustainable relationships towards different stakeholders', Maak and Pless (2006, p. 106) place trust at the heart of responsible leadership. In turn, when leaders are perceived to be acting responsibly by others, they are likely to be trusted (Maak & Pless, 2009). Similarly, a lack of taking responsibility may lead to a decrease in trust (Stahl & DeLuque, 2014). Citing Solomon (1998, p. 45), Maak and Pless (2006) even propose that rather than being a charismatic leader without ethical value, one should shift the focus to trust and trustworthy leadership instead.

Connecting responsible leadership and trust as proposed above requires us to approach the two as relational (Voegtlin *et al.*, 2012), also because trust in itself exists in and develops through relationships. For example, Mayer, Davis, and Schoorman (1995, p. 712) define trust as the 'willingness of a party to be vulnerable to the actions of another party'. Building on this work, Rousseau, Sitkin, Burt, and Camerer (1998, p. 395) suggest that 'trust is a psychological state comprising the intention to accept vulnerability based upon positive expectations of the intentions or behaviour of another'. To both definitions, the relationship between the trustor and the trustee is central, as the trustor makes him- or herself vulnerable to the trustee by accepting risks, including for example the possibility of being hurt, disappointed, and generally challenged in the sense of self (Hardin, 1992; Mayer *et al.*, 1995).

Previous research linking trust and leadership has mainly investigated the processes through which trust in leadership may be developed (e.g. Gillespie & Mann, 2004; Whitener, 1997; Whitener, Brodt, Korsgaard, & Werner, 1998) as well as the outcomes of these behaviours (e.g. Dirks & Ferrin, 2001; Ferrin, Dirks, & Shah, 2003). For example, Whitener *et al.* (1998) attribute a central role to senior members in organisations in developing trust. They define five behaviours that influence how trustworthiness is assessed in interaction: behavioural consistency, behavioural integrity, sharing and delegation of control, communication, and demonstration of concern. They further distinguish several relational factors such as initial interactions between leaders and employees, expectations around reciprocity of behaviours and the cost of exchange between the two parties. All of these emphasise the central meaning of relational dynamics and exchanges in these contexts (Blau, 1964).

Similarly to responsible leadership, there seems to be a strong business imperative for trust. For example, previous studies have suggested that trust increases knowledge sharing and information exchange (Dirks & Ferrin, 2002; Lee, Gillespie, Mann, & Wearing, 2010; Mayer *et al.*, 1995), support for unfavourable decisions (Brockner, Siegel, Daly, & Tyler, 1997), organisational (Davis, Schoorman, Mayer, & Tan, 2000) and team performance (Dirks, 2000; Lee *et al.*, 2010). Trust in senior leaders also influences how survivors respond to downsizing activities (Mishra & Spreitzer, 1998). For example, Mishra and Spreitzer (1998) argue that trust relations influence the sense-making and responses of employees in these critical situations. High trust in top management leads to more constructive responses of survivors embedded in a sense of hope, optimism, and loyalty. On the contrary, survivors who do not trust senior management more often feel threatened by downsizing leading to potentially destructive behaviours caused by fear, anxiety, and anger.

Building on previous studies, several integrative models linking leadership and trust have been proposed. This includes Burke, Sims, Lazzara, and Salas (2007) who developed a multi-level review bringing together the various elements through which trust in leaders is developed as well as its outcomes on various organisational processes. In addition, Dirks and Ferrin (2002) developed a meta-analysis of trust in leadership while Kramer (2011) investigated trust and distrust in the leadership process. Trust has also been linked to particular styles of leadership such as transformational leadership (Bass, 1985; Bass & Avolio, 2006; Diaz-Saenz, 2011). Relevant research found that a transformational approach to leadership, emphasising consultation and collaboration, led to higher trust levels (Dirks & Ferrin, 2002; Gillespie & Mann, 2004; Lee *et al.*, 2010).

Finally, recent research also points us to the 'dark' side of trust. For example, Skinner *et al.* (2014) introduce us to the metaphor of trust being a 'poisoned chalice'. Drawing on social exchange theory and gift-giving research, they propose that in some scenarios trust may indeed be a burden leading to anxiety and dysfunction. This may be the case, for example, when the trust-receiver, such as the employee, may not actually want the trust put in them by the trust-giver, such as their superior, as it may lead to feelings of obligation. These may be contradictory to their own interests or moral compass and cause a sense of being trapped or not being able to fulfil the expectations placed on them.

What then appears from the literature is that responsible leadership and trust are closely intertwined. In this chapter, we propose that it is particularly in situations where we make assessments about someone's trustworthiness that the link between trust and responsible leadership becomes most evident. In the trust literature, the notion of trustworthy behaviour is mainly contained within four elements: ability, benevolence, integrity, and predictability, or, in summary, ABIP (Dietz & Den Hartog, 2006; Mayer *et al.*, 1995). First, ability, or competence, describes the need to perform a leadership role effectively, with skill and competence. Benevolence defines leaders acting with care for the good of others beyond their own egoistical needs. Integrity describes a leader's adherence to principles of fairness and honesty, which are acceptable to the trustor and congruent with his or her own beliefs. Integrity can be distinguished into personal and moral integrity, with the former focusing on abiding with a set of principles and the latter linked to the purpose of behaviours (McFall, 1987). Finally, predictability emphasises the regularity or consistency of leadership behaviour over time. Importantly, these pillars can further be grouped into two types: (1) *morality-based trustworthiness*, leadership as doing the right thing based on a set of acceptable principles of behaviour; and (2) *competency-based trustworthiness*, leadership as behaving in a way that is skilful and competent (Elsbach & Currall, 2012; Kammrath, Ames, & Scholer, 2007). Both of these are important in trust relations. Looking at these elements we may argue that several overlap with what we understand to be responsible leadership. Yet, it seems as if adapting a trust lens also allows us to consider a broader picture of what responsibility may entail, one that emphasises not ony morality but also the importance of showing competence and acting consistently. Given our interest in the role of Human Resource Management (HRM), in the following section we turn our attention to a discussion of the very function itself.

HRM and trust

Extensive research has suggested that HR practices and processes are critical for the development of trust in organisations generally (e.g. Eberl, Clement,

& Moller, 2012; Searle & Dietz, 2012; Searle & Skinner, 2011; Taylor, Tracy, Renard, Harrison, & Carroll, 1995; Whitener, 1997; Whitener *et al.*, 1998). For example, in a comprehensive review, Searle and Dietz (2012) suggest that HRM and trust interact in a variety of ways. As such, trust has been conceptualised as an antecedent of HRM, as a consequence, in a correlation relationship, as a mediator and a moderator. The dominant assumption seems to be that HRM has the potential to influence intra-organisational trust relationships and that trust in HR practices and processes is central for their effectiveness (Robinson, 1996; Robinson & Rousseau, 1994). This is argued not only to be important for trust building but also in situations where trust needs to be repaired following a breach of trust (Gillespie & Dietz, 2009).

However, only a few studies thus far have linked HRM, trust, and leadership, also not always explicitly. For example, Whitener (1997) investigates the impact of HR practices on employee trust. She suggests that trust levels from employees to their superiors will be higher when HR practices encourage fairness, clarity, and openness in their exchange. She also proposes that HRM can increase trust at both group and organisational level when they are designed to develop specific skill sets in group members and communicate organisational benevolence and commitment to employees. In addition, Taylor and colleagues (1995) propose that appraisal systems influence the extent of open communication and employee participation which in turn may lead to higher levels of trust. Similarly, Mayer and Davis (1999) study how performance appraisal systems influence employee trust for management. Their 14-month field study found that following the replacement of a performance appraisal system, which was perceived to be inaccurate and did not allow the measurement of rewards based on performance, trust of top management rose significantly.

Much of the research on trust is built on the assumption that HRM carries strategic importance in organisations, particularly in relation to leadership development. Particularly, with the introduction of the discourse on Strategic Human Resource Management, or SHRM (e.g. Boxall & Purcell, 2011; Lepak & Snell, 1999), HR started to be seen as central in developing key organisational resources. This has not always been the case. Indeed, the HR function finds itself in a continuous struggle for organisational and professional legitimacy, seeking to move beyond being a primarily supportive function (Francis & Keegan, 2006; Guest & King, 2004; Herriot, Hirsh, & Riley, 1998). From an SHRM perspective, developing leaders with the 'right' human capital has become central to creating and sustaining competitive advantage (Boxall & Purcell, 2011; Lepak & Snell, 1999; Ployhart & Moliterno, 2011). This perspective emphasises the role of HR practices in developing the KSAOs (knowledge, skills, abilities, and other characteristics) of leaders through, for example, performance appraisals and competency models.

Yet, linking back to the characteristics of trustworthiness described in the previous sections, we may argue that this strategic role of HRM seems to advocate an emphasis on ability or competence-based trustworthiness, a focus on the 'what' rather than the 'how', driven by the need to perform according to a set of goals. However, it is particularly this focus on performance that has caused us to question the role of HR in those industries that we often think to be the greatest culprits of the last years. Debates around how performance is measured and rewarded in, for example, financial services, particularly investment banking, have raised questions for concern. Assuming that HRM plays an important role in developing leadership, we may argue that HR practices and processes have played a big part in encouraging some, perhaps less responsible, behaviours over others. In addition, given the greater concern for the deontological aspects of leadership, such as moral values and ethical conduct postulated in this book, we seem to lack clarity in regards to the role that HRM plays (Searle & Dietz, 2012).

To further develop previous research and our understanding of the role of HRM in responsible leadership, we present empirical data collected as part of a wider research programme. In total 22 organisations participated in this research study from a range of different sectors including retail, financial services, public service, and others. For illustrative purposes we will examine two of these case organisations, BAE Systems and BBC Worldwide, and present key findings of our research, drawing on empirical material collected during interviews, conversations with HR practitioners from these organisations during multiple workshops, and the analysis of company documents. These organisations have agreed to be named publically, hence we are confident to use their names here while maintaining the anonymity of individual research participants.

Case illustrations

BAE Systems

Background

BAE Systems is a global defence, security, and aerospace company with headquarters in London and home markets in the UK, US, Australia, India, and Saudi Arabia. The organisation was formed in 1999. In 2014 it recorded annual revenue of nearly £17 billion. BAE Systems employs just under 85,000 people, 35,000 of whom are based in the UK. Some of its major projects include the Eurofighter Typhoon and the Astute Class submarines. The organisation is also the UK's largest manufacturing employer and employer of engineers and as such contributes £3.3 billion to the UK's GDP.

Responsible leadership and trust

An analysis of BAE's values shows that behaving responsibly is one BAE's cultural pillars: 'We are honest and take responsibility'. In addition, when we asked what a trustworthy leader should behave like, we recorded responses that made explicit reference to responsibility, such as the following:

Senior leaders have the responsibility of building winning teams, high performing teams. So the perform bit is objective setting. [...] being able to articulate how we go about differentiation of performance, how we classify performance ratings themselves, so we understand what good looks like. We understand what exceptional looks like. You have to hit everything and exceed everything to become exceptional.

(HR Manager 1, BAE Systems)

Importantly, as this quotation shows, responsible leadership here is mainly interpreted in a way that emphasises performance and capability. Thus, the expectation to show how able one is seems to be deeply embedded in how leadership is interpreted in BAE. To some this seemed to be so obvious that they even referred to it as a 'slam dunk'. The company's culture and type of operations as being highly technical and scientific clearly put an emphasis on leadership as 'getting the job done', 'being an expert', and having an awareness of 'processes and products'. Drawing back on the distinction between competence-based and morality-based trustworthiness, we thus see a strong emphasis on the former compared to the latter. Looking more specifically at the relationship between responsible leadership and trust in BAE, we propose that behaving responsibly is one of the antecedents of trust. This is made particularly evident in one of BAE's core values which states the following: 'Trusted – We deliver on our commitments'.

HRM and leadership development

BAE systems summarises its expectations on leadership in a *Total Performance Leadership Framework* which underpins their culture of *Total Performance*. Specific developmental exercises include an individual development plan, developmental assessment centres, a four-quadrant model of development, and a leadership intervention entitled *Leading for Total Performance*. This is built on four key elements: *Perform, Assess, Develop*, and *Reward* and emphasises an image of a leader that is primarily competent and capable:

There is a specific leadership intervention called 'Leading or Total Performance' which introduces line managers to the concept that they're responsible for leading change, for having clarity of direction and purpose and uses storytelling or narrative to convey and rich picture works to convey how organisation, how our mark – how we need to adapt to the current context.

(HR Manager 1, BAE Systems)

Indeed, showing sustained ability over a longer period of time was seen to be a requirement for promotion: 'I think the ability side is – absolutely. We promote on that you know [...] so it is, it's that ability' (HR Manager 2, BAE Systems).

Across all stages of the HR cycle, numerical data played a key role, linking back to BAE's engineering culture. As the following manager describes there is a conscious attempt by the HR function to provide the type of information others in the organisation value and are able to comprehend, such as financial data:

> We're an engineering organisation so I'm trying to be savvy about who my audience is. What is it they typically see, programme schedules, milestones, costs. It's primarily financial data so what I'm trying to is, you know, there is a level of analysis and data that exists already inside HR.
>
> (HR Manager 1, BAE Systems)

The emphasis of HR is then very much on aligning individual leadership behaviours with the aims and goals of the organisation. This is also a central theme in the development of future leaders in which BAE's long-term strategy plays a key role:

> Where we are getting to with that is around defining what the critical capabilities are, so in our resource review process that we have, each of the business produces a sort of insight summary which is saying here is my strategy and here is the people implications for that.
>
> (HR Manager 2, BAE Systems)

HRM and responsible leadership in BAE Systems

Based on our empirical material, we propose that in BAE Systems, responsible leadership is mainly contained in competence-based dimensions of trustworthiness, i.e. ability and predictability. As such, a responsible leader builds trust relations with others by performing his or her role effectively, with skill and proficiency. Leadership development practices do not only fully support but also encourage this interpretation of leadership. In fact, the role of the HR function is mainly to ensure that people align around this dominant image of what it means to be a responsible leader. To do so, it relies heavily on numerical data and statistics. For example, ability is tested frequently, linked to various core competencies, while predictability features strongly in the need for sustained performance, tracked as part of one's performance history within the organisation. What this suggests is a very 'real' perspective of responsible leadership which is postulated by HR's own understanding of itself as a driver of organisational performance.

In the following section, we complement this example with the case of BBC Worldwide, an organisation where trust is similarly explicit as in BAE, but where interpretations of responsible leadership differ.

BBC Worldwide

Background

BBC Worldwide is the commercial arm of the BBC by whom it is fully owned. As such it supports the public service mission of the BBC while maximising its financial contribution in a way that is consistent with the BBC's values. BBC Worldwide operates globally across a range of regions including the UK, Australia and New Zealand, North America, Asia, Latin America, and Europe. Its financial performance has been consistently positive over the last years, with annual returns to the BBC reaching a record high of £226.5 million in 2014–15. During 2012, BBC Worldwide reorganised its business from a geographical to a regional focus. BBC Worldwide is currently led by Tim Davie who became its CEO in April 2013.

Responsible leadership and trust

According to our informants, trust is the 'foundation of the BBC'. Being owned by the BBC, trust in BBC Worldwide also resides in the values that are underpinning BBC's culture more broadly. Generally, organisational trustworthiness was rated highly by our participants, particularly on integrity towards its members internally and external stakeholders. Personal relationships are key and being able to trust one's colleagues is crucial. When being asked what it means to act in a way that would be considered as trustworthy in the organisation, many replied with notions that we would often consider as defining responsible leadership, such as acting with integrity and care towards each other:

> She openly communicates. She's very honest. She's quite transparent with what she does and where she's trying to go. [...] So you're very clear the path you need to follow, rather than perhaps being shrouded in mystery. Even though she sits away from us, she's very approachable and she's also very clear on what she's trying to achieve. She's just open and honest with us, which immediately just creates trust.
>
> (HR Manager 1, BBC Worldwide)

Repeatedly the CEO, Tim Davie, was described as being particularly trustworthy by our respondents. Again, the emphasis was mainly on his level of integrity which manifested itself in being open and honest and avoiding a culture of blame, motivated by a concern for others: 'I think it comes from Tim, of just being 'Hey guys, this is how I want it to be, nothing to hide, not going to beat you up over it, I just need to know what's happening' (HR Manager 2, BBC Worldwide). Linking back to the distinction between competence- and morality-based trustworthiness, in contrast to BAE Systems, here we perceive a greater focus on the notion of morality in doing the right thing. This was further emphasised by recent restructuring efforts, which were aimed at shifting focus from divisional to global lines of business. Building trust relations played an important part in this. Given BBC Worldwide's relational way of working, an image of leadership which was about driving the wider good of the organisation at an international level was emphasised.

HRM and leadership development

There are various leadership development practices in place at BBC Worldwide, with an emphasis on developing leadership from 'within'. These include a corporate leadership programme which is built around multiple tiers and assessment stages. The organisation further distinguishes between four developmental groups: *WEx* – the main top leadership group; *WEx plus* – leaders who have been identified with the potential to join the *WEx* group, as well as *Atlas* and *Inspire* – its emerging leaders' programme. It also offers skill and behaviour focused leadership coaching and has introduced a rather unique development practice. This is a live 360-degree feedback session where future leaders of their *Inspire* programme participated in a live feedback environment involving up to eight peers, superiors, and those reporting to them. Those who took part in this activity received direct feedback which HR professionals suggest to be very 'powerful' and 'insightful'. One of the aims of this session was to create an environment of openness and honesty where trust could be built between those who were receiving and those who were giving the feedback.

The shift towards global integration also meant that the HR function at BBC Worldwide needed to act as a global integrator across the organisation and hence put greater resources into the development of an internationally aligned approach to leadership:

> I think that my aim and intention or one of the things that I want to provide value in is ensuring that in introducing global programmes that they are not UK globally applicable but that they are genuinely global and are effective and reflective as that international piece.
>
> (HR Manager 4, BBC Worldwide)

As a result, BBC Worldwide has introduced a global competency framework and scoring grid which supports the recruitment, development, and assessment of leaders while enforcing its global strategy and cultural values. The perception was that this would help to build trust at the organisational level as well as in the HR function given that transparency, objectivity, and openness would be increased. In addition, the structural shift also brought a greater need for financial accountability. In accordance with this development, more processes and procedures and some 'tough conversations' on performance have started which some found to be in conflict with BBC's relational ways of working: 'Relationship-based people want to be liked and it's hard to find a way to do that tough conversation in a way that you're still liked' (HR Manager 3, BBC Worldwide).

HRM and responsible leadership in BBC Worldwide

While our participants readily talked about the importance of responsible leadership contained in the notion of acting with integrity and following strong moral values, when we asked them how this was assessed, HR professionals struggled to see it expressed explicitly in their practices and processes, quoting ambiguity and a lack of tangibility:

> I think it's quite key but because it can be such an ambiguous term. Trust is one of our values. [...] What are the most tangible things that it can demonstrate? It's probably the same when we do our assessments of leaders as well. Yes, I would say those people are put forward because they are seen as trustworthy but it's not something we specifically evaluate.

Similarly, even though acting with integrity and compassion towards others was seen as important for leadership, existing HR tools such as the nine-box grid for 'star performers' emphasised characteristics such as 'ability', 'drive', and 'ambition':

> The categories we were using, particularly for our stars. [...] It was basically their learning agility, so their ability to basically learn from mistakes and to apply, or apply learnings going forward; their drive and ambition; to be able to act as a leader outside their business areas, so across businesses; and there was a fourth one as well because we had classic definitions for all the nine-box grids but we ended up when we were looking at this top talent programme going back to four core attributes. I think it must have been something about maximising the benefits of everything they do for BBC Worldwide as a whole, not just their discrete business area. Things like benevolence hasn't come up, which is interesting.
>
> (HR Manager 1, BBC Worldwide)

In summary, what these findings suggest is a much more complex picture of the relationship between an organisation's explicitly stated values around trust, contained in notions of responsibility, and how this can be put into practice by the HR function. HR's own struggle for relevance seems to play an important role in this, which we elaborate upon in the following.

Concluding discussion

In this chapter we sought to investigate the role of HRM in responsible leadership, encouraged by the dearth of research in this area and HR's proposed potential to influence leadership behaviours. We have provided a literature review that linked responsible leadership, trust, and the role of HR. Drawing on research conducted in 22 organisations, we have presented empirical material in the form of two case studies for illustration. Our findings inform our understanding of responsible leadership in various ways. Most importantly, they highlight the ambiguity around the role of HR in this context. Also, taking a trust lens, we have thought to open up existing inquiries into responsible leadership, showing how it may encompass different, yet always contextually embedded meanings which can collate around the notion of performance.

First, as our two case studies show, leading responsibly was one of the pre-conditions in order to be perceived as trustworthy and to build trusted relations with others, supporting existing claims on the two as interlinked (e.g. Maak & Pless, 2006). Importantly, what the findings suggest is that the meaning of responsible leadership does not exist in vacuum but is very much contextually embedded. In BAE systems a responsible leader was someone who accepted the responsibility that the role carried and who would perform according to the goals set for her or him. Hence the focus was on competence and ability. In BBC Worldwide on the other hand, it was someone who would show responsibility in acting with integrity, someone who is open and honest and 'walks the talk'. This differentiation was informed by the organisation's heritage, culture, and strategy, and the industry itself. Importantly, particularly in BBC Worldwide, responsible leadership as being honest, transparent, and acting with integrity was not only important in order to build trust relations internally in the organisation but also provided it with discursive resources to communicate its trustworthiness to its external audience. This was perceived to be of high importance, specifically as the BBC had been through some challenging times and public trust had been tested.

Context and the dominant meaning of responsibility consequently informed HR's approach to leadership development. In BAE Systems, guided by its culture of *Total Performance*, leadership development practices emphasised the particular skills and competencies that were required in order for leaders to be perceived as 'high performers'. The ideal image was that of a 'red cape' style leader, a hero with super powers who provides safety to those in need of his protection while brimming with strength. In BBC Worldwide, the approach was different, more relational, informed by a culture which is characterised by working in and through relationships. Live 360-degree feedback sessions were supposed to foster an environment of openness and mutual exchange that would help to strengthen these relations and create environments of trust.

In both cases we perceived the role of HR as mainly embedding and aligning behaviours with the dominant interpretation of what a responsible leader should be like, informed by strategic prerogatives. By weaving this meaning into development practices, HR tried to create a common language and hence a sense of alignment across the organisation more widely. In the case of BBC Worldwide this purpose was specifically global given that organisation's concern for international integration. The discourse on alignment also meant that individual national differences were moved to the background. Instead, leadership that would be considered to be trustworthy by a range of diverse cultures and nationalities was favoured. This in turn did leave less room for individual interpretation and judgement. Rather competence became the decisive factor.

We propose that this may have implications for our understanding of the mutual constitution of trust and responsibility (Maak & Pless, 2006, 2009; Stahl & DeLuque, 2014; Voegtlin *et al.*, 2012). First, it postulates a specific interpretation of responsible leadership as superior or better equipped in building sustainable trust relations. This type of leadership encompasses capability, competence, and consistency. Most importantly, it can be evidenced numerically and over extended periods of time. Second, from the perspective of the trustor, the one who makes him- or herself vulnerable in deciding to trust, a trustee who does not show these behaviours and does not have the evidence to prove it will be considered less trustworthy. Responsible leadership and trust are then not only mutually constitutive but also mutually constructed in a space which is primarily built around the importance of performance.

Our findings also suggest a sense of ambiguity around the role of HR, informed by what seems to be its own struggle for legitimacy and wanting to be perceived as trustworthy by those in power. While on the one hand HR was able to create conversations around trust and helped to communicate the importance of responsibility in developing trust relationships, there were 'grey areas' which it did not penetrate. These appeared particularly in the context of morality-based understandings of responsible leadership. Captured by their need to demonstrate themselves as strategically important, HR professionals continuously rely on existing tools, processes, and procedures which ultimately had a performance focus, or what we have identified as competence-based trustworthiness. As result, they were either lacking or reluctant to deploy a discursive repertoire which might address or develop deontological aspects of leadership.

Linking in with the theme of this book, its distinction between the real and the romantic, our inquiry into trust and the role of HR thus postulates a story of realism, told by HR professionals themselves. It is a story that is informed by organisational imperatives on the expectations of responsible leadership on the one hand, and HR's struggle to understand, communicate, and develop these on the other. In order to do so, HR professionals draw on tangible empirical evidence created through established HR procedures and practices. In this story, a trusted leader is one who takes his/her responsibility to *perform* seriously and uses it as part of his repertoire to build trust relationships with others.

In summary, we may ask ourselves how the HR function went from being the 'conscience' of the organisation (Sissons, 1995), concerned with morality and justice, to the 'enforcer' of dominant competence-based paradigms? In its search for strategic legitimacy (and therefore power) has the function become solely a loyal enforcer and reproducer of the means deemed necessary to deliver short-term business goals (Hope Hailey, Farndale, and Truss, 2005)? This contrasts with the seemingly old-fashioned views of commentators such as Charles Handy, who perceived HR as a visionary activity, a conscience and thought-leader around the fairness and morality of employers, concerned with building workplace cultures which inspired leaders to be virtuous in their pursuit of the common good. The long-term implications of this retreat into solely producing leaders who serve the present commercial reality may be that we cannot look to HR as a function to answer the call for the exploration of responsible ways of leading. Others may have to take up that visioning instead of them.

References

Balogun, J., Hope Hailey, V., & Gustafsson, S. (2015). *Exploring strategic change* (4th edn). Harlow: Pearson Education.

Bass, B. M. (1985). *Leadership and performance beyond expectations* (1st edn). New York: Free Press.

Bass, B. M., & Avolio, B. J. (2006). *Transformational leadership* (2nd edn). Mahwan, NJ: Lawrence Erlbaum Associates.

Blau, P. M. (1964). *Exchange and power in social life*. New York: Wiley.

Boxall, P., & Purcell, J. (2011). *Strategy and human resource management* (3rd edn). Basingstoke: Palgrave Macmillan.

Brockner, J., Siegel, P. A., Daly, J. P., & Tyler, T. (1997). When trust matters: The moderating effects of outcome favourability. *Administrative Science Quarterly, 43,* 558–583.

Burke, C. S., Sims, D. E., Lazzara, E. H., & Salas, E. (2007). Trust in leadership: A multi-level review and integration. *Leadership Quarterly, 18*(6), 606–632.

Davis, J. H., Schoorman, F. D., Mayer, R. C., & Tan, H. H. (2000). The trusted general manager and business unit performance: Empirical evidence of a competitive advantage. *Strategic Management Journal, 21*(5), 563–576.

Day, D. V. (2000). Leadership development: A review in context. *Leadership Quarterly, 11*(4), 581–613.

Day, D. V. (2011). Leadership development. In A. Bryman, D. Collinson, K. Grint, B. Jackson, & M. Uhl-Bien (Eds.), *The Sage handbook of leadership*. London: Sage.

Diaz-Saenz, H. R. (2011). Transformational leadership. In A. Bryman, D. Collinson, K. Grint, B. Jackson, & M. Uhl-Bien (Eds.), *The Sage handbook of leadership*. London: Sage.

Dietz, G., & Den Hartog, D. N. (2006). Measuring trust inside organisations. *Personnel Review, 35*(5), 557–588.

Dirks, K. T. (2000). Trust in leadership and team performance: Evidence from NCAA basketball. *Journal of Applied Psychology, 85*(6), 1004.

Dirks, K. T., & Ferrin, D. L. (2001). The role of trust in organizational settings. *Organization Science, 12*(4), 450–467.

Dirks, K. T., & Ferrin, D. L. (2002). Trust in leadership: Meta-analytic findings and implications for research and practice. *Journal of Applied Psychology, 87*(4), 611–628.

Eberl, P., Clement, U., & Moller, H. (2012). Socialising employees' trust in the organisation: An exploration of apprentices' socialisation in two highly trusted companies. *Human Resource Management Journal, 22*(4), 343–359.

Elsbach, K. D., & Currall, S. C. (2012). Understanding threats to leader trustworthiness. In R. M. Kramer & T. L. Pittinsky (Eds.), *Restoring trust in organizations and leaders.* New York: Oxford University Press.

Ferrin, D. L., Dirks, K. T., & Shah, P. P. (2003). Many routes toward trust: A social network analysis of the determinants of interpersonal trust. Paper presented at the *Academy of Management Proceedings,* 1 August, Seattle.

Francis, H., & Keegan, A. (2006). The changing face of HRM: In search of balance. *Human Resource Management Journal, 16*(3), 231–249.

Gillespie, N. A., & Dietz, G. (2009). Trust repair after organization-level failure. *Academy of Management Review, 34*(1), 127–145.

Gillespie, N. A., & Mann, L. (2004). Transformational leadership and shared values: The building blocks of trust. *Journal of Managerial Psychology, 19*(6), 588–607.

Guest, D., & King, Z. (2004). Power, innovation and problem-solving: The personnel managers' three steps to heaven? *Journal of Management Studies, 41*(3), 401–423.

Hardin, R. (1992). The street-level epistemology of trust. *Analyse & Kritik, 14*(2), 152–176.

Herriot, P., Hirsh, W., & Riley, P. (1998). *Trust and transition: Managing today's employment relationship.* Chichester: Wiley.

Hope Hailey, V., Farndale, E., & Truss, K. (2005). The HR department's role in organisational performance. *Human Resource Management Journal, 15*(3), 49–66.

Kammrath, L. K., Ames, D. R., & Scholer, A. A. (2007). Keeping up impressions: Inferential rules for impression change across the Big Five. *Journal of Experimental Social Psychology, 43*(3), 450–457.

Kramer, R. M. (2011). Trust and distrust in the leadership process: A review and assessment of theory and evidence. In A. Bryman, D. L. Collinson, K. Grint, B. Jackson, & M. Uhl-Bien (Eds.), *The Sage handbook of leadership.* London: Sage.

Lee, P., Gillespie, N., Mann, L., & Wearing, A. (2010). Leadership and trust: Their effect on knowledge sharing and team performance. *Management Learning, 41*(4), 473–491.

Lepak, D. P., & Snell, S. A. (1999). The human resource architecture: Toward a theory of human capital allocation and development. *Academy of Management Review, 24*(1), 31–48.

Maak, T., & Pless, N. M. (2006). Responsible leadership in a stakeholder society: A relational perspective. *Journal of Business Ethics, 66*(1), 99–115.

Maak, R., & Pless, N. M. (2009). Business leaders as citizens of the world: Advancing humanism on a global scale. *Journal of Busienss Ethics, 88*(3), 537–550.

Mayer, R. C., & Davis, J. H. (1999). The effect of the performance appraisal system on trust for management: A field quasi-experiment. *Journal of Applied Psychology, 84*(1), 123–136.

Mayer, R. C., Davis, J. H., & Schoorman, F. D. (1995). An integrative model of organizational trust. *Academy of Management Review, 20*(3), 709–734.

McFall, L. (1987). Integrity. *Ethics, 98*(1), 5–20.

Mishra, A. K., & Spreitzer, G. M. (1998). Explaining how survivors respond to downsizing: The roles of trust, empowerment, justice, and work redesign. *Academy of Management Review, 23*(3), 567–588.

Pless, N. M. & Maak, T. (2011). Responsible leadership: Pathways to the future. *Journal of Business Ethics, 98*, 3–13.

Ployhart, R. E., & Moliterno, T. P. (2011). Emergence of the human capital resource: A multilevel model. *Academy of Management Review, 36*(1), 127–150.

Robinson, S. L. (1996). Trust and breach of the psychological contract. *Administrative Science Quarterly, 41*(4), 574–599.

Robinson, S. L., & Rousseau, D. M. (1994). Violating the psychological contract: Not the exception but the norm. *Journal of Organizational Behavior, 15*(3), 245–259.

Rousseau, D. M., Sitkin, S. B., Burt, R. S., & Camerer, C. (1998). Not so different after all: A cross-discipline view of trust. *Academy of Management Review, 23*(3), 393–404.

Searle, R. H., & Dietz, G. (2012). Editorial. Trust and HRM: Current insights and future directions. *Human Resource Management Journal, 22*(4), 333–342.

Searle, R. H., & Skinner, D. (Eds.). (2011). *Trust and HRM*. Cheltenham: Edward Edgar.

Sissons, K. (1995). Human resource management and the personnel function. In J. Storey (Ed.), *Human resource management: A critical text*. London: Routledge.

Skinner, D., Dietz, G., & Weibel, A. (2014). The dark side of trust: When trust becomes a 'poisoned chalice'. *Organization, 21*(2), 206–224.

Solomon, R. C. (1998). Ethical leadership, emotions, and trust: Beyond 'charisma'. In J. Ciulla (Ed.), *Ethics: The heart of leadership*. Santa Barbara, CA: Praeger.

Stahl, G. K., & DeLuque, M. S. (2014). Antecedents of responsible leader behavior: A research synthesis, conceptual framework, and agenda for future research. *Academy of Management Perspectives, 28*(3), 235–254.

Taylor, M. S., Tracy, K. B., Renard, M. K., Harrison, J. K., & Carroll, S. J. (1995). Due process in performance appraisal: A quasi-experiment in procedural justice. *Administrative Science Quarterly, 40*, 495–523.

Voegtlin, C., Patzer, M., & Scherer, A. G. (2012). Responsible leadership in global business: A new approach to leadership and its multi-level outcomes. *Journal of Business Ethics, 105*, 1–16.

Whitener, E. M. (1997). The impact of human resource activities on employee trust. *Human Resource Management Review, 7*(4), 389–404.

Whitener, E. M., Brodt, S. E., Korsgaard, M. A., & Werner, J. M. (1998). Managers as initiators of trust: An exchange relationship framework for understanding managerial trustworthy behavior. *Academy of Management Review, 23*(3), 513–530.

8 Promoting responsibility, purpose, and romanticism in business schools

Ken Parry and Brad Jackson

Leadership responsibility can and should be differentiated from leadership accountability. Our assertion is that responsible leadership involves the generation of sense-making within the minds and hearts of those who are being led. Sense-making is the essence of leadership, according to Pye (2005), Smircich and Morgan (1982), and Parry (1999). Yukl (2012) and others, including Parry (2001) before him, have concluded that sense-making will have an impact upon the actions and behaviours of followers such that the bottom-line outcomes can be achieved for the organisation or community for which the persons in the leadership positions are responsible. This plausible and practically adequate consensus about the role of leadership is represented in Figure 8.1.

In this chapter we will argue that the responsibility of 'leadership' is to generate the sense-making that is the essence of leadership. Furthermore, the bottom-line outcomes are those for which leadership of any organisation is held accountable. We also suggest that when responsible leadership generates shared sense-making, long-term sustainability is generated such that the outcomes for the broader community can be achieved over time.

The accountability of leadership might reflect the plausible and practically adequate outcomes for which leadership is generally held accountable. However, in order to achieve those outcomes, responsible leadership has a degree of latitude in how it might go about generating shared sense-making. Responsible leadership should draw upon inspiration, beauty, and subjectivity as it stimulates the imagination and the emotion of the 'follower' audience. In short, responsible leadership can and must draw upon romanticism at least as

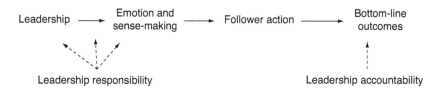

Figure 8.1 Leadership responsibility and accountability (source: based on Parry, 2001 and Yukl, 2012).

much as it draws upon the realism for which it is held accountable, in order to generate sense-making and emotion. The balance between romanticism and realism must be ethically, virtuously, and morally rooted and resonant with a nobility of purpose, if it is to generate the sustained following from any audience. This is the leadership challenge that we will address in this chapter. In particular, we highlight the role of business schools in ensuring that this delicate balance is struck through the students, immediate stake-holders, and the wider society that they serve.

In our account we are guided by Pless and Maak's (2011) conception of 'responsible leadership' as a multilevel response to deficiencies in existing leadership frameworks and theories. It is a response to high-profile scandals on individual, organisational, and systemic levels. And it is a response to new and emerging social, ethical, and environmental challenges in an increasingly interconnected world. Responsible leadership is geared toward the concerns of others and asks for what and to whom those leaders are responsible. Accordingly, responsible leaders are trusted. If they are trusted, they are seen as ethical. This comment may seem to be stating the obvious, but it is arguably one of the most under-researched concepts in this field, as well as one of the most relevant. At its core, this discussion seeks to identify the purpose of leadership for those people in those senior positions, in business and in society.

Students in business schools might be learning how to be unethical

Given the extensive recent media coverage of wide-ranging corporate scandals and misdeeds, public sentiment has increasingly called into question business leaders' willingness to put the public good above the company bottom line. As Michael Porter said in a recent interview: 'High unemployment, rising poverty, and the public's dismay over corporate greed continue to challenge the market system and the legitimacy of business itself' (Porter, 2010: 1). Businesses appear to be facing yet another crisis of public confidence brought on in part by an apparent lack of moral character in some executive suites – the widely perceived domain of 'leadership'. This crisis of public confidence has recently become more visible as thousands of Americans took to the streets early in the twenty-first century in the 'Occupy Wall Street' protests directed at corporate greed – protests that expanded to other cities nationwide. We suggest that the resultant low public confidence in business leadership leads to reduced trust, which in turn diminishes following. Disengaged following identifies poor quality leadership.

Corporations are commonly perceived to be prospering at the expense of the broader community, and the general legitimacy of business has fallen to worryingly low levels, say Porter and Kramer (2011). This low perceived legitimacy reduces trust considerably. After all, who would put their life in the hands of an illegitimate business-person? Kochan has observed that the main cause of 'recent' corporate scandals in the United States lies in the 'over-emphasis American corporations have been forced to give in recent years to maximising shareholder value without regard for the effects of their actions on other stakeholders' (2002, p. 139, in Ghoshal, 2005, p. 81). This claim is still relevant, we feel.

We are witnessing a growing discussion about the appropriateness of current leadership theories to address pertinent leadership challenges. This discussion often cites the role and responsibilities of business leaders in society, frequently in light of social and environmental crises. Despite the strong push for reforms, irresponsible leadership was a primary cause of the global economic crisis of 2008. As Jeffrey Sachs (2011, p. 3) argues, 'Without restoring an ethos of social responsibility, there can be no meaningful and sustained economic recovery'.

Leadership is about trust

A vital part of success in any business is the leadership responsibility of building public trust. In order to maintain the metaphorical licence to operate that society provides to businesses, and to maintain a reputation as a good corporate citizen, we suggest that people in business must have the trust of that society, or community. Parry and Fiskerud (2015) describe this as 'community trust'. Mayer, Davis, and Schoorman (1995) define 'trust' as putting oneself in a position of vulnerability, at the discretion of another person. In other words, if you trust someone, yes truly trust them, you will put your life in their hands. Putting your life in the hands of another person is commonplace. Children do it with their parents all the time. Trust accounts are there to protect the interest of people who cannot look after it themselves. For the rest of us, it might be a metaphor, but extreme examples do make a point. People are much more likely to follow people whom they trust. If trust is lost, 'followers' might obey, but willing following is jeopardised severely. And, if willing following is lost, we suggest that leadership is lost. So, the point is that people in the community will trust people who help them; and they are less likely to trust people who make money from them without then feeding that profit back into their community. Taking without giving back will generate mistrust and will damage willing following. Perhaps the responsibility of leadership is to weave an inclusive web where those 'in charge' engage themselves among equals; giving and taking becomes matched by all the members of the community, business-people, and customers alike. Ciulla (2004a) has noted that Plato expressed this critical task of leadership in his depiction of the 'Statesman', that leaders should be weavers, whose core task is to weave different people and groups together into the fabric of society (or community). People will be willing to be woven if they trust in the weaver.

If a company exploits its community, then that community will not trust the company or the people who run it. Of course, we differentiate exploitation from legitimately making a profit. We also differentiate 'our' community from another community. As customers, many of us purchased the same brands of clothing after April 2013, knowing that they probably were made at Rana Plaza in Bangladesh. However, we would not tolerate dangerous sweat-shops in our own country. Communities have the same ethical dilemmas as business leaders. Nonetheless, we suggest that communities will not patronise the business of managers who exploit those communities. Assuming they had a choice, responsible followers will not follow irresponsible leaders. There-fore, those business-people are less likely to succeed financially. Who would put their life in the hands of a business that worked only for the benefit of its shareholders, and not for the benefit of its community, for the benefit of its customers? Assuming that customers had a choice, they would not put their lives in the hands of someone who worked just for corporate purpose and not for societal purpose (Kempster, Jackson, & Conroy, 2011).

Maak and Pless (2006) propose that a responsible leader must be a steward and a custodian of values and resources; a good citizen and a caring and active member of communities; a servant to various others; and a visionary by offering inspiration and perspective about a desirable future. They do not mention 'bottom-line' accountability. This might seem like a tall order, but not really. The concept of the leader as a 'great person' (OK, 'great man') is arguably no longer particularly valid. Rather, leaders should be regarded as equals who earn from their followers a license to lead. Relational notions of leadership (Cunliffe & Eriksen, 2011; Uhl-Bien, 2006) emphasise the interchangeability of leadership and followership. People are concurrently leader and follower. Perhaps leadership should no longer be thought of as actions by senior managers within their companies. Rather, Parry and Fiskerud (2015) suggest that it could be thought of as leadership by companies (that just happen to be run by individual people) within their communities. The key to leadership might just be about helping the community (of which the company happens to be just one member). Every person in that business/company has a leadership responsibility; and that leadership responsibility cannot easily be passed off to the 'company' or the 'boss'.

Traditional business curricula in colleges usually state that individuals lead 'subordinates', within the context of a company. Perhaps, new business curricula could state that companies (led by people) lead their communities. The romance of leadership (Meindl, 1995) and our understanding of charismatic attributions (Parry & Kempster, 2014) will help us to conclude that the person in charge will be attributed with leadership. The story of Richard Branson comes to mind as an exemplar of this narrative. Virgin is somehow seen as a charismatic company to work for, as much as Richard Branson is seen as a charismatic person to work for. Implicitly, everyone knows that they will not actually work for Richard Branson. Instead, they will work for Virgin. Richard Branson is seen as a hard-nosed businessman who is accountable for the business outcomes of his company. Yet, at the same time, he is seen as being responsible for the positive emotions of the workforce and the sense-making that employees internalise about the more noble purpose of the company than just making money.

Sins vis-à-vis virtues in the study of leadership

Well, one reflection of the loss of purpose is the proposition that we have introduced into the business curriculum sinful notions like greed, anger, pride, envy, and gluttony. Giacalone and Promislo (2013) claim persuasively that this outcome is implicit rather than explicit, and that it is a function of the discourse that is used around business communication. Indeed, the morality of leadership is a very contestable discourse, as much as the accountability of business leadership is almost uncontestable. The transformational leadership gurus, Bernie Bass and Paul Steidlmeier, differentiated between pseudo-transformational and authentic transformational leadership (Bass and Steidlmeier, 1999). More recently, Bruce Avolio, Bill Gardner and others (Walumbwa, Avolio, Gardner, Wernsing, & Peterson, 2008) have differentiated authentic from inauthentic leadership. Quite recently, there is still an empirical investigation into destructive leadership, the implication being that even though it is destructive, it still is leadership. These pejorative dimensions are still seen as leadership.

The immediacy with which Adolf Hitler emerges in classroom discussion about leadership illustrates the contestability of morality within notions of leadership. To be fair, he is used as an extreme example in order to make a point. However, many people still use him as a benchmark for leadership. However, as Giacalone and Promislo (2013) have argued, to dialogue virtuous notions within organisations is often seen as weakness. Altruism is dialogued as putting others' interests ahead of the organisation's interests; compassion reduces the ability to make tough decisions; morals might be unwilling to do the 'dirty work' that is necessary. Sinful leadership is still leadership, often 'strong' leadership, while virtuous leadership often is seen as weakness.

Amoral neoliberalism

A less confrontational and more amoral advocate of this message was Milton Friedman (1970), one of the most prominent exponents of free-market, neoliberal economics. We call him amoral because he was not immoral. He did not advocate doing immoral things. He just washed his hands of moral questions. He proposed that a corporation's social responsibility is to increase its profits; working within legal and social norms, but generally left to pursue its own self-interest as much as it likes. It is government's role to look after the welfare of society and to legislate accordingly. Within this narrative, morality and ethics are the responsibility of government. Friedman was not writing about leadership. Rather, he was writing about people who run companies; people who are accountable for the performance of those companies; people who have often become known as 'leaders'. He was writing about the purpose of business; and the purpose of business was to be an efficient and successful business and that this was the best thing that business could do for society. This traditional view of the role of corporations has permeated management theory and practice for decades, and such a narrative for business is still a reality in the minds of many managers today. This traditional view is being seen as Brute Capitalism, vis-à-vis Moral capitalism (Young, 2003). Young wrote about Brute Capitalism as a flawed system but also as a challenge for individuals to respond to. It is from the latter perspective that he writes his book. This traditional view has dominated business curricula for decades. Arguably, it still does.

What we are experiencing at the moment is the devastation of societal systems around the world, as well as frequent business scandals resulting from a dominant amoral management ideology. Note the use of the word amoral, meaning acting without regard for morality, as opposed to immoral, meaning violating moral principles. The important question is whether corporations do in fact have moral duties. Current influential business, management, and leadership theories cover a wide range of academic disciplines including psychology, sociology, and economics. Sumantra Ghoshal (2005) reminds us that, collectively, these theories have converged on a negative view of human nature and of the role and responsibilities of corporations in our society. Ghoshal also speaks freely and cogently about these issues on YouTube. Leadership practices in both private and public sector institutions seem to have succumbed to the corrupting influence of money, status, and power. Moreover, leadership is still pitched at the person who is at the very head of these responsibilities – the senior manager – 'leader'.

The majority of business schools appear largely to base what they teach on the principles of Brute Capitalism, despite an increasing number of their graduates yearning for a greater sense of purpose and being drawn towards social entrepreneurship (Porter and Kramer, 2011). Indeed, most business schools are co-opted into neoliberalist ways of thinking. However, we would still have a dominant block of students looking for traditional business education as opposed to anything like social entrepreneurship. Perhaps through no fault of their own, they neither know nor care for a greater sense of noble purpose in what they learn and practice.

Power and responsibility

The mission statement of Harvard Business School is: 'We educate leaders who make a difference in the world'. The more verbose mission statement of the Wharton School of the University of Pennsylvania is:

> In a world defined by global markets and hyper-speed communications, the challenges of leadership have changed. Wharton is committed to devoting our wide-ranging resources and innovative energy to build and

share the knowledge needed by individuals, businesses, and public institutions to excel in this evolving global arena.

Leadership is central to the mission statements of most (if not all) business schools. These mission statements often mention ethics and morality, but they all mention leaders and/or leadership. Romantically, they say the right things. However, we suggest a critical and a realist interpretation by looking at the reality of the values and principles that emerge from the discourse and practices of business schools. In effect, the outcomes from business school learning often are about accountability and not responsibility. By concentrating on the accountability of leadership, we suggest that business schools often generate irresponsible leadership. Worse, we sense the ominous suggestion of Brute Capitalism as the outcome of business schools. By 'leaders' these business school statements refer to 'captains of industry'. By 'leadership', they refer to the accountability for which people run their businesses, whether public or private sector. The question that remains is 'for what purpose?'

The results of Brute Capitalism have included missed opportunities and public distrust, and business school curricula will need to broaden in several areas, suggest Porter and Kramer. Many of the worst instances of misconduct of recent business practices arguably stem from a set of ideals which have emerged from business school academicians over the last few decades. Ghoshal (2005) also suggests that business schools do not necessarily need to create new courses; they need to simply stop teaching several of the old ones. Leadership might be one example. Regrettably, by propagating ideologically inspired amoral theories, often under the heading of 'leadership', business schools have removed any sense of moral responsibility or societal purpose from their students, said Ghoshal. At best we are misleading the students. At worst, we might be creating monsters.

By contrast, in company with societal purpose as well as corporate purpose, leadership fosters contributions to society. Apart from more passive actions such as charity and various forms of corporate giving, these corporations should inspire active engagement for the wellbeing of their communities (Maak and Pless, 2006). It appears that good relationships with all stakeholders are vital to the success of businesses. Such a relationship is heading toward a new understanding of 'moral' and 'ethical' leadership, and of societal purpose.

Possession of power places people in office: in political office, in social office, in public office, and in commercial office. Similarly, people in office are attributed with power. With office comes accountability. With the privilege of holding office also come a range of responsibilities. Some of these responsibilities are ethical. Craig and Gustafson (1998) said that integrity is about *not* doing unethical things, rather than just doing the ethical things. Moreover, they also recognised the value of supererogatory behaviours, wherein one goes above and beyond normal expectations of altruism or citizenship, even though such behaviour is not specifically called for. The metaphor for the supererogatory behaviour is to go into the burning building to rescue someone. To do it is extremely ethical and is to be lauded. Not to do it is not seen as unethical. Indeed, to do it is to put oneself at risk. It is acceptable not to do it (Craig & Gustafson, 1998). We suggest that supererogatory behaviours might be the key to ethical leadership and societal purpose – doing more for the community rather than merely doing enough for the organisation. Notions like this do not yet appear to be in leadership curricula. We have recently witnessed calls for a change of focus in leadership theory, away from the 'hero' to more of a 'host'. Joanne Ciulla (2004b) has reminded us that leadership is increasingly becoming a practice of ethics and the careful exercise of responsibility.

Consequences of the loss of virtue

To be fair, all the ills of Brute Capitalism cannot be blamed on business schools. However, the discourse of the teaching of business schools falls too easily into sinful notions of greed, pride, anger, and gluttony (Giacalone & Promislo, 2013), among others. By contrast, the discourse of business schools should fall more readily into messages of benevolence, wisdom, prudence, and courage, among other virtuous and desirable tactics. Perhaps a responsible leadership message would integrate the realism of power, greed, control, and lust with the romanticism of charity, benevolence, and prudence. Perhaps a responsible leadership message coming from business schools will integrate the goals of societal purpose and corporate purpose. Perhaps accountability will be matched with responsibility.

Studies have found that business students are actually less ethical than students in other disciplines. Ferraro and colleagues note that a 'growing body of evidence suggests that self-interested behaviour is learned behaviour, and people learn it by studying economics and business' (Ferraro, Pfeffer, & Sutton, 2005, p. 14). Clegg (2014) bemoans the hegemony of managerialism, and its origins from statisticians, lawyers, and economists. Business and economics majors are more likely to 'free-ride'; are more likely to keep more resources for themselves; and are more corruptible than others. Further, Nonis and Swift (2001) found that students who engaged in unethical behaviour in college were more likely to engage in unethical behaviour at work. Wang, Malhotra, and Murnighan (2011) found a positive relationship between economics education and students' attitudes toward greed, and McCabe, Butterfield, and Treviño (2006) found that MBA students cheat more than non-business students.

Miller (1999) has proposed that business students do not come into business schools this way, and argues that they learn about the principle of rational self-interest and believe that they are supposed to behave this way. Findings such as these have led some scholars to go so far as to propose that the entire paradigm underlying business education needs to change if we are to overcome the ethical difficulties we are currently facing. There is the possibility at the moment that learning leadership in business schools actually reinforces the semiotic connotation of 'economics' and 'business' as being one that reflects Brute Capitalism. Giacalone and Promislo's (2013) notions of econophonics and potensiphonics, discourses that pervade business school curricula, reflect and reinforce Brute Capitalism. Econophonics is the language of quantification and financial valuation. Potensiphonics is the language of power and domination. These languages eschew virtue and destroy trust.

The summation of our argument is this. Business schools presently treat leadership as influence by individuals over organisations for the benefit of stockholders and other like-minded stakeholders. The authors in this book do not, but the implicit connotation in most courses is accountability, not responsibility. We suggest that the message which students get from a business school is something like this: 'Leaders are accountable for profit; therefore leadership is accountability for profit; along the way, you leaders should also be ethical and moral, but don't forget what you are mainly here for!' Consequently, the accountability of leadership is emphasised at the expense of the responsibility of leadership. Responsible leadership is usually a cameo role in the main drama – a replacement player hoping to get a run in the main game.

Instead, perhaps leadership should be treated as ethical influence by organisations over their communities and within their communities for the benefit of those communities. In so doing, business leadership can be both accountable and responsible. Therefore, business schools can play an assertive role in this by being more reflexive in the way they teach and model leadership. Also, we suggest that changing the discourse of leadership, in particular, will aid this.

Address the gap through discourse

Our propositions reflect a vaccine more than an antidote (Parry & Fiskerud, 2015). An antidote will instantly fix the symptoms; but a vaccine will reduce the possibility of the disease occurring at all. These issues cannot be fixed instantly. After all, business students will still have to study strategy and finance and accounting and 'bottom-line' outcomes. Businesses still have to make money and be financially resilient. We need to massage the discourses that students engage in so that they are sympathetic to something other than making money for shareholders. We must manage a discourse of societal purpose to replace the discourse for corporate purpose. Here are some suggestions:

- Business as community must be emphasised instead of business vis-à-vis community.
- Societal purpose must be a criterion for success in addition to corporate purpose.

- Ask 'How much money did we make *for* the client?' rather than 'How much money did we make *from* the client?'
- Happy workers cost less rather than employ fewer people.
- Engage in civil discourse rather than aggressive discourse.
- Dialogue family and community metaphors rather than military and horticultural metaphors.
- Leader as 'host' rather than leader as 'hero'.

In short, we need to match the rational/realist discourse with a romantic/responsible discourse. We should not engage in the mythology of the hero leader, because the hero leader does not exist. After all, he or she is a myth. Instead, to complement the criterion of corporate purpose, we must articulate responsible, romantic, and virtuous notions of noble societal purpose and community values.

Parry and Fiskerud (2015) claim that changing the curriculum might be just a change in terminology and be seen as a platitude, just as in the past with emasculated terms like 'communication' and 'ethics'. There is more to this problem than just having a new ethics course. This has already been done. We do need more sociology and philosophy to enrich the psychology and finance and accounting and strategy that are still necessary. However, we cannot just add more courses. Also, we will fight a losing political battle to substitute sociology for (for example) psychology. Rather than changing through the forced implementation of actual systemic power, which will generate resistance, we should use symbolic power to our advantage. We should change the discourse of business, rather than changing the structural content of business.

Reorient leadership in business school programmes

We have been teaching leadership in MBA and other business programmes for over 20 years. Over that time we have evolved our approach to teaching leadership from a primary focus upon promoting accountable leadership to promoting responsible leadership. In making this adjustment, we have been mindful of the changing foci and priorities of leadership scholarship, the broader shifts in society and the needs and priorities of a different generation of business school students. Our students have responded positively and encouraged the shift in emphasis in our leadership teaching. This has definitely been a case of shared leadership! Every year we have been impressed by how our students begin our classes either struggling to identify their core leadership purpose when asked or pointing to an immediate operational challenge such as implementing a new IT system, meeting this year's sale targets or getting promoted. After only ten short weeks, they tend to emerge with a sharpened personal focus, a keener sense of possibilities about where they can work, and a zest to make a positive change beyond their immediate work context. This heightened sense of responsible leadership is invariably a keynote of their graduation dinner speeches in which they remark with surprise that they came into the MBA to get promoted and to move up and now they have a profound desire to move beyond.

We are sure that many of the token 'hopeless romantics' like us who lecture in leadership in business schools throughout the world can well relate to this experience and have many examples of personal and professional transformations that they can point to, including their own. We wish to point to some of the things that we believe have been most important in our work.

First, for at least the first half of the semester, the context for leadership should be taken out of the exclusive domain of the corporate organisation. Leadership should be explicitly decoupled from business to something that takes a societal perspective. Indeed leadership should be viewed as a critical means of bridging disparate groups within society to achieve broader worthy societal goals. This became the central focus of an entire Master's-level course that was entitled 'The Geography of Leadership' that one of the co-authors co-taught with Eric Guthey at the Copenhagen Business School. A central feature of this course was the role of place in enabling and constraining leadership and a correspondent shift in concern away from developing intra-sectoral to cross-sectoral leadership, and from intra-organisational to inter-organisational leadership.

While the scope of leadership widens and the complexity intensifies significantly, it is just as vital to ensure that leadership becomes the domain of the student, not of their or exemplary 'heroic' organisations they work for or study. The student needs to become an active and responsible player in the various scripts that are presented to them through readings, cases, simulations, and guest speakers. The primary discourse becomes one of helping the community such that the community will follow you (and your organisation). The suggestion is that one should help the community and all people will follow. We suggest that this will be the responsibility of leadership.

Second, students need also to reflect upon their own critical experiences and notable people in their life. Perhaps as an assignment or as an internship, they must actually serve the wider community with the business that they are learning about. This reflexivity becomes important to understanding their own traits, implicit theories, personality, skills, beliefs, and habitus. Teachers start to build in examples from history. The example of the BP Gulf Oil Spill of 2010 might be introduced. The experience of the Philippines tsunami or the Fukushima tsunami-induced meltdown can be investigated. The success of the mutuals and co-operatives in the UK in the early twenty-first century might be examined. The following and community support generated by Cadbury in the UK from the mid-1800s might be explored. In these ways, the core discourse of leadership is not really changed. Rather, the language has virtue built into it. The role of econophonics – dictated by money – and potensiphonics – verbalised through power and domination (Giacalone & Promislo, 2013) – is reduced. Therefore, the leadership discourse is less reflected by greed, symbolic violence, gluttony, and domination. Societal purpose is highlighted.

Third, greater reflexivity should be introduced into the teaching of management, organisational behaviour, and leadership. Students need to experience 'discontent' and 'unease' (Vaara & Faÿ, 2012). The study of leadership will include research about the theory of leadership. At the same time it should focus on students' own experiences. As an MBA student of ours said in support of these notions, 'Don't discredit negative events, adversity, and tragedy. We should embrace them and realise that sometimes important lessons and revelations can come only from these.' Students learn from their own experiences, as well as from the Cadbury experience, as well as from the experience of a journalist who is encouraged to engage in phone hacking. Undergraduate students have had at least 19 years of experience of leadership. So, all students have had much experience upon which to anchor a new discourse about leadership. Indeed, by disengaging leadership from the KPIs (key performance indicators) of senior management, educators are able to unleash a nobler and more reliable understanding of leadership within students, and then to teach it more effectively.

Fourth, as Vaara and Faÿ argue, we should problematise current ideas, values, and practices, rather than taking them for granted and reproducing them within teaching. When leadership is taken out of the organisation and given back to the community, students will develop their own ethical consciousness. As a skill-building exercise, students will learn how to construct an inspirational leadership speech. They are in the leadership role, and they speak to an audience about a matter that is close to their heart. It need not be a business speech. It is preferable if it is not a business speech. The students could be a representative of the youth community speaking to their parliament about 'boat people' or 'migrants' or 'refugees' or 'illegals', who have to pay people smugglers money to make a dangerous voyage across the sea. In this way, the students develop their own discourse of passion, empathy, emotion, sense-making, sense-giving, and ethically defensible influence.

Finally, we have found that students can learn leadership by looking at movies and current affairs in new and different ways. Movies dramatise leadership. Examples might be *Whale Rider* or *Milk* or *Hotel Rwanda* or *Moneyball* or *American Gangster* or *The Queen*. Current affairs show leadership in action, including how the community reacts to business decisions. Examples might be the UK phone hacking trial in the second decade of the twenty-first century, or world reaction to the typhoon that hit the Philippines in 2013, or President Hollande's reaction to the Charlie Hebdo massacre in Paris in 2015; or almost anything that is happening in the world. All the core elements of leadership theory and of leadership curriculum are identified in these dramas. These case studies emphasise the responsibility of leadership for communities, rather than the accountability of leadership for outcomes.

But, here's the thing!

To conclude, our discourse about learning and developing leadership should include a new criterion for the success of any strategy or decision in any business. This criterion should be: 'How will this decision help the community?' This criterion is not just responsible but also romantic. Hitherto, the criterion has been merely: 'How will this decision help the bottom-line of our business?' People in leadership roles must be accountable for that realist criterion. However, because our company is just one member of our community, the hegemony of that criterion must change. Now we hope that readers will understand the difference between the responsibility of leadership and the accountability of leadership. We suggest that to concentrate solely upon on the accountability of leadership will be just plain irresponsible.

References

Bass, B. M., & Steidlmeier, P. (1999). Ethics, character, and authentic transformational leadership behavior. *The Leadership Quarterly, 10*(2), 181–217.

Ciulla, J. (2004a). Ethics and leadership effectiveness. In J. Antonakis, A. T. Cianciolo, & R. J. Sternberg (Eds.), *The Nature of Leadership* (pp. 508–542). London: Sage.

Ciulla, J. (2004b). *Ethics: The heart of leadership* (2nd edn). London: Praeger.

Clegg, S. (2014). Managerialism: Born in the USA. *Academy of Management Review, 39*(4), 566–585.

Craig, S. B., & Gustafson, S. B. (1998). Perceived leader integrity scale: An instrument for assessing employee perceptions of leader integrity. *The Leadership Quarterly, 9*(2), 127–45.

Cunliffe, A. L., & Eriksen, M. (2011). Relational leadership. *Human Relations, 64*(11), 1425–1449.

Ferraro, F., Pfeffer, J., & Sutton, R. I. (2005) Economics language and assumptions: How theories can become self-fulfilling. *Academy of Management Review, 30*, 8–24.

Friedman, M. (1970, 13 September). The social responsibility of business is to increase its profits. *New York Times Magazine*, p. 32.

Ghoshal, S. (2005). Bad management theories are destroying good management practices. *Academy of Management Learning and Education, 4*(1), 75–91.

Giacalone, R. A., & Promislo, M. D. (2013). Broken when entering: The stigmatization of goodness and business ethics education. *Academy of Management Learning and Education, 12*(1), 86–101.

Kempster, S., Jackson, B., & Conroy, M. (2011). Leadership as purpose: Exploring the role of purpose in leadership practice. *Leadership Journal, 7*(3), 317–334.

Maak, T., & Pless, N. M. (2006). Responsible leadership in a stakeholder society: A relational perspective. *Journal of Business Ethics, 66*, 99–115.

Mayer, R. C., Davis, J. H., & Schoorman, F. D. (1995). An integrative model of organizational trust. *Academy of Management Review, 20*(3), 709–774.

McCabe, D. L., Butterfield, K. D., & Treviño, L. K. (2006). Academic dishonesty in graduate business programs: Prevalence, causes, and proposed action. *Academy of Management Learning and Education, 5*, 294–305.

Meindl, J. R. (1995). The romance of leadership as a follower-centric theory: A social constructionist approach. *The Leadership Quarterly, 6*(3), 329–341.

Miller, D. T. (1999). The norm of self-interest. *American Psychologist, 54*, 1053–1060.

Nonis, S., & Swift, C. O. (2001). An examination of the relationship between academic dishonesty and workplace dishonesty: A multicampus investigation. *Journal of Education for Business, 77*, 69–77.

Parry, K. W. (1999). Enhancing adaptability: Leadership strategies to accommodate change in local government settings. *Journal of Organizational Change Management, 12*(2), 134–156.

Parry, K. W. (2001). Could leadership theory be generalised? In R. Wiesner & B. Millett (Eds.), *Management and organisational behaviour: Contemporary challenges and future directions* (Chapter 14, pp. 161–173). Brisbane: John Wiley & Sons.

Parry, K. W., & Fiskerud, A. (2015). Can leadership be value free? In C. Mabey & W. Mayrhofer (Eds.), *Developing leadership: Questions business schools don't ask* (Chapter 7, pp. 98–107). London: Sage.

Parry, K. W., & Kempster, S. J. (2014). Love and leadership: Constructing follower narrative identities of charismatic leadership. *Management Learning Journal, 45*(1), 21–38.

Pless, N. M., & Maak, T. (2011). Responsible leadership: Pathways to the future. *Journal of Business Ethics, 98*, 3–13.

Porter, M. E. (2010). How big business can regain legitimacy. *Bloomberg Business Week.* Retrieved 19 December 2014, from www.businessweek.com/stories/2010-05-06/how-big-business-can-regain-legitimacybusinessweek-business-news-stock-market-and-financial-advice.

Porter, M. E., & Kramer, M. R. (2011). Creating shared value. *Harvard Business Review, 89*(1/2), 62–77.

Pye, A. (2005). Leadership and organizing: Sensemaking in action. *Leadership, 1*(1), 31–49.

Sachs, J. D. (2011). *The price of civilization: Reawakening American virtue and prosperity.* New York: Random House.

Smircich, L., & Morgan, G. (1982). Leadership: The management of meaning. *Journal of Applied Behavioral Science, 18*(3), 257–273.

Uhl-Bien, M. (2006). Relational leadership theory: Exploring the social processes of leadership and organizing. *The Leadership Quarterly, 17*, 654–676.

Vaara, E., & Faÿ, E. (2012). Reproduction and change on the global scale: A Bourdieusian perspective on management education. *Journal of Management Studies, 49*(6), 1023–51.

Walumbwa, F. O., Avolio, B. J., Gardner, W. L., Wernsing, T. S., & Peterson, S. J. (2008). Authentic leadership: Development and validation of a theory-based measure? *Journal of Management, 34*, 89–126.

Wang, L., Malhotra, D., & Murnighan, J. K. (2011). Economics education and greed. *Academy of Management Learning and Education, 10*: 643–660.

Young, S. (2003). *Moral capitalism: Reconciling private interest with the public good.* San Francisco: Berret-Koehler Publishers.

Yukl, G. (2012). *Leadership in organizations* (8th edn). Upper Saddle River, NJ: Prentice Hall.

9 Developing responsible leadership through discourse ethics

Steve Kempster, Sarah Gregory, and Emma Watton

The nature of responsible leadership has been outlined in previous chapters and it is the ethical aspects within responsible leadership that we examine in this chapter. We seek to outline how ethics within responsible leadership can be made salient through the notion of discourse ethics – enabling managers to explore how ethical or unethical behaviour becomes manifest in the contexts in which they practice leadership. It is uncommon in many organisational contexts for managers to examine ethics within their decision-making; it is simply not part of everyday organisational discourse. We outline why this is so, and the implications of this for the hopes for establishing responsible leadership; and we place such hopes alongside a critique of those ethical leadership theories that underestimate the difficulty of drawing ethical expectations into leadership practice within an organisational context. To do this we consider how ethics are typically explored in the educational context through the use of hypothetical case studies in the classroom and we problematise such an approach in light of our critique of ethical leadership literature. Whilst hypothetical case studies can have pedagogical value in catalysing discourse, they have limited resonance with the complexity of everyday managerial context – they lack the necessary nuance of lived experience which is provided by real life cases. This chapter explores how real life cases can be created within management education through the use of the critical incident technique, and how such incidents enable rich debate in the classroom. We consider what practical action is needed to bring ethics within everyday pragmatic discourse on decision-making in the organisation. The chapter suggests that engaging in discourse ethics is a mechanism for enabling responsible leadership to become manifest and so provide a sense of connecting grounded and framed realism of the organisational context with romantic possibilities of what it might be to improve everyday practices.

'We don't often talk about this'

The above quotation is taken from an interview with a manager who was reflecting on an ethical incident that they had faced in their organisation. It was one of a number of comments presented by managers in a research study undertaken by Sarah Gregory (2010) which highlighted that ethics is not part of the everyday organisational discourse. Little conversation appears to occur regarding ethics in such managerial life. It is uncommon for decisions to factor in an ethical lens.

Within the context of examining responsibilities in everyday leadership practice the limited salience of ethics poses some fundamental questions: How do 'leaders' make judgements on the impact of decisions on diverse and often competing stakeholder interests? How do they act for the greatest good and what might be the greatest good? How do they judge right from wrong? Is the fiduciary duty only to shareholders or to stakeholders, or is it as extensive as a duty of care for the human condition? Exploring such questions makes ethics as a central responsibility within leadership (Voegtlin, Patzer, & Scherer, 2012). Waldman and Galvin assert that responsible leadership fundamentally is a *moral* 'inner obligation to do the right thing toward others ... to act on this obligation and to be accountable for the consequences of one's actions' (2012, p. 328).

Buchholtz and Carroll (2012) have asserted that organisations are dominated by *amoral* behaviour, where morality is outside the realm of business, and managers do not consciously consider the ethical implications of their decisions and actions. It is not that people are immoral. Rather, research shows that outside of the organisational context they are able to draw on an ethical compass (Brown & Treviño, 2014). So, why not within the organisation? Anand, Ashforth, and Joshi (2004) provide a helpful synthesis. They suggest that the prevalence of amoral behaviour is a consequence of the dual processes of socialisation and rationalisation. In terms of socialisation managers and employees engage in activities with historic cultural antecedents reinforced by role modelling behaviour, the outcome of which is that conduct is perceived as normal. Through a series of rationalisations – 'denial of responsibility', 'denial of harm', and 'denial of victims' (2004, p. 41) – individuals are able to separate such conduct from personal morality. Detert, Treviño, and Sweitzer point to the impact of moral disengagement, where individuals deactivate their 'moral self-regulatory processes that normally inhibit unethical behaviour' (2008, p. 374), and to the lowering of an individual's moral impulse and diluted sense of moral identity (Shao, Aquino, & Freeman, 2008) as part of this process. In essence employees and managers have a low sense of ethical awareness – it is simply not salient with regard to everyday activity.

The target for leadership development then is to tune people back into becoming responsible and ethically aware, allowing their moral impulse to become alive and, through high salience of ethics, strengthen their moral identity. With all these aspects prominent we assert that discourse ethics would become highly prevalent. So, if we view ethical responsibility as 'the set of rules, principles, or ways of thinking that guide, or claim authority to guide, the actions of a particular group' (Singer, 1994, p. 4), and an ethical issue as a situation where 'two or more important values, rights and responsibilities conflict' (Treviño & Nelson, 2014, p. 39), then the importance of being able to engage in discourse ethics concerning these issues becomes paramount for responsible leadership. However, comments such as 'ethics is still considered one of the least important skills necessary in manager's daily work' (Velthouse & Kandogan, 2007, p. 151) highlight again the importance of the development of responsible leadership, with leaders who will bring ethics to the fore in their own practice and that of others.

We shall outline the nature of discourse ethics further on; however, first we explore how leadership development has sought to intervene in this area. The primary vehicle has been through the use of case situations.

Hypothetical case studies are still prevalent in the teaching of business ethics (Maclagan & Campbell, 2011), and their purpose is to catalyse discussion on business ethics and ethical behaviour. In a related research project (Gregory, 2010), Sarah Gregory showed that middle managers faced numerous ethical dilemmas in their working lives but often felt unable to raise these within the organisational context. However, within her teaching of business ethics using hypothetical cases, the class discussion often lacked depth and reflection when exploring the nature of these dilemmas. Gregory experimented with using anonymous 'real life' cases drawn from her research. The difference in discussion was palpable. As a consequence we are exploring the notion of linking leadership learning lived experience (Kempster, 2006, 2009) and ethical dilemmas from such lived experience using the critical incident technique in the classroom, with the primary goals of stimulating discourse ethics and interrelated management learning. This chapter seeks to elaborate the theoretical argument of why such an approach of real life cases in the classroom may gain greater learning and reflection than hypothetical cases.

We now outline the structure of the chapter. We begin by first critiquing the nature of business ethics and ethical behaviour linked to the notion of 'real' and 'hypothetical' discussions. The discussion of 'real' experienced ethical issues links strongly with discourse ethics. We outline the nature of discourse ethics and suggest that exploration of discourse ethics in the educational context of executive programmes has considerable scope for developing reflexive awareness of the nature and impact of business ethics on managerial practice. We suggest that such discourse ethics can be developed in the classroom through the use of the critical incident technique (CIT) (Flanagan, 1954). Building on Steve Kempster's work on exploring experiences of leadership learning that draw on lived experience, we outline a method we have used in executive education and leadership development contexts. A brief case from the classroom is outlined where we explore the process of discourse ethics alongside the content of the discussion. We assert that the palpable richness and insight of engaging in discourse ethics provides a most important process for the emergence and development of responsible leadership. Yet we situate this discussion within the complexity of seeking to enable discourse ethics in the everyday practices of business leadership. We conclude with a research agenda intertwined with a discussion on leadership development of responsible leadership in practice focused on discourse ethics.

Ethics: practice or theory?

The study of ethics can be viewed from two perspectives: as a form of practice or action; and from a philosophical perspective. The first perspective focuses on the way that employees practice, or do not practice, ethical behaviour within organisations (see, for example, Clegg, Kornberger, & Rhodes, 2007; Velthouse & Kandogan, 2007), in terms of taking some form of action in order to be ethical (Connolly, Cox-White, Keller, & Leever, 2009; Sekerka & Bagozzi, 2007), as well as a behavioural orientation on ethical decision-making (Kish-Gephart, Harrison, & Treviño, 2010; Treviño, Weaver, & Reynolds, 2006). For all three areas the focus is on asking questions such as: 'What would you do in this situation?' A common generic educational approach reflects the notion of presenting the managers with models and concepts that provide a guide for reflection on their everyday actions, or perhaps giving them a framework to consider when faced with an ethical dilemma.

In contrast, the second perspective on ethics has a philosophical and theoretical focus, where the emphasis is on understanding the philosophies and theories which help to illustrate ethical situations. Academics identified with this perspective include MacIntyre (1985), Hosmer (1995), and Hinman (1998). This is not saying that theoretical ethics does not consider the practice of ethics, but it does so in relation to the philosophical theory, hence the focus is on the theory and on asking questions such as: 'What should you do in this situation?'

The approach that has resonated with Gregory's teaching in terms of enabling rich discussion of ethical issues by managers is the practice-based perspective. The resonance with managers of the practice approach reflects Toffler's (1986/reprinted 1991) early research. Toffler examined 'what people working in organizations, particularly managers, were experiencing as ethical concerns' (1991, p. vii). Their own words or voices were then used to present ethical situations in which they were personally involved: in essence, 'an empirical approach to understanding social and moral problems in corporate life' (Norton, 1992, p. 75). Giving voice to the ethical experience connects strongly with notions of discourse. Notwithstanding Fairclough's comment that 'discourse is a difficult concept, largely because there are so many conflicting and overlapping definitions' (1992, p. 3), Wetherell, Taylor, and Yates helpfully describe discourse as a form of 'social action' which involves 'talk, language in use and human meaning-making activities' (2001, p. 27). We suggest that exploring discourse ethics may have an important contribution in terms of teaching business ethics to managers on executive education and leadership development programmes.

Discourse ethics

A definition of discourse ethics is provided by Griseri and Seppala as 'the idea that ethics should be based on processes of dialogue between different parties'

(2010, p. 464). Crane and Matten explore the notion of discourse ethics and propose that at its heart is the issue that 'norms ultimately cannot be justified by rational arguments, but that they have to be generated and applied to solve ethical conflicts on a day-to-day basis ... ethical reflection has to start from real life experience' (2010, p. 122).

In this way a purpose of discourse ethics could be seen as encouraging the resolution of ethical conflicts through discourse and reflection. For Stansbury, discourse ethics is a 'form of valid collective moral deliberation' (2009, p. 33). He states that it is a 'normative framework that is appropriate for deliberating on the moral problems that emerge in a pluralistic business context' (2009, p. 34). So although a focus of discourse ethics is on the collective and the resolving of conflicts between distinct parties, we are seeking to ask the question whether discourse ethics could also be a way for an individual to resolve a personal ethical dilemma, by talking about and reflecting on what had happened.

Bird, Westley, and Waters (1989) considered a form of discourse ethics when they presented their findings on the uses of 'moral talk' by employees, viewing it as a 'social exchange'. They developed three groupings that illustrated when employees would discuss ethics, the first two being what they termed 'functional uses' which include the clarification of issues to determine relevant norms and the consideration of structures of authority. The third grouping they saw as being 'dysfunctional', as this involved the rationalising of 'morally ambiguous behaviour' with the consequent expression of frustrations (1989, p. 75). They concluded that some forms of moral talking about ethics perform useful functions that ought to be encouraged, whilst other forms are dysfunctional in terms of social interactions.

A critical perspective on discourse ethics is provided by Clegg et al. (2007). They comment that 'discourse is a powerful way through which social reality is shaped' (2007, p. 113), as it provides a means through which reality can be explored. They link discourse to 'ethics in practice' as: 'ethics in practice focuses on the discourses that make sense of behaviour and often categorise practices as more or less ethical, whereas discourse is considered as a resource that legitimises behaviour and constructs frameworks (including vocabulary) to justify practices' (2007, p. 113).

The notion of legitimisation connects with Fisher and Lovell's work which considers how an individual constructs a rationalisation for their actions or behaviour, but suggests that this process can be 'untenable because it requires decisions about what ought to be, to be derived from descriptions of how things actually are' which could be seen as 'illogical' (2009, p. 127). The response that they put forward is that it is not the purpose of discourse to 'establish ultimate values but to arrive at pragmatic resolutions through a rigorous process that is not anchored in immutable values' (ibid.). This is an important aspect in the context of leadership development. Discourse ethics needs to be anchored with practice ethics and provide guidance for making sense of ethical issues and dilemmas and also legitimising behaviours.

The key for us is how to enable discourse ethics in developing responsible leadership? How to surface dialogue on ethical behaviour within the organisational contexts of the managers? We briefly explore the opportunity that the critical incident technique can bring to leadership development as a proposed way of developing participant case studies that have a 'real' ethical perspective. Yet we are cautioned by Jackall's conclusion that 'managers do not generally discuss ethics, morality, or moral rules-in-use in a direct way with each other' (1988, p. 6). In this sense, will discourse ethics work in the classroom if it does not work in organisations? It is not that morality is outside of leadership responsibility, but rather that managers' experience of exploring ethics in the organisational context is rare and therefore would this disable managers from exploring ethics within leadership development?

Discourse ethics and the critical incident technique

The Critical Incident Technique (CIT) was developed by Flanagan as 'a procedure for gathering [...] facts concerning behaviour in defined situations' (1954, p. 335). Focusing on organisational contexts, Bryman and Bell (2003) see CIT as an opportunity for people to tell their incidents in a way that could be described as stories or narratives; while for Snell the CIT can enable insight that is 'grounded in the complexities of actual practice, [...] rather than being based on mere espousals and generalisations by respondents' (1999, p. 511). Finally, for Easterby-Smith, Thorpe, and Jackson (2008, p. 150) it 'offers an opportunity to go straight to the heart of an issue and collect information about what is really being sought'. The above reasons indicate that the CIT could be an appropriate technique to obtain ethical real life case studies that have participant resonance in the classroom context. The CIT has been used successfully in a number of research studies in areas such as: health and nursing (Norman, Redfern, Tomalin, & Oliver, 1992); education (Brookfield, 1990; Preskill, 1996; Woods, 1993); the restaurant and café industry (Chell & Pittaway, 1998); and entrepreneurs and small businesses (Chell, 1998; Cope & Watts, 2000; Kaulio, 2003; Tjosvold & Weicker, 1993). But we have not found evidence of use in educational contexts to explore business ethics or ethical behaviour.

From Gregory's research (2010), applying the CIT usefully focused managers on recalling what happened, how it happened, and why. Sarah also found a significant advantage that recalling critical incidents provided what Chell described as a 'rich source of information on conscious reflections of the incumbent, their frame of reference, feelings, attitudes and perspective on matters which are of critical importance to them' (1998, p. 62). Adapting the use of the CIT from a research instrument to an educational technique to aid reflective recall of ethical incidents may 'obtain [reflection] of specific behaviours from those in the best position to make the necessary observations and evaluations' (Flanagan, 1954, p. 340). Again adapting comments from Nyquist and Bloom (taken from Gummesson), the CIT 'generates [reflection] with the level of detail and richness that puts the [delegate] close to the realities of the process [experienced]' (2000, p. 136).

In this sense the technique is most helpful in the context of leadership development where the managers have 'difficulty in expressing an opinion' (Collis & Hussey, 2009, p. 198) as it encourages them to discuss their own experiences through the recalling of the incidents, rather than commenting on a hypothetical situation or answering specific interview questions, which can be daunting. Perhaps one of the main advantages of the CIT is that it 'enables the development of case based theory grounded in actual critical events' (Chell, 1998, p. 71).

To summarise the advantages of the CIT, this is a technique that is a method of data collection which 'enables one to understand the context of action, the tactics, strategies and coping mechanisms adopted and the outcomes, results or consequences of people's actions and the new situation with which they are faced' (Chell, 1998, p. 62). It is this link between context and outcome through action that provides such a rich opportunity for the initiation of discourse ethics and practice-based ethics within the development of responsible leadership.

Developing discourse ethics in the classroom: personal critical incidents

The use of critical incidents/critical episodes is more common in leadership development. For example, Steve Kempster has used a time-line approach to leadership learning in the 'classroom' for many years. The approach has been captured as the 'Tents Exercise' (Kempster, 2009, p. 114) and evaluation has shown that during this exercise, managers make conscious the incidents and episodes that are formative in the development of leadership practice. Such classroom learning makes conscious learning from lived experience that managers have not previously drawn into a cohesive frame; a sense of a new picture on their development that has been hidden or at best been simply glimpses of their recall of disconnected mountain peaks of events. The process brings to the fore prominent significant others whose impact on an individual in terms of their leadership practice is most pronounced. Recent work by Brown and Treviño (2014) confirms the importance of role models to the development of ethical leadership. Their research has shown that ethical leadership is developed through social comparison. This is most prominent in the early stages of leadership learning – the formative years in organisational participation (Kempster & Parry, 2013), for example the supervisor-follower relationship. Interestingly, Brown and Treviño (2014) showed that ethical role models become significantly less available as people progress through their careers, indeed the 'direct impact of top managers as role models for managers at lower levels of the organisation is limited'; however these managers are 'likely to be important role models for their own direct reports' (2014, p. 595). In a sense they give support to Anand *et al*'s (2004) argument for processes of socialisation that lessen moral identity and lead to an increasing sense of moral disengagement (Detert *et al.*, 2008).

The Tents exercise generates for each individual a portfolio of significant others at various stages of their career. People are able to recall the people, the situations in which they engaged with them, the behaviours and emotions generated (Mackay, 2012). In a sense, they are developing a series of personal case studies. It was our intention to use these personal case studies as the focus of discourse ethics. In particular we wished to address two questions:

1   Does an examination of personal case studies enable participants to become reflexively aware of their experiences of business ethics?
2   Can the process engender a rich exploration of ethics in practice? For example, might it show the complexities of engaging in ethical practice and the contextual constraints on such an orientation?

We were running the Tents exercise in the first module of our Master's course in Leadership Practice and Responsibility – perhaps unsurprisingly titled 'Responsible Leadership'. Sarah Gregory and Steve Kempster had piloted the use of the CIT in the classroom six months earlier on an Executive MBA programme. The learning from the pilot was that managers readily engaged in the conversation if they were in groups of at least three: if there were two managers in the group, the discussion lacked depth of questioning. The design for the Responsible Leadership module sought to undertake the Tents exercise as the first element. This was in order to be able to draw on the detail generated by each delegate of their significant others, alongside their own enactments of leading that could be used throughout the module. In this way theory could be applied to their lived experience to give reflective practice insights. Theory relating to ethics in practice, ethical decision-making, and ethical leadership was then explored in plenary. With the critical incident technique as the core process we asked the managers to do the following:

> Looking through your time-lines identify leadership relationships that featured an ethical issue. Bring to the fore particular incidents. Select at least one positive incident and at least one negative incident. Consider the nature of your relationship, what happened in the incident, and the impact this had on you (and others) at the time, how you think the issue could have been handled, and the effect on your understanding of ethics in the practice of leading. After 30 minutes explore what you have captured in groups of three.

The outcome of the exercise enabled discourse ethics to occur in the small groups. Discourse ethics was much less effective in plenary. Feedback on the module indicated this to be one of the most highly valued processes of the week, which was surprising. We followed up on the feedback using the online forum and subsequently, through interviews with the managers, asking for detail about their learning from the critical incidents. The following message was posted onto the online forum:

> After receiving the feedback on the module we noticed the positive value placed on the session on ethical leadership of significant others. We are wishing to capture your insights on the process for on-going research, and to inform the development of the process. Here is the brief you undertook from the module. Please could you kindly recall the conversations you had in your groups of three, as well as your subsequent reflections on ethical leadership in your context. Please comment on whether you have witnessed or engaged in ethical discussions related to subsequent decisions and actions? If this has occurred could you outline what has enabled this or if it hasn't what do you think has constrained it? If the latter, what practical action do you think is needed to bring ethics within everyday conversations within leadership practice. Please be assured that we will anonymise the feedback.

We then approached a selection of the managers to see if they would be willing to talk about this further and four agreed to take part in interviews to consider their ethical dilemmas in more depth. The interview questions were based on those asked in the online message. The information obtained in the interviews related both to their ethical dilemmas and to the impact of the process that had been undertaken in the module on their organisational leadership practice. We offer up two examples of incidents using the manager's own words, following which we examine the reflections of the managers on the process of talking about their dilemmas.

Incident 1 'I was put in a very difficult situation'

William described an incident which was 'very difficult' and concerned an initiative in the organisation for which his boss was responsible:

> I knew and had heard feedback from others that the initiative wasn't going quite well and was not on track with regards to the outputs. My boss and the delivery team didn't want to hear that feedback; they wanted it to be successful. Part of that, I think, was linked to the practice of the organisation. Normally a person was given a new initiative to run for two years and they have two years to demonstrate a good result from the initiative and this then usually guarantees them their next good posting. So, really the organisation is driving this behaviour. In this incident my boss was at the end of his two years with this initiative when my boss's superior stepped in and took him off the initiative and he asked me to take over. I felt like this had put me in an awkward position. I wanted to stand up to do the right thing but I also knew that my job was on the

line. I ended up turning the initiative round and because of that I gained new friendships and respect from people. The reporting structure stayed the same so I still reported to my boss and he took the changes very personally.

When asked about what happened next, William responded that

Ultimately my boss left the organisation. He was very intelligent but with this particular initiative his thoughts seemed to be clouded by other things. He was under serious pressure to perform well and this was partly driven by some stakeholder changes that had happened part way through the project. I learnt to try to make sure that I didn't make the same mistake.

It is interesting that William had not included this boss on his timeline because of his *mixed feelings* about him. What this example illustrates is the way that the combination of producing the timeline (even though this boss was not cited on it) and use of the CIT enabled William to discuss and reflect on his ethical behaviour within a 'difficult' organisational situation.

Incident 2 'It was totally unprofessional and unethical'

Another incident was discussed by Richard and was taken from his timeline. It concerned his manager and he saw it as an example of *how not to lead*. His description of the incident is below:

This one example stood out for me as an example of how you can manipulate people to do things and for people to feel like they have no choice but to follow. At the time I worked in an organisation where we would hold a client seminar every few months. For the seminar we were asked to invite 20 to 30 clients to come along and hear news updates. By doing this, the organisation was hoping to bring clients together and to also generate new business. In principle it was a great idea. However, what happened was that there were very few clients who wanted to attend. My manager at the time would put pressure on us to fill the room with people who weren't clients and sometimes other colleagues from the business. People who attended under these false pretexts didn't know what they were doing there. When it came to the Q&A part of the seminar, my manager would pick on colleagues to ask questions. This put us all in an awkward situation and none of us liked doing it, but because the manager was close to the chairman of the company, none of us could protest openly. It used to happen a fair bit. It's wrong and I would feel bad about it for my clients. In the end colleagues would lie and say they had no suitable clients to invite. The manager used to play one of us off against another.

When asked how the situation was resolved, Richard responded:

> A bunch of us left the organisation. It was a kind of mutiny. We wrote to the senior management team of the company and said we couldn't carry on working like this and so most of us left. It had produced such a lot of negative energy. The whole thing dragged on for about 12 months and it was totally unprofessional and unethical. People didn't know who they could trust anymore.

Again, this incident illustrates the way that the managers were expressing their ethical dilemmas and also reflecting on what they saw as being unethical behaviour in the organisation.

The process in practice

Regarding the impact of the process, one manager commented that 'this was an ethical dilemma that I've thought through more as a result of the module at Lancaster' (Nick). What is interesting is that Nick goes on to say that he hadn't felt that the discussion with colleagues at the module helped him at the time, but 'what it did do though was make me think about things more clearly and to put it into context. I've thought about this type of thing much more since I started doing the course.'

For another manager, the discussion at the module had resulted in the development of his own model: 'I've thought about this and developed a model to show the forces I think that people go through with ethical dilemmas' (Mo). Mo then proceeded to use his model as a framework for the discussion of his ethical dilemma.

As discussed above, William considered an ethical dilemma where he was asked to take over an 'initiative' from his boss. He commented that this 'put him in an awkward position' especially as he still reported to his boss 'who took the changes very personally'. When asked if this boss had appeared on his timeline, William responded as follows:

> no actually he didn't. I think that's because I had mixed feelings about him. He had some good and bad qualities and he didn't particularly stand out for me as someone to include on the timeline.

This example illustrates how the follow-up through the online forum and interviews encouraged the manager to engage in discourse ethics to draw out additional reflections which had not been considered in the module. The interviews also provided the opportunity for the managers to reflect on their leadership practice and whether they had subsequently engaged in discourse ethics within their organisations. For Nick, conversations about ethics are now occurring within the business, partly as a result of the module but also because his new manager is 'extremely ethical'. As he commented: 'ethical decision-making is much more salient to me now. These conversations are now happening in the business and I feel much more confident in being able to raise concerns.'

For Richard there was a further ethical dilemma to the one presented in the previous section, which he felt unable to discuss within the organisation as it would be 'uncomfortable' for colleagues to know what had happened, however he did discuss the dilemma with a couple of his close friends who 'understood the situation and had empathy for me'. Mo took a different approach to discourse ethics within his organisation as he described a situation where the Vice President of the company had instructed him to pay invoices for services that the company had not received. He refused but then discovered that the invoices had been paid and his access to the invoices removed. As he said:

> My line manager told me not to pursue it anymore. Since then we have a new VP come in. I have raised the issue with him and he has supported me to get things back on track. Sometimes the power in organisations creates the dilemma, power is dangerous. I felt like I was having to fight this on my own until the new VP came in. He only took it seriously because I told him I was going to escalate the situation to the Ethics Committee in my organisation.
>
> (Mo)

This example illustrates how the manager had found a way to engage in discourse ethics within a difficult environment, although he had to resort to almost threatening behaviour to have it taken 'seriously'!

The module broadly sought to engage the managers in becoming reflective of their context with regard to ethical responsibility in the practice of leading. On examining the feedback, the subsequent online forum discussions, and the interviews, it struck us how the process of enabling discourse ethics is far from straightforward – even in the classroom where levels of trust, support, and confidentiality had been established. However, examining the process longitudinally we could see that discourse ethics could be prompted, stimulated, and nurtured within the context of leadership development. More significantly, we do not know whether it has persisted and flourished in the minds and actions of the managers as they continue in their everyday endeavours within their practice of leading. The sense of realism rather takes a firm hold of us here and we rather believe that the organisational context may greatly disable such flourishing. Drawing from the well of romanticism and linked to Nick's comment, given the right environment with an ethical management team in place, the module creates the opportunity for students to have these conversations.

Discussion: in search of discourse ethics

We have outlined earlier that the awareness of ethics in everyday leadership practice is restricted. Further exploration of ethics within decision-making in the organisational context is understandably also very restricted. We have mentioned that Brown and Treviño (2014) have recently shown the limited number of positive role models as ethical leaders. Yet the timelines of the participating managers in the responsible leadership module (and similarly with the Executive MBA module) illustrates the prominence of incidents and the associations of such incidents with significant others in leadership roles. Brown and Treviño hinted at this, pointing towards a greater proportion of negative significant others at ever increasing senior levels: 'research on role modelling in general suggests that older employees tend to learn from both positive (i.e. learn what to do) and negative (i.e. learn what "not" to do) role models' (2014, p. 596), therefore reflecting a declining presence of overt moral responsibility as observed from followers. They suggest further research is required to examine this dynamic in terms of the manifestation on ethical leadership practice.

We now offer some provocations as stimuli for exploring ethical responsibility in leadership. Our first three interrelated provocative statements draw out from our extant review and are reinforced through our empirical data. These are rather overshadowed by the lens of realism:

(1) *Timelines of managers will have increasing numbers of reported negative ethical role models in association with escalating levels of seniority.*
(2) *The increasing levels of negative role models will lead to higher levels of moral disengagement, lower moral identity, and higher prevalence of amoral leadership behaviour.*
(3) *Higher levels of moral disengagement will lead to low levels of discourse ethics within the practice of leading.*

Our supposition associated with these three statements suggests that there is a decline in the salience of moral identity, leading to moral disengagement within the practice of managers as they move to higher levels of authority and associated responsibility. Our propositions seek to direct future research to explore the plausibility of this supposition. What are the underlying influences that may shape the emergence of a lowering of ethical responsibility? Is it the processes of socialisation and rationalisation that Anand *et al.* (2004) point to or is there something more? These aspects ground debates in ethics and responsible leadership into a realism of significant dynamics that need to be understood in much greater illumination if traction is to be gained, to allow the flourishing of ethics and enable the manifestation of responsible leadership.

However, the data with our managers suggests there is scope for hope; space for romanticism to get a toe hold into practice. The process of reflecting on critical incidents appears to enable explorations of ethics within the practice of leading to become more salient. We suggest that exploring critical incidents provides a means for enabling managers to engage in discussions in the classroom context. The critical incidents are drawn from real life experiences of the managers. In the process of sharing and examining these experiences there appears to be a sense of collective permission to talk about aspects of organisational life that are normally subterranean. Further, our subsequent research has shown that some of the managers have begun to engage in discourse ethics within their organisational context, or have reflected more deeply on the notion of ethics in everyday practice of leading, yet their context may not be conducive to allow such conversations. We need to know more about the contexts that are enabling or restricting such discussions, for example: the nature of the relationships in which they are situated, the hierarchical level of such relationships and associated sense of responsibilities, the histories, rituals, and routines of past practices, and perhaps the degree of influence of key role models – what they seek to reward and what they seek to punish. Taken collectively these aspects have a morphostasis impact – sustaining a predominantly amoral orientation.

We wish to draw attention to the important role discourse ethics might have in addressing this dominant amoral perspective. As previously discussed, discourse ethics provokes managers into 'collective moral deliberation' (Stansbury, 2009, p. 33) and is 'based on processes of dialogue between different parties' (Griseri & Seppala, 2010, p. 464). However, we are suggesting that discourse ethics can be a way for an individual to resolve a personal ethical dilemma, by talking about and reflecting on what happened with those who are outside the incident. Ultimately, discourse can be viewed as providing one way of making sense of ethical issues and also legitimising behaviours.

Discourse ethics is central to our ongoing research as it enables us to understand the ways in which managers make sense of their ethical incidents. Importantly it also has significant opportunity for development by enabling the manager to become conscious of the level of moral engagement/ disengagement or sense of moral identity prevalent in their particular context. We assert that it has the potential to enable managers to move from being unintentionally amoral to the development of moral awareness, moral imagination, and moral judgment (Buchholtz & Carroll, 2012). Accordingly we suggest our fourth statement that perhaps has a hint of romanticism within it:

(4) Managers' ethical expectations of leadership practice can be made salient through examining critical incidents from their timelines.

So can discourse ethics become prevalent in the organisational context? Voegtlin *et al.* (2012) suggest it can. They suggest a process of societal deliberation where business leaders secure moral 'legitimacy of decisions through proactive [...] inclusion and mobilization of stakeholders' (2012, p. 3). However, Voegtlin *et al.* do not outline explicitly the mechanisms by which this can occur. We suggest that applying the CIT with managers could be a most useful mechanism.

The CIT would allow managers to tell their incidents in a way that could be described as stories or narratives (Bryman & Bell, 2003). The CIT usefully focuses employees on recalling what happened, how it happened, and why. There also is the advantage that recalling critical incidents can often provide a 'rich source of information on conscious reflections of the incumbent, their frame of reference, feelings, attitudes and perspective on matters which are of critical importance to them' (Chell, 1998, p. 62). Chell has identified that at the heart of the CIT is the issue that:

> people immersed in these situation and circumstances are trying to make sense of them. Their accounts are partial; but partial or not, biased or not, such accounts constitute *their* reality, and, arguably, it is the way they view the world which shapes their future actions.
>
> (2004, p. 58)

The importance of future action is significant. We suggest that the reflexive process of coming to know a situation anew through examining past incidents would greatly address Anand *et al.*'s call to assist managers to remain aware and vigilant of the 'occupational pressures and temptations to cut ethical corners and continue questionable practices instigated by others' (2004, p. 51). We suggest our final 'romanticised' statements:

(5) *The use of the CIT with managers will stimulate the manifestation of discourse ethics.*

(6) *The use of CIT will lead to a heightened awareness of organisational ethics within everyday leadership practice.*

We have outlined six statements that draw from the predominantly theoretical arguments of the chapter. Collectively these enable us to structure a research agenda, to which we now turn.

The research agenda

Based on our learning from the pilot study and the Responsible Leadership module, we now suggest a research agenda to be undertaken in three successive steps with three clear foci: step 1 – exploring organisational contexts to illuminate an understanding of the nature and manifestation of discourse ethics (a form of base-lining); step 2 – developing discourse ethics in the classroom; step 3 – exploring how stimulating the salience of ethics in a classroom activity impacts on the manifestation of discourse ethics in the everyday practice of responsible leadership. Through these three foci we suggested research that can begin to understand the realism of the context in which leadership practice is situated, that can inform both leadership development interventions and interrelated development of theory on responsible leadership through the lens of ethical responsibility.

Step 1   Exploring organisational contexts

A vital first stage is understanding what is presently going on in terms of ethics within leadership practice. Sarah Gregory's original research examined middle manager decision-making and the way ethics impacted on such decisions (2010). It was clear that the impact of ethics was very limited. We suggest a thorough exploration of leadership practice in context is required: an exploration from the top to the bottom of the organisation in terms of hierarchical levels. This would involve combining an ethnographic approach with a phenomenographic method (Marton, 1981) to map out what managers at all levels are experiencing in terms of everyday practice, and outlining the interconnections and influences with a view to providing a deep contextual examination of leader-follower relationships: relationships that are embedded in rich histories of practice alongside current manifestations of practice; highlighting key role models from the past and present, the stories associated with them; how work is structured, and the assumptions and espoused beliefs of how the work of leading (and following) is done; and how these dynamics impact on individual activity in terms of the manifestation of ethics in this everyday milieu. The contexts would be of managers engaged in studying responsible leadership.

Step 2   In the classroom

The way that we will approach developing discourse ethics in the classroom is to use the following process: A week prior to the module the managers will be sent an online message asking them to think about and make notes on an incident which presented them with an ethical dilemma. A copy of the message is below:

> Activity:
> Think of an incident at work where ethics have become relevant to you, either at the time of the incident or afterwards.
>   Briefly describe the incident and then examine it through the following questions:
> 1   What scope for acting in an ethical way do you have?
> 2   What informs/influences your ethical leadership practice?

Through the Tents exercise on the module, the managers will develop their timelines and subsequently they will be allocated into groups of between three and six in the classroom and asked to share their incidents, referring to leaders identified on the timeline. The following questions will be provided as a guide for further developing their consideration of the incident and encouraging discourse ethics, especially in relation to their responsible leadership practice:

- Point of realisation – when did you realise that there was an ethical issue?
- Response to the realisation – what did you then do?

- Conflicts of interest that arose – were there personal or organisational conflicts of interest?
- Outcomes from the incident – what was the outcome for yourself and others connected to the incident?
- Reflections on the incident – was there any learning from this incident? Did you change your behaviour or were there changes in the organisation?
- Overall, does your examination of this incident give you insight into aspects of ethical responsibility within leadership practice?

This part of the process will take up to an hour and can be followed with an opportunity for the managers to share their discussions in a plenary setting if they choose.

Finally, a message will be sent to the managers one month after the completion of the module, via the online forum, asking for feedback on whether the above process has had an impact on their leadership practice within the organisation.

Step 3 The impact on the manifestation of discourse ethics in the everyday practice of leading

A longitudinal research agenda would follow the leadership development intervention through maintaining relationships with the managers. It would seek to see whether the new awareness of ethics in responsible leadership practice can be sustained within their organisational contexts. Has increased salience of discourse ethics had an impact on responsible leadership practice? The baseline understanding of step 1 can provide a guiding frame to explore which influences limit or enable the emergence of discourse ethics. In this way the research of step 3 would give empirical insight into the challenges of developing responsible leadership practice; but would also illuminate the processes of socialisation and rationalisation seeking to suppress, or even extinguish such micro-relational engagement in the fledgling flames of discourse ethics. Research might reveal a story of little fires taking hold and give insight into processes of how and when they combine to make an impact on the organisation, for example, by spreading through different levels of management until certain role models take a lead in exploring ethics within visible decision-making.

We argue that this interconnected research agenda would address our six statements. The inter-connectivity of research and leadership development may enable greater effectiveness of both activities in understanding the responsible leadership practice of middle managers.

The challenge of developing responsible leadership is in no small way encapsulated in the necessity of ethics being a central aspect in the everyday practice of leading. Yet we have argued that this is no small feat. The realism of organisational activity manifests in the predominance of amoral habitus. Changing learned occupational practices of leading within such a context requires much hope, creative desire, and imagination of the possibility in which ethics shape everyday relational discourses regarding decisions and actions within the leadership relationships between employees, suppliers, customers, and communities. Such romanticism set against the contextual realism is a broad chasm. Stimulating discourse ethics through applying the CIT to personal ethical dilemmas is a most realistic bridge, but research is needed to see if the mechanism of classroom discussions can stimulate lasting changes in the development of responsible leadership.

References

Anand, V., Ashforth, B. E., & Joshi, M. (2004). Business as usual: The acceptance and perpetuation of corruption in organizations. *Academy of Management Executive, 18*(2), 39–53.

Bird, F., Westley, F., & Waters, J. A. (1989). The uses of moral talk: Why do managers talk ethics? *Journal of Business Ethics, 8*(1), 75–89.

Brookfield, S. (1990). Using critical incidents to explore learners' assumptions. In J. Mezirow (Ed.), *Fostering critical reflection in adulthood: A guide to transformative and emancipatory learning* (pp. 177–193). San Francisco: Jossey-Bass.

Brown, M. E., & Treviño, L. K. (2014). Do role models matter? An investigation of role modelling as an antecedent of perceived ethical leadership. *Journal of Business Ethics, 122*(4), 578–598.

Bryman, A., & Bell, E. (2003). *Business research methods.* Oxford: Oxford University Press.

Buchholtz, A. K., & Carroll, A. B. (2012). *Business and society: Ethics and stakeholder management* (8th edn). Andover: South-Western Cengage Learning.

Chell, E. (1998). Critical incident technique. In G. Symon & C. Cassell (Eds.), *Qualitative methods and analysis in organisational research: A practical guide* (2nd edn) (pp. 51–72). London: Sage Publications.

Chell, E. (2004). Critical incident technique. In C. Cassell & G. Symon (Eds.), *Essential guide to qualitative methods in organizational research* (pp. 45–60). London: Sage Publications.

Chell, E., & Pittaway, L. (1998). A study of entrepreneurship in the restaurant and café industry: Exploratory work using the critical incident technique as a methodology. *Hospitality Management, 17*(1), 23–32.

Clegg, S., Kornberger, M., & Rhodes, C. (2007). Business ethics as practice. *British Journal of Management, 18*(2), 107–122.

Collis, J., & Hussey, R. (2009). *Business research: A practical guide for undergraduate and postgraduate students* (3rd edn). New York: Palgrave Macmillan.

Connolly, P., Cox-White, B., Keller, D. R., & Leever, M. G. (2009). *Ethics in action: A case-based approach.* Malden, MA: Wiley-Blackwell.

Cope, J., & Watts, G. (2000). Learning by doing: An exploration of experience, critical incidents and reflection in entrepreneurial learning. *International Journal of Entrepreneurial Behaviour and Research, 6*(3), 104–124.

Crane, A., & Matten, D. (2010). *Business ethics: Managing corporate citizenship and sustainability in the age of globalisation* (3rd edn). Oxford: Oxford University Press.

Detert, J. R., Treviño, L. K., & Sweitzer, V. L. (2008). Moral disengagement in ethical decision making: A study of antecedents and outcomes. *Journal of Applied Psychology, 92*(2), 374–391.

Easterby-Smith, M., Thorpe, R., & Jackson, P. R. (2008). *Management research* (3rd ed.). London: Sage Publications.

Fairclough, N. (1992). *Discourse and social change*. Cambridge, UK: Polity.

Fisher, C., & Lovell, A. (2009). *Business ethics and values: Individual, corporate and international perspective* (3rd edn). Harlow, UK: FT Prentice Hall.

Flanagan, J. C. (1954). The critical incident technique. *Psychological Bulletin, 51*(4), 327–358.

Gregory, S. (2010). Purchasing prostitutes in Paris: An exploration of the influence of ethics on the decisions of middle managers. Unpublished PhD thesis, Lancaster University.

Griseri, P., & Seppala, N. (2010). *Business ethics and corporate social responsibility*. Australia: South-Western Cengage Learning.

Gummesson, E. (2000). *Qualitative methods in management research* (2nd edn). London: Sage Publications.

Hinman, L. M. (1998). *Ethics: A pluralistic approach to moral theory* (2nd edn). Fort Worth, TX: Harcourt Brace.

Hosmer, L. T. (1995). Trust: The connecting link between organizational theory and philosophical ethics. *The Academy of Management Review, 20*(2), 379–403.

Jackall, R. (1988). *Moral mazes: The world of corporate managers*. Oxford: Oxford University Press.

Kaulio, M. A. (2003). Initial conditions *or* process of development? Critical incidents in the early stages of new ventures. *R&D Management, 33*(2), 165–175.

Kempster, S. (2006). Leadership learning through lived experience: A process of apprenticeship? *Journal of Management and Organization, 12*(1), 4–22.

Kempster, S. (2009). *How managers have learnt to lead*. Basingstoke: Palgrave Macmillan.

Kempster, S., & Parry, K. (2013). Exploring observational learning in leadership development for managers. *Journal of Management Development, 33*(3), 164–181.

Kish-Gephart, J. J., Harrison, D. A., & Treviño, L. K. (2010). Bad apples, bad cases and bad barrels: Meta-analytic evidence about sources of unethical decisions at work. *Journal of Applied Psychology, 95*(1), 1–31.

MacIntyre, A. (1985). *After virtue: A study in moral theory* (2nd edn). London: Duckworth.

Mackay, F. (2012). 'I don't have to be like my principal': Learning to lead in the post-compulsory sector. *Educational Management Administration and Leadership, 40*(3), 392–409.

Maclagan, P., & Campbell, T. (2011). Focusing on individuals' ethical judgement in corporate social responsibility curricula. *Business Ethics: A European Review, 20*(4), 392–404.

Marton, F. (1981). Phenomenography: Describing conceptions of the world around us. *Instructional Science, 10*(2), 177–200.

Norman, I. J., Redfern, S. J., Tomalin, D. A., & Oliver, S. (1992). Developing Flanagan's critical incident technique to elicit indicators of high and low quality nursing care from patients and their nurses. *Journal of Advanced Nursing, 17*(5), 590–600.

Norton, T. W. (1992). The narcissism and moral mazes of corporate life: A comment on the writings of Howard Schwartz and Robert Jackall. *Business Ethics Quarterly, 2*(1), 75–81.

Preskill, H. (1996). The use of critical incidents to foster reflection and learning in HRD. *Human Resource Development Quarterly, 7*(4), 335–347.

Sekerka, L. E., & Bagozzi, R. P. (2007). Moral courage in the workplace: Moving to and from the desire and decision to act. *Business Ethics: A European Review, 16*(2), 132–149.

Shao, R., Aquino, K., & Freeman, D. (2008). Beyond moral reasoning: A review of moral identity research and its implications for business ethics. *Business Ethics Quarterly, 18*(4), 513–540.

Singer, P. (Ed.). (1994). *Ethics*. Oxford: Oxford University Press.

Snell, R. S. (1999). Obedience to authority and ethical dilemmas in Hong Kong companies. *Business Ethics Quarterly, 9*(3), 507–526.

Stansbury, J. (2009). Reasoned moral agreement: Applying discourse ethics within organizations. *Business Ethics Quarterly, 19*(1), 33–56.

Tjosvold, D. & Weicker, D. (1993). Cooperative and competitive networking by entrepreneurs: A critical incident study. *Journal of Small Business Management, 31*(1), 11–21.

Toffler, B. L. (1986/1991). *Managers talk ethics: Making tough choices in a competitive business world*. New York: John Wiley and Sons.

Treviño, L. K., & Nelson, K. A. (2014). *Managing business ethics: Straight talk about how to do it right* (6th ed.). New York: John Wiley & Sons.

Treviño, L. K., Weaver, G. R., & Reynolds, S. J. (2006). Behavioural ethics in organisations: A review. *Journal of Management, 32*(6), 951–990.

Velthouse, B., & Kandogan, Y. (2007). Ethics in practice: What are managers really doing? *Journal of Business Ethics, 70*(2), 151–163.

Voegtlin, C., Patzer, M., & Scherer, A. G. (2012). Responsible leadership in global business: A new approach to leadership and its multi-level outcomes. *Journal of Business Ethics, 105*(1), 1–16.

Waldman, D. A., & Galvin, B. M. (2012). Alternative perspectives of responsible leadership. *Organizational Dynamics, 37*(4), 327–341.

Wetherell, M., Taylor, S., & Yates, S. J. (2001). *Discourse theory and practice: A Reader*. London: Sage Publications.

Woods, P. (1993). *Critical events in teaching and learning*. London: Falmer Press.

10 Developing 'next generation' globally responsible leadership

Generation Y perspectives on global responsibility, leadership, and integrity

Sharon Turnbull and Sue Williams

Introduction

This paper focuses on the crucial role of 'Generation Y' leaders in building a responsible global society for the future. Generation Y is usually taken as referring to the generation born between the early 1980s and 2000. Although the notion of generation is a problematic construct, as we will discuss later, we believe that there is value in focusing on this broad cohort of young people for this study, and we have therefore adopted the mainstream descriptor of this group for ease. We recognise, however, that many of the behaviours and values captured by the US-based literature to describe these young people may not apply to the same generation living in other parts of the globe, nor indeed to many young people in more marginalised communities in the West. This generation is important, however, as many young people in this age bracket are now arguably on the brink of taking up senior leadership roles in public institutions, corporations, government, and in society as a whole. Our chapter argues that a better understanding of the experiences, attitudes, values, and behaviours of this generation will enable employers, educators, and leadership developers to focus on how best to support them to develop their leadership skills, and to focus on developing the ethos, capability, resilience, values, and behaviours that will enable them to actively promote and enact globally responsible leadership as they enter leadership roles. Many commentators have noted that the workforce is set to lose large numbers of Baby Boomers and Generation X employees as they take up retirement. People born within the 'Gen Y' generation (1982–2000) will inevitably be the next generation to take responsibility for our planet, businesses, and society.

Leadership itself may be seen as a discourse that has now achieved universal status, fuelled by the globalisation of capitalism, as brought about by technological and digital advances. In this chapter we therefore pay particular attention to how the dominant leadership discourses, as well as other contested discourses such as 'sustainable', 'responsible', and 'integrity' are currently constructed by Gen Y. Understanding these perceptions will, we argue, enable employers and educators to better understand how best to work with the next generation of senior leaders to promote responsible leadership.

We recognise that without a significant shift in business school curricula as well as leadership development agendas, it will not be possible to break with the individualistic short-term behaviours of today's organisations and businesses. This research, therefore, also raises some important questions about whether the current research into Gen Y, which is highly Western-centric and almost exclusively US-based, is replicated when we look at the wider global cohort, and what our own primary data reveals about a more globally dispersed cohort of Gen Y future leaders and the alternative insights that our own research participants reveal for the future of responsible leadership development.

In 2011 a global manufacturer's Corporate Academy invited 125 next-generation leaders from across the globe to a World Students' Dialogue. The essay that they were asked to write for selection to the event was entitled 'What does globally responsible leadership and integrity mean to you?' This event was designed to inform the 50 + 20 project, a collaborative initiative that 'seeks to learn of new ways and opportunities for management education to transform and reinvent itself' (www. 50plus20.org).

Also, in 2012–13, the University of Gloucestershire incorporated a final-year undergraduate module on Global Responsible Leadership (GRL). The students were also asked to write a similar essay, although there was a more traditional academic approach in the request to draw on the GRL, business ethics, and corporate social responsibility (CSR) literature. The most highly graded 22 essays were selected for analysis.

Our research set out to analyse the mindsets of the young people who wrote these essays. Our purpose was thereby to inform the theory and practice of globally responsible leadership development, and in turn to support GRLI's (Globally Responsible Leadership Initiative, www.grli.org) agenda to reframe the purpose and practice of management education.

The research confirmed that the vast majority of current research into Generation Y (otherwise known as the Millennial Generation, Nexters, or Echo Boomers) has been conducted in the US with a little in Europe. In the US they are thought to represent 30 per cent of their population (Baldano and Spangenburg, 2009). Gen Y has typically been characterized in such recent studies as self-centred and narcissistic. They are known by some as 'Generation Me' (Twenge, 2010; Twenge, Campbell, Hoffman, & Lance, 2010) and have been portrayed as having a 'myopic tendency toward self gratification' (Boyd, 2010). Others have found that they have a sense of entitlement and are used to getting their way (VanMeter, Grisaffe, Chonko, & Roberts, 2013). Part of the explanation for this appears to be that in the West at least, Gen Y appears to have been educated by their parents from very young to seek approval and affirmation (Dries, Pepermans, & De Kerpel, 2008; Hewlett, Sherbin, & Sumberg, 2009; Kowske, Rasch, & Wiley, 2010). In addition, for many, it seems that involvement in family decisions was part of their upbringing, as their parents communicated with them much more than the previous generation of parents (Lancaster & Stillman, 2002). In summary, Gen Y children in Western countries have tended to experience a more democratic relationship with their parents than previous generations, and now appear to find authoritarian managers difficult to work with.

Furthermore, Gen Y also seems to have a high need for structure and reassurance, and the desire for a family feeling at work that may also be the result of their upbringing (Flander, 2008). Many have revealed that they like to be led by a manager who will also play the role of confidant, friend, and coach (Hershatter & Epstein, 2010). Baldano and Spangenberg (2009) also noted that Gen Y appears to be more idealistic than Gen X, but a little more realistic than Baby Boomers.

A strong desire to achieve a much greater work–life balance than their parents has also been revealed in many studies. Although they are broadly engaged at work, these US-centric studies found that this does not translate into a long-term commitment to their employer. Instead, Generation Y tends to assume responsibility for their own career management and employability. They value a high degree of freedom and autonomy in the way they carry out work as highlighted by the ILM/Ashridge survey (2013). The survey continues by suggesting that they want their managers to respect and value them, support with career progression, trust them to get on with things, and communicate well with them. Izzo (2002) supports this finding by suggesting that they are entrepreneurial, independent, digitally savvy, reject micromanagement, and value empowerment and excitement. A further study highlights that Gen Y are likely to be 'skeptical, mistrustful and apathetic towards traditional hierarchies and authority' (Martin & Tulgan, 2002). This could create problems for multinational, globally based large organisations, as working for such corporations has limited appeal. Generation Y would seem to wish for a workplace that allows them to be imaginative, creative, and demonstrative, enabling them to be part of an ever-changing scenario. Schlichtemeier-Nutzman (2002, p. 49) also commented that Gen Y is 'considerably more optimistic and more interested in volunteerism than Generation X'. In short, they appear to possess a more romanticised approach to work than previous generations which is demonstrated in their aspirations for a better society.

In terms of their relationships at work, Gen Y prefers working in teams, wanting work that really matters to them. The advice from Baldano and Spangenburg (2009) is that part of developing job satisfaction for Gen Y employees is to make the workplace fun, comfortable, and safe. This unrealistic and romanticised notion of the workplace tends to pervade the expectations of this generation, whilst today's realities indicate a very different experience of work. This generation's early work experiences of an upswing in the economy now contrasts with the current recessional experiences of the workplace in many Western countries.

Possibly as a result of being born in the digital age, Gen Y appears to be good at multi-tasking, being comfortable with contacting internet 'friends' across the globe, using Facebook and other social networking sites to find out about individuals from all types of cultures. This may create future leaders who can communicate well across differing cultures but who are perhaps less good than previous generations at face-to-face interaction and deciphering non-verbal cues.

A study of recent Gen Y undergraduates in their final year (some with work experiences) using Implicit Leadership Theory (Lord, Foti, & Phillips, 1982) suggests that they already have 'clearly defined expectations of traits, qualities and behaviours needed by senior management' (Curtis, Loon, & Williams, 2014) but lower expectations of those in supervisory or general line management. However, when these more vaguely expressed expectations were met these young people reported a more positive view towards the organisation that employed them. Equally a more negative perception of their line managers led to negative feelings about the organisation.

This echoes some of the characteristics identified in a study of both senior leaders and Gen Y employees conducted by Munro (2012). Here, Gen Y leaders expected to develop a much more values-based approach to leadership than previous generations, to harmonise, and to make more transparent the connections between organisational values and organisational initiatives. Munro (2012) suggests that cultural as well as emotional intelligence is likely to be seen as a competency for future Gen Y leaders. Her study of Gen Y employees found that they placed importance on mentoring, and in line with other research, a desire to 'discard the ... phrase "think outside the box" and replace it with "burn the box ... and recycle the ashes"' (Munro, 2012, p. 5). Gen Y would seek to remove many company policies and procedures, especially those showing lack of trust. Gen Y tends to seek a more collaborative approach to workplace relationships. However, despite evidence of strong collectivist views, other research suggests that they can be narcissistic and self-focused. These tensions and values paradoxes mean that managing, educating, and developing this generation is a complex challenge.

Little has been written about the approach that Gen Y takes towards the planet, society, community, and responsibility. However, research (for example, Munro, 2012) has suggested that Generation Y employees do expect to move quickly into leadership positions, and are often society-minded, eco-aware, and socially conscious, displaying respect and tolerance for diversity, and a focus on human rights.

Despite the US-centric nature of the Gen Y literature, we did identify a number of fertile discussions that raised many important questions for our study. Our research examined the narratives of globally responsible leadership embedded in the two sets of essays outlined above, focusing on what underlying meaning and assumptions about the economic and social world, the planet, and the nature of responsibility and integrity are found within them, and how these young people might lead our society into the future. We sought to identify within the texts the underlying meanings and assumptions about the economic and social world, the planet, the nature of responsibility, and how this group of Generation Y young people perceive their future leadership roles in the workplace. Our data analysis found many puzzling and contradictory patterns, values, and beliefs exhibited by these future leaders from across the globe.

We acknowledge that both groups were to some extent self-selecting. The corporate conference applicant group was largely MBA students and graduates who had chosen to apply to join an event on globally responsible leadership, and the Gloucestershire cohort of undergraduates were studying business and management and had chosen to study this particular module. Given the particular focus and nature of these young people, we wanted to understand what was driving them to want to focus on responsible leadership, and what these narratives were adding to our understanding of Generation Y as a whole, and their perspectives on globally responsible leadership and integrity in particular. As noted earlier, the notion of generation is generally a Western-centric construct and has been defined in a number of ways, clustering many diverse groups of people whose behaviours will vary widely according to culture, experience, education, background into a single 'generation'. Clearly such a clustering is highly problematic, but despite this we found much of value to our inquiry in this literature that helps us to understand the voices of the young people themselves.

Narrative themes and trends in our two groups

It was noteworthy that the biggest national group within the corporate event essays was from China. Also represented were India, southeast Asia, the Middle East, Africa, Europe, and Scandinavia. Only a few came from the US, where most previous research has been undertaken. We are not able to give a reason for the prevalence of Chinese applicants for the event, but are content that the voices represented are much broader than the group most commonly surveyed in the US-centric literature. The undergraduates were mostly from the UK, with small numbers of Chinese, Malaysian, American, and European students. Many of these latter groups had studied at degree level in their own countries prior to coming to the UK to complete or broaden their studies.

A number of core themes were found within their narratives. They are discussed here in order of frequency.

Fighting injustice

Despite the portrayal of Gen Y in the published research discussed above as being self-centred, and known as Generation Me, the essays indicated a strong focus on human rights and fighting injustice in the workplace, and a sense of what is right. Significant global issues were identified frequently such as corruption, child labour, and inequalities:

> A responsible business must identify major problems in an organization, like corruption, inequalities between men and women, forced labour,

racial discrimination, children labour and fight against for the image of its business.

These comments came from across the globe, and were not exclusive to one culture or nationality. These young writers also advocated tolerance of diversity, and trust building:

> Firstly, a good globally responsible leader should tolerate others' opinions and combine different forces. This will help people build mutual trust and confidence to break down barriers, which is helpful or even crucial for the establishment of a tolerable and pluralistic society.

For some of the authors, and in particular those from developing countries, we saw how first-hand experience of oppression and injustice had led to a strong desire to contribute to leading society toward achieving a better world.

> I had lived for thirteen years in an underdeveloped country, where injustices and societal flaws were covered up by the fraudulent action of a few very powerful men. These same powerful people were the ones who most likely hired the team of criminals who kidnapped my brothers and me, leaving us with agonizing and painful memories. After this harrowing experience, how could I not be enraged enough to understand that I had to do something to moderate the world in which I live.

Similar ideas were expressed by the undergraduate students and, although their own experiences were less dramatic and raw, they had nonetheless shaped their values directly as illustrated below:

> I notice that I need to develop the ability to recognise when someone is treated unfairly and also of how to cope with conflict situations.

> Being an intern for a construction company ... it was not uncommon for subcontractors to take quantity surveyors out for the day to cricket as a 'good will' gesture. They would be rewarded with lucrative contracts. It might be argued this is not direct bribery but ... a sweetener. If I had understood the four moral codes at the time it may have caused me to look at this from a number of different perspectives.

> Cultural dilemmas ... are becoming more and more common because of globalization. This makes it difficult for a leader to act responsibly in the eyes of all stakeholders.

Integrity, trust, and the meaning of responsibility

The question posed to both groups asked the writers to consider the meaning of integrity for globally responsible leadership. Most held a broad view of what this means in practice, although recognising that organisational and national cultures may often play a part in the way that integrity is enacted. For many, therefore, integrity has to be culturally embedded:

> When business integrity is present throughout the deepest layers of a company and not just at its surface, it becomes the heart and soul of the company's culture and can mean the difference between a company that succeeds and a company that falters.

Others equated the word 'integrity' with ethical behaviour and business ethics.

> What is business integrity? In my opinion, it is very similar to business ethics. Business ethics, in other word, business integrity, has a wide definition. Firstly it means fair play, no cheats, no briberies, and no monopolies.

> I regard integrity in a multinational company as sticking to laws and regulations, social morality and business ethics.

A third focus of integrity was on fair treatment of employees.

> Thirdly business integrity has something to do with employees.

Finally, some saw integrity as being about responsibility for society. Whereas the US-centric research on Gen Y discussed above showed a tension between self-obsession and societal focus, this group was far more outwardly focused on taking responsibility for society. For many of them integrity and responsibility were interrelated:

> Integrity is not just to be responsible for the organization itself, but also responsible for the society. Individuals and organizations have the obligation to act to benefit society at large. A company must develop its own understanding of how its principles or behaviour relate to external expectations or to external codes or guidelines in the society.

> An organisation's leadership is not only defined by how the organisation contributes some percentage of its after tax profits to social development but also needs to be responsible as to how profits are made in the first place.

> The blame [for unethical corporate behaviour] will be put on a leader if a case of misconduct falls on those at the helm, when it is obvious to those

who understand how big organisations work that it takes more than one person to make decisions.

For one student, learning more about business ethics and integrity was saddening. Seen from a Chinese perspective it appears Western-centric and inequitable:

> In my viewpoint business ethics may be the special right of well-developed entities accompanied by well-developed legislations.... For Chinese farmers pesticide abuse is a must because if they do not they would not be living ... they will not survive ... the fierce competition. Ethical western organisations seem to be double-dealers.

These comments concerning integrity and trust highlight a recognition of a tension between what is felt to be practical and reasonable in a local setting, especially where survival is at stake, and what might be ideal in terms of holding and enacting the values of a globally responsible perspective. They are also indicative of the difficulties of trying to be realistic on the one hand, but wanting a 'better' world on the other, within what is seen as a highly competitive and complex commercial world, in which leaders are responsible for a range of stakeholders.

In terms of the word 'responsibility' there were a range of views as to what this means, but many saw it as their duty and accountability to serve future generations:

> We, as global leaders, have the duty and responsibility to ensure that we preserve this earth for the benefit of future generations.

This surface view was held by many, although some were a little more sceptical and aware of the problems and tensions associated with this word.

The following extract demonstrates that the tensions and paradoxes of working towards responsible leadership can be experienced as highly problematic when moving from principles to practice and are then often seen as intractable:

> Then responsibility comes into play. *Being accountable for the harmful effects of their own or of others' actions.* Unfortunately it is not always the case. How many times have the different forms of the media informed us about environmental tragedies and other human errors such as loss of millions of gallons of oil in the open ocean, radiation leaks, 'poisoned' food exported around the world without controls? Then after a short time ending up in oblivion from the media and a legal point of view.... We suffer the consequences of a paradoxical model: we live in an era of greater well-being, that ensures unprecedented growth, but also in a period of more pollution and social injustice. This is due to fact that the

sole purpose of the game is profit. Economic progress, however, is not reflected in the progress of all humanity, but it remains a privilege due to the few. Those who work for the common good with morality and political ethics will be 'responsible'. But who should 'acquire' more responsibility? Leaders, who must have the ability to direct, guide and inspire. Leaders are the heads of state, the rulers, and above all the heads of corporations and industries around the world (often with more power and less visibility than others). But leaders can also be the companies themselves for inspiring the necessary changes of tomorrow.

Technological advancement: optimising resources, energy efficiency, and protecting environment

In addition to a broad focus on society, many of the young people in our study, from the corporate applicant group in particular, felt that without a focus on technological advancement in order to optimise resources, generate energy, and protect the environment there could not be responsible leadership. This view is also a more pragmatic one than their often more romanticised notions of responsibility.

Innovation, for example, was often mentioned as being important:

> A worthy 'globally responsible leadership' is obliged to continually push forward technological advance and conceptual innovation within its industry.

Collaboration and connectivity were also cited as key to such efforts being both local as well as joined up across the globe in order to make a real difference.

> They would devote themselves in helping local economic booming, to participate in globally joined efforts in goals like lowering down CO_2 emission, eliminating poverty and so on.

The management of risk was seen by some as another significant factor in globally responsible leadership.

> The capability of risk control and subsequently crisis management also counts in determining whether a company lives up to 'globally responsible leadership' or not. Neither in manufacturing nor business running should this issue be of less importance. Actually risk control is attracting unprecedented attention since the world has seen a series of catastrophes e.g. the atomic disaster in Fukushima power plant and the oil spill in Deepwater Horizon offshore oil drilling rig.

And not surprisingly many focused their attention on optimising global resources:

The globally responsible leadership will guide to optimize the allocation of resources in the global scope, and to reduce the improper utilization or the waste of natural resources. The most important task of this leadership is to unite the people to create a more secure, more comfortable and more sustainable world.

We have to face the fact that we have an unequal distribution of resources of the planet especially the renewable ones, which leads to a lot of problems and challenges for all humans from the smallest one of us to the biggest.

The undergraduates rarely commented specifically on resources or technology as this was not the main demand of the assignment. One or two commented on sustainability and the environment in the context of corporate social responsibility being the responsibility of leaders, but there was clearly much less awareness of responsibility for planetary resources in the narratives of this group.

Global orientation

The participants in the corporate event had consciously chosen to join an international event with a diverse group of participants from many cultures and backgrounds. Consequently it was unsurprising that their global orientation appeared to be much more developed than many of their peer group. However, it was heartening that responsibility for them extends to the whole of our planet:

More important for me is, that a global leader acts in the interest of the entire world, by making decisions which are fair for all involved parties.

A responsible leader always acts in balance with the needs and demands of the surrounding area on a local as well as on a global ground.

Such leadership functions as a bridge linking different cultures and faiths, which enables people all around the world to go across the chasm and then to promote economic and social progress characterized by sustainable development.

When running a company it is not just about satisfying stakeholders but about caring about the world.

It is a responsibility of corporate leaders to have intelligence in other cultures.

Community and society focus

At the same time, this broad global orientation was frequently seen as needing to be balanced with a local community focus and the needs of all stakeholders as indicated in the quotations below.

> To assume responsibility for the local community and the global society as well, either out of their noble spirits or concerns for sustainable development.

> Think globally, act locally, measure the impacts and consequences of his actions.... Play fairly with responsibility so the sustainable limits are not broken.

> In terms of my own decision making I must take a more considered view based on the impacts of decisions on all stakeholders.

> The success of the organisation should then have a positive impact on the community that the organisation operates in.

A number of the undergraduate students identified in their writing examples of role model leaders and companies who focused on more creative and societally friendly forms of business and capitalism, i.e. more likely to include the needs of all stakeholders in their business activities. These included the John Lewis Partnership, Innocent, L'Oreal, Richard Branson from Virgin, and Bill Gates from Microsoft.

The nature of leadership

The term 'leadership' in the questions posed sparked little debate and few ideas when compared with the discussions and understanding of the complexities of integrity and responsibility. Whilst there was much focus on the vision of a globally responsible leader, there was little sign that the participants had considered how this type of leadership could be conceptualized or enacted. In other words, their focus was more on global responsibility than on leadership itself. This concerned us as the question posed asked about globally responsible *leadership*, and not just about global responsibility.

Within the undergraduate assignments it was evident that their reading of the literature had led them to perceive that ethical leadership generally is linked to the fairness, honesty, and effectiveness of leaders and employee wellbeing, ideas which they felt were key to their own future career and work. One or two of the more perceptive students did suggest that sustainable and successful globally responsible leadership must be present throughout the organisation to develop the sense of shared responsibility, but this was not a commonplace idea, nor was it developed in the essays of those who mentioned it. We will return to this omission later, as we believe that it is a fundamental finding, and an important limitation in Gen Y's education and experience.

Vision, ambition, and future orientation

With their limited and relatively superficial conception of leadership drawn, we believe, from the voluminous and shallow leadership literature ranging from business books to accounts in the popular press, the most popular ideas given was that a globally responsible leader should have a clear vision. The participants were almost without exception referring here to the most senior organisational leaders in organisations, often still portrayed as heroic leaders residing at the top. This discourse appears to reflect the tenacity of traditional notions of all-knowing leaders, who are able to predict and control, and ultimately save the organisation. This is a further example of the paradox that most of our writers repeatedly demonstrated very shallow perceptions of leadership in their narratives compared with relatively well developed notions of responsibility and the global problems that require globally responsible leadership. Examples of this narrow, simplistic and underdeveloped view are given below:

> The leader should have a long-term vision, recognizing that our current behavior has a lasting effect on the development of human society.

> Globally responsible leadership is to have a sustainable vision, balancing the financial interests with the responsibility and the environment.

> In my opinion, global responsible leadership means that key people from the field of politics, business and industry stand for a worldwide vision. This vision should include a sustainable handling with our natural resources as well as human resources.

> Indeed I think that being able to embrace paradox, change and complexity are pathways for successful leadership.

> A global leader has many challenges and one of them is now to incorporate CSR (corporate social responsibility) into their business. This has led to the creation of globally responsible leaders ... and so shaped the definition of a good 21st century leader.

Whilst we do not wish to detract from the importance of the sentiments outlined above regarding setting and enacting a responsible vision, there is little evidence in these statements of how this might be achieved within an organisational setting. The idea seems to be that the omniscient top leader sets a vision and the rest of the organisation will follow. The top leader will, like a knight in shining armour in a fairy tale, rescue society from the evils that would otherwise befall it.

Some of the more perceptive writers recognised that globally responsible leadership is a conundrum at many levels, and argued for greater clarity as to what GRL should mean, and be, in order to help these potential leaders understand what is expected of them, but it as rare to find questions from the writers that went any further than this:

> I take from this that responsible leadership is still yet to be globally defined and with different theorists and organisations viewing it differently, it is almost impossible to define it in one sentence.

Leader as inspirer, teacher, champion, steward, and global citizen

Perhaps the most thoughtful comments on leadership were found in the more experienced corporate application group and were derived from old wisdoms, such as the leader's role as teacher, a role that even Confucius identified for leadership or as a steward for society, a notion found within many ancient tribal customs and traditions.

> Inspiring others to have a high level of commitment and dedication to produce results collectively and make a difference which will impact generations to come.

> A key element should also be his/her ability to teach by example, so that the vision can be authentic, credible and sustainable.

> It is a leadership that fulfills on its expectations and acts as a good steward for the planet and a contributing global citizen.

> Introduced by the context of global responsibility there is also the idea of statesmanship – that a corporate leader should lead by example.

> The role of leader is developed by removing obstacles, as well as developing leadership in others by building confidence.

In the undergraduate work, in particular, although this was evident across both groups, there was a much stronger leaning towards the transformational idea of leadership, the need for such leaders to have charisma without necessarily perceiving the limitations of these ideas.

In a similar vein, a paper presented at the 2014 UFHRD conference by Tymon argued that despite the wealth of academic literature about the adoption of new forms of leadership in organisations, the trait theory still remains alarmingly strong, and especially the old 'Great Man theory' with its gender stereotype. We found much evidence that these notions remain dominant amongst the young people in our study irrespective of their cultural backgrounds.

Commentary on the two sets of essays

Our findings indicate a thoughtful approach and fairly developed understanding of many of the challenges that threaten our globe, and today's society. These differed somewhat depending on the society in which the individuals had grown up, but showed perceptiveness around the complexity of today's world, shortage of resources, and the massive changes that were being brought about as a result of advances in digital technology. Therefore an understanding of the responsibility, trust, and integrity that will be required to transform our globe was relatively well developed, especially in the slightly more mature corporate applicant group, some of whom were already in the workplace.

However, by contrast, we were struck by the limitations in conceptions of leadership, and how responsible leadership might be understood and enacted within and across organisations, communities, and societies. Many of the narratives seem to suggest that this generation is limited to a desire for a 'wish list' for how their leaders behave. Many appear to hold the romanticised ideology that responsible leadership is about caring (or even paternalism), the idea that you do everything you can, without limit, to do what's best for the people around you.

Some went a little further by recognising the stakeholder view of responsible leadership, i.e. the idea that to be both ethical and successful you need to recognise the value of stakeholder-led business – the R. E. Freeman (1984) view of business not just shareholder led – the M. Friedman (2002) view. This perspective was also strongly influenced by the discourse of caring:

> We mentioned a lot of external and internal stakeholders, which in turn means that it is simply impossible for an organisation to focus on only one group. This is a significant aspect and should definitely be borne in mind by me in the future.

For these participants a trustworthy and accountable corporation is about caring for all its stakeholders, as well as for the environment. Such an organisation needs to be people-oriented all the time. It cares for clients, and shows consideration for every customer in product design and service arrangement. It cherishes talents, and knows how to make maximum and best use of every employee. Its leaders and managers are perceived to be ones that encourage collaboration, know what their employees are thinking, engage them in decisions, empower them, and develop their strengths. To encourage the involvement of people, a qualified global responsible leader, it appears, should spare no efforts to raise the awareness that 'man and man', as well as 'man and nature' are an integral whole.

This romanticism, however, is inevitably always balanced with pragmatism, along with some recognition of the ethical conundrums associated with working in organisations, and organisations' ability to control or influence personal values:

> Although one issue is that as I do not have strong leadership values of my own, working in a large organisation could quite easily shape my leadership style to that of the organisation, which may not be seen as being ethical or as ethical as I would like.

Similarly there was some recognition that the local community and the environment in which the business or organisation operates is of equal importance to the wider global picture. For example, some recognised that they were about to go into the workplace in the middle of a recession brought about in many respects by individualistic profit driven leaders, who were running organisations with a global reach but without the concern for local or global ethical decision-making

Unsurprisingly it was clear that many of the undergraduates in the second group were unfamiliar with the concepts associated with globally responsible leadership, and for some it was the first time that they had considered the issues. Consequently their essays were self-evidently more dependent on the literature and drew less on their own experiences. This may also have contributed to the limitations associated with their conceptions of leadership. However, for many it was clear that the messages in the course had made a real impact. This was particularly seen in the final section of their work where they reflected on what they had learnt and how they might use that learning in their future roles. A number were from non-UK, generally Asiatic countries and there was a desire to take these ideas back into their own future careers too. In summary, the undergraduates did show signs of genuine awakening and engagement with the topic once readings and discussions are introduced. However, as discussed above, this was not matched by a realistic view of leadership.

A number reflected on the importance to their thinking of the idea of the stakeholder perspectives as being the key driver for organisations these days. This has resonance with the research on Gen Y's wish for a more collaborative approach to the workplace. This is an important insight for educators, indicating that it is never too early to start the sensitisation process and to help young people to articulate their ideas in a more usable way, in order to take early responsibility for their own actions as soon as they join the workplace. However, there was limited evidence of awareness and understanding of how to enact leadership at all organisational levels and across society in order to make the changes they envision happen. The recognition by some that help is needed to establish the values they seek means that educators have a task or responsibility to provide as much of that help as they can through intellectual and emotional confidence building, but more than this by helping the next generation to understand how to build organisational leadership capacity and to ensure that this is focused on responsible action. It is clear from the narratives of both groups that this is missing from the education and experiences of the next generation in all corners of the globe, as it was a general deficit in the majority of the essays.

The life experiences of those who applied for the corporate event were clearly shaping their thinking, and who were much more passionate about their views and values. This was even more evident, especially in those people from unstable countries (where human rights were considered a priority) and where energy and environmental pollution was also seen as an issue. Those writing from developing countries or fast growing countries such as China frequently referred to the need to manage resources and technology as being a priority. This is heartening given the very real needs in these countries for awareness and action. However, even amongst the most passionate of the writers, there was little to be found in their narratives that indicated to us that they personally had a sense of how to take up their own leadership roles and make a real difference. In short, idealism and romanticism were not supported by a sound understanding of organisational culture, nor political structures, nor how to lead change. It appears that we are seeing in these essays (and in particular in their under-developed ideas about the leadership of others) a worrying blend of idealism, passivity, individualism, and social naivety.

Many of them argue that for change to happen, vision and a global mindset are key. Both sets of writers saw leadership as being about setting vision. Possessing a 'global mindset' and cultural intelligence were also seen by both groups as critical. However, beyond these steps there was little to reassure us that these next generation leaders had the capacity to deal with organisational and societal resistance to change, nor how to connect with others to enact leadership. Human resources, technological advancement, societal and community initiatives, setting an example to others were all seen to be relatively important, but these ideas were not supported by a sense of personal responsibility for change, and more usually they were written as imperatives for top leaders, or existing organisations. In other words they were a 'wish list' as we suggested earlier.

Both groups displayed a very unidimensional and limited understanding of leadership, organisations, and society. There was little understanding of leadership as a dispersed activity. Few of the writers from either group thought that globally responsible leadership applied to them or their own actions. There was in both groups a naivety too about the difficulties of being ethical, values driven and globally fair in our shareholder-focused capitalist structures, although this was even more marked in the undergraduate group.

Recommendations for business school educators and leadership developers

The narratives found in both sets of essays indicate a comprehensive grasp of many of the key aspects of global responsibility that we would seek to develop in the next generation of leaders. The issues were clearly better understood by the MBA students, having first-hand work experience in most cases, but intellectually both groups had a wide interpretation of the issues facing our planet.

However, the essays of both groups tended to be predominantly *issue*-based, instead of *leadership*-based. Leadership was shown in both groups to be a very weak and superficially understood construct. Leadership in most cases was written as referring to others (he, they, leaders should...) and not to themselves (I, we should...). This detachment was striking and indicates a severe deficit in the education of our young people in today's networked digital world. That there was little difference evident in the prevailing beliefs across the cultures represented in the two groups leads us to wonder whether globalisation and social networking is already homogenising the beliefs and values of the next generation. An obsolete and redundant Westernised-biased view of leadership was dominant across both groups, a problem that had clearly not been addressed in any of their education systems.

We believe, therefore, that it will be imperative for educators focusing on building globally responsible leadership to further develop Gen Y's critical thinking beyond sterile notions of leadership, organisations, and society. Awareness of distributed and complexity leadership will follow if we can teach our young people to think and question, and not to simply repeat dominant ideas, that many would argue have led to the economic and planetary crisis in which we now find ourselves. For change to happen, and Gen Y to lead a revolution in leadership action, the next generation must first question and if necessary reject old models of organisation, and develop a deeper and less romaticised understanding of organisational dynamics, power, and engagement that will enable deeper change to take place across society. Social networks and other modes of instant communication have enabled Western ideologies to take root and flourish across the globe. If we do not revisit our education models we must take responsibility for educating a new generation who will fall into the failed patterns of their predecessors

We believe that in order to develop a global leadership mindset that will extend the awareness of the next generation around issues facing the planet to a more informed understanding of how to enact responsible leadership, educators should consider adopting more creative experiential approaches for understanding the leadership of business, society, and disadvantaged communities, and in particular approaches that enable leadership development through deep immersion in real first-hand experiences.

We believe that Generation X and the Baby Boomers have a role to play in teaching the next generation to recognise the mistakes they and their predecessors made in the past leadership of the planet and society. Learning from experience of the previous generations is rarely done well, but it is imperative that this learning is passed on to the next generation of leaders.

Old models of leadership such as hierarchical and charismatic models have been a deterrent to Gen Y taking up leadership roles. They have shown a marked reluctance to take up formal leadership positions. It is important therefore that Gen Y finds alternative and more effective modes of leadership that have more relevance for leading in today's complex and fast changing world. Educators have a duty to move away from teaching out of date and Western stereotypical models of hierarchical leadership and to embrace the many leadership wisdoms that can be found around the globe that reinforce role-modeling, stewardship, and the teaching responsibilities of leadership. A start has been made with the creation of the Globally Responsible Leadership Initiative with its founding partners of the Global Compact and European Foundation for Management Development. Its demands are for changing mindsets in three areas, reconsidering the role of the 'firm', changing our views of leadership into one that focuses on values and responsibilities within organisations, and an idea that they call corporate statesmanship which would broaden the debates and dialogues with the wider society. Through their dialogues to date the partners have developed some tools and communities in which to engage others in this discussion. Similarly the alternatives expressed in dialogues such as 'worldly leadership', 'distributed leadership', 'complexity leadership', and 'servant leadership', for example, should receive greater promotion and attention. We should be starting even earlier with such education, at pre-university levels as one undergraduate commented:

> After University I intend to become a business teacher ... as a result (of this module) ... I would attempt to enhance and increase relationships that the school has with its stakeholders to generate sustainable and influential leadership.

The Gen Y narratives we have studied show a willingness to engage and to be challenged in understanding ethical approaches, business ethics, and philosophical writers who focus on the issues of consideration for others. However, as we have discussed we must find a way to assist young people to better understand the structures of power and society that sustain the status quo. As one young writer commented 'self-awareness and continued reflection will be vitally important for me in my future workplace'. This engagement needs to be built and the tools provided for Gen Y to develop their leadership capabilities. The development of greater and deeper awareness of these issues should help these potential senior leaders to have the tools and confidence to be less romantic, more practical, and more deeply and critically reflective, less dominated by mainstream discourses of business and society, and more able to think and act in alternative ways to bring about responsible shifts. In this way this generation might also provide for themselves and others the sense of safety, resilience, and even fun that they seek in their organisations.

Whilst educators will need to reinforce the global mindset and develop cultural awareness early in curriculum, and across all aspects of it, they must now go further. If we can tap into Gen Y's natural romanticism preferences for a family feeling at work, teamwork, autonomy, and early leadership responsibility in our inducting processes we may start to reduce their belief that leadership is something others do and should do and facilitate their ownership of the responsible leadership agenda. Gen Y seeks human flourishing, but now they need a grounded and ambitious approach to leadership, based on deep awareness and critical thinking

References

Baldano, A. M., & Spangenburg, J. (2009). Leadership and the future: Gen Y workers and two-dactor theory. *Journal of American Academy of Business, 15*(1), 99–103.

Boyd, D. (2010). Ethical determinants for generations X and Y. *Journal of Business Ethics, 93*(3), 465–469.

Curtis, R., Loon, M., & Williams, S. (2014). In the eye of the beholder: A study of implicit leadership theories among undergraduate business management students. *Conference presentation, 15th International Conference on Human Resource Development Research and Practice across Europe.* Napier University, Edinburgh.

Dries, N., Pepermans, R., & De Kerpel, E. (2008). Exploring four generations' beliefs about career: Is 'satisfied' the new 'successful'? *Journal of Managerial Psychology, 23,* 907–928.

Flander, S. (2008). Millennial magnets. *Human Resource Executive Online.* www. hreonline.com/HRE/view/story.jhtml?id=84159035.

Freeman, R. E. (1984). *Strategic management: A stakeholder approach.* Boston: Pitman.

Friedman, M. (2002). *Capitalism and freedom.* Chicago, IL: University of Chicago Press.

Hershatter, A., & Epstein, M. (2010). Millennials and the world of work: An organization and management perspective. *Journal of Business and Psychology, 25,* 211–212.

Hewlett, S. A., Sherbin, L., & Sumberg, K. (2009). How Gen Y and Boomers will reshape your agenda. *Harvard Business Review, 87*(7/8).

ILM/Ashridge Survey. (2013). *Great expectations.* Berkhamsted, UK: Ashridge University.

Izzo, J. (2002). *Values shift: The new work ethic and what it means for business.* Toronto: Prentice Hall Canada.

Kowske, B. J., Rasch, R., & Wiley, J. (2010). Millennials' (lack of) attitude problem: An empirical examination of generation effects on work attitudes. *Journal of Business and Psychology, 25,* 265–279.

Lancaster, L., & Stillman, D. (2002). *When generations collide: Who they are, why they clash. How to solve the generational puzzle at work.* New York: Collins Business.

Lord, R. G., Foti, R. J., & Phillips, J. S. (1982). A theory of leadership categorization. In J. G. Hunt, U. Sekeran, & C. Schriesheim (Eds.), *Leadership: Beyond establishment views.* Carbondale, IL: Southern Illinois University.

Martin, C. A., & Tulgan, B. (2002). *Managing the generation mix.* Amerherst, MA: HRD Press.

Munro, C. (2012). Preparing the next generation of leaders: The emerging organizational landscape with Generation Y at the helm. *International Conference on Human Resource Management and Professional Development for the Digital Age Proceedings.* Global Science and Technology Forum, Singapore.

Schlichtemeier-Nutzman, S. E. (2002). Linearity across generations: An exploratory study of training techniques. (Doctoral dissertation, University of Nebraska Lincoln 2001). *Dissertation Abstracts International, 62,* 09.

Twenge, J. M. (2010). A review of the empirical evidence on generational differences in work attitudes. *Journal of Business and Psychology, 25*, 201–210.

Twenge. J. M., Campbell, S. M., Hoffman, B. J., & Lance, C. E. (2010). Generational differences in work values: Leisure and extrinsic values increasing, social and intrinsic values decreasing. *Journal of Management, 36*(5), 1117–1142.

Tymon, A. (2014). 80 years on and the Great Men are still with us. *Proceedings of 15th International Conference on Human Resource Development Research and Practice across Europe.* Napier University Edinburgh.

VanMeter, R., Grisaffe, D., Chonko, L., & Roberts, J. (2013). Generation Y's ethical ideology and its potential workplace implications. *Journal of Business Ethics, 117*(1), 93–109.

11 Romanticism, antimodernism, and a pluralistic perspective on responsible leadership

Eric Guthey

Cultural historian T. J. Jackson Lears has recounted how, towards the end of the nineteeenth century, many educated and affluent beneficiaries of modern American progress began to feel like they were actually its victims. As he describes in his book, *No place of grace: Antimodernism and the transformation of American culture, 1880–1920*, a significant number of artists, authors, intellectuals, and cultural figures during this period gave voice to a common sense of dissatisfaction with the ways that modern technological and industrial advancements had left them feeling 'overcivilized', empty, and disconnected from authentic physical sensation, emotional intensity, and spiritual transcendence (Lears, 1994).

Some of these Victorian malcontents sought out more intensive forms of direct experience by celebrating medieval chivalry and military ideals, by joining religious revivals, or by exploring literary fantasies of violence and primal irrationality. Others tried to counteract industrial and commercial alienation by launching an arts and crafts movement or by elevating the simple life of the artisan as a cultural ideal. According to Lears (1994), the various, often highly romantic ways that these individuals and groups responded to and acted upon their feelings of disconnection and weightlessness generated a set of distinctively *antimodernist* patterns of thought and expression that continue to frame cultural reactions to capitalist modernity and technological progress even up to the present day.

Because antimodernism is shot through with the spirit of romanticism, in this concluding chapter I will build on Lears' (1994) argument to revisit the theme introduced by the editors at the beginning of the book, and to highlight both the promise and the peril of approaching responsible leadership through the lens of romanticism. I will also use the concept of antimodernism to touch on some of the subsequent chapters of the book, and to point out how they exemplify these same potentialities, as well as some of these pitfalls. Throughout this exercise I will argue the point that leadership discourse itself is heavily influenced by antimodernist sentiments – again, both for good and for ill.

As with antimodernism, so with romanticism, and so with responsible leadership: all three discourses seek on some level to challenge the status quo, to question the dominant priorities of the present, and to recapture a sense of connection, authenticity, and moral value that is perceived to be in peril, if not already lost, amidst the rush of progress and modernity. But all three discourses also balance on a razor's edge. While they can provide resources and energies for protest and perhaps even change, they can also tip in the other direction, and end up reinforcing the realities they promise to transform. As Lears (1994) explains, in fact, the antimodernist movement ultimately failed as a form of protest because it accommodated itself to the very source of its dissatisfaction in the first place. The reason for this, he argues, was that the discourse of antimodernism shared too many of the foundational assumptions that buttressed and nurtured the same modern developments it sought to protest against. In particular, the antimodernist emphasis on intense individual experience comported too well with the kind of possessive individualism that paved the way for market capitalism and a consumer society. Despite their best intentions, Lears (1994) argues, the antimodernists helped usher in precisely the type of society they sought to avoid.

With this argument in mind, I will conclude this chapter and this book with a discussion of how responsible leadership can benefit from the energy and spark of the romantic impulse towards antimodern protest, while avoiding the romantic trap of foregrounding individual experience and self-fulfilment to the point of reinforcing the status quo rather than mobilizing change. As I will argue, several chapters in this book point the way towards a sustainable form of responsible leadership, especially when they adopt a radical perspective on the relational and collective dynamics of leadership over more conventional, individual and leader-centred perspectives. Brigid Carroll describes what such a perspective would look like in her chapter, and proposes that we move from an emphasis on responsibility in the singular to an understanding of the multiplicity of shared responsibilities, or *co-responsibilities*, in the plural. The outline of the dimensions of responsible leadership provided by the editors in the first chapter also suggests that it is important to take multiple stakeholders and responsibilities into account. If we want to use the notion of responsible leadership to mount an effective and sustainable critique of conventional approaches to leadership, and ultimately to critique modern corporate capitalism itself, we would do well to fundamentally reconceive of leadership as a social, collective, and interactive activity that functions much more like a social movement than a personal romantic challenge or quest.

Romanticism and antimodernism

Romanticism is fraught with contradictions and difficult to pin down. Leaving aside its defining content and subject matter for a moment, what is it, really? A literary genre? An aesthetic ideal? A cultural movement? While many scholars would define romanticism as a specific canon of novels, poems, and paintings, Thomas Streeter points out that the great romantic artists may have been responding to a broader, symptomatic impulse towards romanticism in the culture at large, rather than creating it (2011). As Streeter also points out, many people who have never read Byron nor appreciated Blake have celebrated the power of spontaneous emotions, the thrill of heroic tales of outcast wanderers on desperate quests, the appeal of iconoclastic ideas about authentic experience, and the lure of impulsive protests against history and tradition – all familiar characteristics of the romantic ideal. For this reason Streeter concludes that romanticism is best understood as a sort of 'cultural toolkit', a grab-bag of loosely coupled sentiments, tropes, discursive practices, and habits at one and the same time diffuse and somehow familiar (Streeter, 2011, p. 46).

This helps to specify the genus of romanticism, but not necessarily its species. For many, the distinctive content of romanticism remains elusive precisely because of the aforementioned contradictions at its core. In *Romanticism against the tide of modernity*, for example, Michael Löwy and Robert Sayre describe romanticism as 'simultaneously (or alternately) revolutionary and counterrevolutionary, individualistic and communitarian, cosmopolitan and nationalistic, realist and fantastic, retrograde and utopian, rebellious and melancholic, democratic and aristocratic, activist and contemplative, republican and monarchist, red and white, mystical and sensual' (Löwy & Sayre, 2001, p. 1). As these authors point out, some critics have concluded on this basis that contradiction and dissonance are the only things that hold romanticism together as a coherent whole. Already in 1924 the literary scholar Arthur O. Lovejoy went so far as to declare that the term romanticism meant so many different things that it meant nothing at all, and that it had 'ceased to perform the function of a verbal sign' (quoted in Löwy & Sayre, 2001, p. 2).

Löwy and Sayre (2001) do not agree. After an exhaustive review of the vast literature on romanticism they conclude that both the aristocratic/retrograde and revolutionary/utopian extremes of the movement share at their core a common sense of longing, alienation, and loss. As they put it, 'the Romantic vision is characterized by the painful and melancholic conviction that in modern reality something precious has been lost, at the level of both individuals and humanity at large' (2001, p. 21). Echoing Jackson Lears' argument, and invoking Max Weber, they point out that the rise of industrial capitalism had a lot to do with generating this negative reaction against modernity. 'The principal characteristics of modernity – the calculating spirit (*Rechnenhaftigkeit*), the disenchantment of the world (*Entzauberung der Welt*), instrumental rationality (*Zweckrationalität*), and bureaucratic domination – are inseparable from the advent of the "spirit of capitalism"' (Löwy & Sayre, 2001, p. 18). Löwy and Sayre conclude that at its core, Romanticism represents a revolt against the kind of modern civilization created by capitalism.

In his book, *The net effect: Romanticism, capitalism, and the internet*, Thomas Streeter also invokes Weber to explain this same sense of loss at the heart of the romantic impulse, and to explain its continued relevance in the present day:

Faced with the dull weight of a highly specialized, technologically and bureaucratically organized world, at various moments, many of us go off in search of ways to bring elation to our lives, to bring the magic back, to recover what Max Weber described as enchantment; and on this quest we expend energy, careers, lives. Sometimes this impulse simply peppers the social fabric of industrialized societies and comes out in random instances of individuals suddenly turning to, say, mountain climbing or abrupt changes of careers or spouses. But at times the impulse becomes organized and can lead to paroxysm of social change, such as the diverse religious movements that currently convulse our world.

(Streeter, 2011, p. 45)

Streeter details how romantic patterns of thought have helped frame the internet and computer culture as anarchic and liberating sources of freedom, power, and rebellion. As he points out, the news media and countless pop-biographies have reinforced these perceptions by seizing upon recognizably romantic tropes to render figures like Silicon Valley entrepreneur Steve Jobs as heroic paragons on noble quests against insurmountable odds. Related romantic narratives portray the lone computer hacker standing up against the stultifying tyranny of the bureaucratic machine, or the open source software movement providing a utopian communitarian alternative to the monopolistic regimes of powerful corporate interests. In a similar vein, I have described and analysed what I call 'New Economy romanticism', and traced its links with a persistent strain of anti-managerialism in American public business discourse (Guthey, 2004).

Of course, as Streeter also points out, the internet and computer culture have provided a fertile nesting ground for these same powerful commercial interests. Arguably, companies like Google, Apple, Amazon, Microsoft, and Facebook channel and control the supposedly autonomous individual experiences of most internet users, all the while tracking their purchases, their contacts, their credit histories, and even their physical location. From this perspective the consumer fantasy of unlimited free choice and instant gratification appears more like Weber's iron cage or Foucault's panopticon. And this is not just *in spite of*, but also in large part *because of* the romantic individualism that pervades computer discourse. The reasons for this are twofold. First, as Streeter and others have pointed out, romantic individualism does not provide an effective or sustainable basis for challenging powerful corporate interests because it does not address, or even really comprehend, the political and social dynamics that invest them with their power in the first place. 'If romanticism's great strength is its critique of rationalist fantasies of predictability, its blind spots concern social relations and historical context', he explains. 'With its focus on heroic narratives, romanticism obscures the broad social relations that make those "heroic" acts possible' (Streeter, 2011, p. 178).

At a deeper level, romantic individualism aids and abets the entrenchment of powerful commercial interests by providing the foundational logic for a culture of consumption. This is counterintuitive, because as Colin Campbell has argued in *The romantic ethic and the spirit of modern consumerism* (2005) and elsewhere, 'the Romantics were correct to perceive their philosophy as fundamentally opposed to those essentially mundane and utilitarian attitudes which characteristically accompany consumption'. But as the title of his book would indicate, Campbell is also quick to point out that that 'those self-same Romantics actually aided the emergence of modern consumerism since their advocacy of a romantic world-view unwittingly served to legitimize auto-nomous illusory hedonism' (Campbell, 1997, p. 169, 2005).

This was also the legacy of the antimodernists as described by Jackson Lears – their idealisation of possessive individualism, and their emphasis on the therapeutic virtues of intense experience and emotions, paved the way for the very kind of society they sought to avoid. 'By exalting "authentic" experi-ences as an end in itself, antimodern impulses reinforced the shift from a Prot-estant ethos of salvation through self-denial to a therapeutic ideal of self-fulfillment in *this* world through exuberant health and intense experi-ence', Lears concludes. 'The older morality embodied the "producer culture" of an industrializing, entrepreneurial society; the newer non-morality embod-ied the "consumer culture" of a bureaucratic corporate state' (Lears, 1994, p. xvi). Dana Cloud has extended Lears' critique of antimodernism to deliver a wholesale indictment of the pervasive, personalising rhetoric of therapy and self-help in American culture, charging that it 'dislocates social and political conflicts onto individuals or families, privatizes both the experience of oppression and possible modes of resistance to it, and translates political ques-tions into psychological issues to be resolved through personal, psychological change' (Cloud, 1998, p. xviii).

The antimodern impulse in leadership discourse

If the family resemblances between romanticism, antimodernism, and indi-vidualised leadership discourse have not yet become fully apparent, mention of a few prominent, popularised leadership texts should help bring them into sharper focus. Rob Goffee and Gareth Jones make the connections very explicit in their popular book *Why should anyone be led by you? What it takes to be an authentic leader* (2006). In fact, they open their book with an extended discussion of Weber's diagnosis of the alienating effects of modernity and instrumental reasoning, and they propose authentic leadership as the cure to this malaise. After cataloguing the degrading nature of meaningless labour and the corrosion of traditional sources of meaning and value, they conjecture that 'Max Weber's grim predictions of the "disenchantment of the world" may be fulfilled' (Goffee & Jones, 2006, p. 7). Goffee and Jones recount their many conversations and interviews with executives who should ostensibly feel like the primary beneficiaries of the triumph of corporate capitalism, but who have instead begun to feel – just like the antimodernists – that they are actually the victims of a pervasive banality and hollowing out of meaning:

Executives are not immune to this. Interviewed at work about what gives their lives meaning, they mouth the latest corporate propaganda: 'increasing shareholder value,' 'delighting customers.' Asked the same questions at home, they admit to profound symptoms of meaninglessness as they struggle with work–related stress and dysfunctional family lives. We face an epidemic of anomie.

(Goffee & Jones, 2006, p. 7)

It may seem odd to encounter a popular business text that delivers so withering a condemnation of the deleterious effects of capitalist work practices and 'corporate propaganda'. But just this kind of critique of the empty, rationalising logic of workplace bureaucracies has become a mainstay of mass market and popularised leadership literature. In *Leading with soul: An uncommon journey of spirit*, for example, Lee Bolman and Terrance Deal (2001) launch a similarly moral and emotional campaign against the negative consequences of formally rational imperatives to increase efficiency, productivity, or sales. 'Too many workplaces … are ruled by technology, efficiency, and the bottom line, with little regard for what human beings need in order to experience personal fulfillment and success', they charge. In classic antimodernist fashion, their diatribe includes an indictment of the hollow array of products on offer in a consumer society driven by technological progress. 'Does this dazzling array satisfy our hunger for a richer, fuller, more meaningful life?' they ask (Bolman & Deal, 2001, p. 4).

In order to restore a greater sense of meaning, control, and connection in the face of the alienation and weightlessness brought on by large managerial bureaucracies and modern consumer society, these two sets of authors advocate characteristically romantic and antimodernist solutions. Goffee and Jones (2006) argue that leaders must learn to be their authentic selves, while Bolman and Deal (2001) call for leaders to rediscover spiritual basics. Both approaches essentially advocate a turn inward towards personal and individual sources of leadership strength.

Goffee and Jones actually claim that they have a very social and interactive understanding of leadership (2006). In the introduction to their book, they insist that leadership is above all else situational, non–hierarchical, and relational. But they go on to talk exclusively about leadership as something *leaders do*. Consequently they define authentic leadership in exceedingly individualist, leader-centred terms, not as a relational process or a social phenomenon but as a set of qualities that leaders have. For them, authentic leaders display a consistency between words and deeds, they display a 'real self' that holds together the various roles they have to perform, and they have an inner sense of 'comfort with self' that serves as the source of their consistency and coherence. Goffee and Jones conclude that 'to be a more effective leader, you must be yourself – more – with skill'. Or as they also put it, 'LEADERSHIP BEGINS WITH YOU – and you will not succeed as a leader unless you have some sense of who you are' (Goffee & Jones, 2006, p. 29).

Part of the reason for the contradiction stems from the distinction between two very different understandings of the word 'relational' as applied to leadership. As Mary Uhl-Bien has explained, the more traditional, or entity perspective, 'considers relationships from the standpoint of individuals as independent, discrete entities' who then enter into relationships, while a more fundamentally relational perspective 'starts with processes and not persons, and views persons, leadership and other relational realities as made in processes' (Uhl-Bien, 2006, p. 655). This latter perspective does not focus on the perceptions, intentions, behaviours, personalities, expectations, or skills that leaders have with respect to their relationships with others. Instead, a more radical relational perspective 'changes the focus from the individual to the collective dynamic' and 'sees an appointed leader as one voice among many in a larger coordinated social process' (Uhl-Bien, 2006, p. 662).

With this distinction in mind, it becomes clear that Goffee and Jones may think that they adopt a radically relational perspective on leadership, when in fact they retain a very traditional entity perspective in which individual leaders have to be skilled at managing relationships with other individuals, primarily followers (2006). Indeed, the chapter subheading for the section of their book in which they insist that leadership is relational reads 'How can we become more effective as leaders and as developers of leaders?', clearly indicating the authors' allegiance to a leader-centred approach whereby individuals understood as self-possessed entities enter into relationships, rather than being constituted by a set of social processes.

In a similar manner, the notion of spiritual leadership often appears to reinforce an entity perspective that channels a romantic element of protest in the direction of individualist accommodation. Bolman and Deal, for example, work hard to remove the notion of leadership from the complicated fray of social and organisational interaction, and to place it firmly in the hearts of individual leaders (2001). 'Perhaps we lost our way when we forgot that the heart of leadership lies in the hearts of leaders', observe Bolman and Deal. 'We lost touch with a most precious human gift – our spirit' (Bolman & Deal, 2001, p. 6). These authors propose that the pervasive malaise in workplace organisations calls for a turn inward to recapture a sense of moral grounding and transcendence. 'Leading with soul returns us to ancient spiritual basics – reclaiming the enduring human capacity that gives our lives passion and purpose' (2001, p. 6). For Bolman and Deal, the ultimate point of spiritual leadership is to help 'our society to rediscover it's ethical and spiritual center', and 'to enrich your life and leave a better legacy for those who come after you' (Bolman & Deal, 2001, p. 12). While this sounds very moving, it effectively channels their own very cogent critique into a form of self-enrichment that is not capable of addressing the complex social and political realities that lead them to critique the soullessness of commercial organizations in the first place.

Other variants of spiritual leadership push their romantic critique of the workplace in even more rationalising and profit-maximising directions. For example, Louis Fry maintains that the purpose of spiritual leadership is 'to foster higher levels of organizational commitment and productivity' (Fry, 2003, p. 693). The Spiritual Leadership Survey tool distributed commercially by Fry's International Spiritual Leadership Institute subjects the notion of spirituality to a quantitative, formally rational calculus, and concludes that 'results to date support a significant positive influence of organizational spiritual leadership on employee and unit performance, life satisfaction, organizational commitment and productivity, and sales growth' (International Institute for Spiritual Leadership, 2011). Peter Case and Jonathan Gosling have argued that Fry's approach places human spirituality at the service of productivity and profit-maximisation in a manner that exemplifies 'the instrumental appropriation of spiritual energy' and that threatens to hollow out the distinctive nature of the concept of spirituality itself (Case & Gosling, 2010, p. 274).

Conclusion

The chapters collected in this volume exemplify the promise and the power behind a romantic critique of contemporary work organisations – and perhaps also a few of the pitfalls that lurk behind that critique. I will conclude my own contribution to this volume by returning to some of the key themes raised throughout the book in order to reiterate my central point – that the very admirable element of romantic critique inherent in the notion of responsible leadership risks merely reinforcing the status quo if it does not come part and parcel with a radically relational notion of what leadership is and how leadership works. There is not sufficient space here at the end of this book to touch upon each of the chapters in turn. Fortunately, three of the chapters in particular speak to the point I have made here in ways that exemplify the connections at play within the volume as a whole.

In 'Promoting responsibility, purpose, and romanticism in business schools', Ken Parry and Brad Jackson contribute to this volume a bracing indictment of the notion of shareholder value and of the complicity of business school education in promoting that often very unfortunate ideal. They argue cogently that we have become too enamoured of corporate purpose, and far too taken with the idea that persons who work for corporations should and must be accountable for the purpose of profit maximisation first and foremost. They propose, quite convincingly, that this is precisely where the notion of accountability falls short, and where the notion of responsibility for societal purpose comes to the fore. Ultimately, Parry and Jackson argue, we should be teaching that the purpose of leadership is to integrate corporate and societal purpose in a manner that gives priority to the latter. 'Perhaps a responsible leadership message coming from business schools will integrate the goals of societal purpose and corporate purpose', they conclude. 'Perhaps accountability will be matched with responsibility.'

This is a powerful argument, one to which I would suggest one important rejoinder on the basis of the argument I have presented in this chapter. A radically relational perspective on responsible leadership would emphasise not just one *purpose*, but many *purposes*. Or as Brigid Carroll suggests in her chapter, and as the editors convey in their outline of the dimensions of responsible leadership, not just one responsibility, but multiple, competing, sometimes conflicting, and often complementary *responsibilities*, in the plural. My colleagues Ken Parry and Brad Jackson use these two terms almost exclusively in the singular. But the bulwark of a healthy society is a multiplicity of different purposes, competing visions of responsibility, different political perspectives, diverse ethnic, racial, cultural, regional, and gendered identities and interests, along with a vital and functioning political system that allows for debate, negotiation, and compromise among these different groups and interests. From this pluralist perspective, the notion of corporate or societal purpose is not quite adequate to address the multiple purposes attached to either business, or society, or the combination of the two. This is not to argue that there is no point in talking about shared purposes and responsibilities – but these are ideals to be sought after and fought for in a crowded public and civic sphere. In short, a radically relational approach to responsible leadership would begin from a recognition of the social, political, and often contentious give-and-take between different purposes and interests at play in a pluralistic democratic society.

Karen Blakely delivers a radical critique of responsible leadership in her chapter, 'Responsible leadership: a radical view'. It is an exciting chapter to read, primarily because Karen does not appear afraid to jump into the political fray, to speak frankly about competing interests and contentious contemporary debates, or to speak truth to power. Reflecting concerns voiced in Parry and Jackson's chapter, as well as elsewhere in this book, Karen calls into question the profit-maximising interests of large, multinational corporations, and she catalogues the social and environmental degradation such heedless interests can cause. In a manner reflected in my own argument, Karen emphasises also the importance of the democratisation of institutions, and the crucial task of reconceiving of leadership as something more akin to an organisational, social, and political movement.

From the perspective I have developed in this chapter, however, even Karen's compelling argument could be carried in a more radical direction, because the language she uses to define responsible leadership still draws heavily on an entity perspective that assumes the primacy of the leader as person. Granted, she emphasises the importance of the notions of shared or distributed leadership, but she phrases her list of the key elements of responsible leadership as a description of what responsible leaders are like, not an analysis of how responsible and relational leadership *processes* unfold. This is why Brigid Carroll's contribution to this volume performs such a valuable service for us all. In her chapter, 'From responsibility to responsibilities: towards a theory of co-responsible leadership', she outlines the concept of *co-responsibility* as a new paradigm for reconceiving of responsible leadership, and she articulates a clear and compelling argument for why it is important to move from a notion of responsibility in the singular to an emphasis on *responsibilities* in the plural. Her argument builds on a radically relational understanding of leadership, and on a rejection of an individualising, entity perspective in favour of an emphasis on the primacy of interaction and even political contention.

Appropriately, Brigid's argument for this approach to the notion of plural co-responsibilities builds on an analysis of leadership events and processes in the public and political sphere, rather than just within the confines of commercial organisations. For this reason, she brings into sharp focus the interplay of multiple interests and the centrality of contention and dissent. From this standpoint Brigid argues that responsible leadership theory 'appears far less a radical shift than one might hope'. As she points out, 'it remains a leader-centric theory with an assumption that responsibility lies in "the inner theatre" … or "good character" … of an individual, usually with formal positional authority in an organization'. The editors of the present volume correctly cite Maak and Pless's article 'Responsible leadership in a stakeholder society: A relational perspective' as a foundational work for developing a fresh approach to responsible leadership (Maak & Pless, 2006). But in spite of their emphasis on relationality, Maak and Pless adopt an entity perspective that leads them to ask questions like 'what makes a responsible leader?' and 'what qualities do responsible leaders need?'. As my analysis of romanticism and antimodernism makes clear, these kinds of individualist, entity-based assumptions can subvert the potential for radical critique or meaningful change. As Brigid Carroll also points out in Chapter 3, some approaches to responsible leadership may not even have meaningful change at the top of their agenda. Instead, they foreground the need to orchestrate a 'balancing act' among stakeholder interests in a manner that would seem to indicate 'harmony and consensus might be underlying drivers of this theory'.

As Carroll's argument and as my own chapter has made clear, it is difficult to talk about responsible leadership in relational and pluralist terms. The default position in popular 'leadership speak', reinforced by whole libraries full of more sombre and scientific leadership research, is to reinforce a leader-centred perspective that emphasises the centrality of individual leaders understood as separate entities who then enter into relationships. This is where a whole host of various leadership theories and approaches end up, from authentic to spiritual to responsible leadership and beyond. As I have made clear, this individualising and overly romanticising pattern of thought risks taking the critical edge off of the romantic impulse towards protest, and risks accommodating us to contemporary realities with vague promises of self-fulfilment, harmony, and consensus. This raises the question: how can we retain the romantic spark of protest at the heart of responsible leadership without shading over into platitudes about great responsible leaders and what responsible leadership qualities they possess?

I have pointed towards one possible answer to this question at the start of this chapter, and I will elaborate only briefly here. There is a form of collective, relational, and often contentious human interaction that manages to combine the romantic spark with an emphasis on radical relationality, political contention, and the plurality of interests and co-responsibilities. Moreover, this form of interaction most often has a strong moral component at its core, and often results in sweeping social change. The gay rights movement, the civil rights movement, the Occupy movement, the Tiananmen Uprising, and the Arab Spring are all good examples of this kind of interaction. They are moving. They are romantic. They are often mind-changing, life-changing, and society-changing. Social movements provide a model for understanding leadership from a radically relational perspective with a romantic twist.

For many years now, organisational sociologists like Gerald F. Davis have studied the relational dynamics of social movements, and their relevance for how we understand the dynamics of organisations and organising processes more generally (Davis & McAdam, 2000; Davis, McAdam, Scott, & Zald, 2005). As Davis has argued, social movements can be understood and analysed as a function of opportunity structures, framing processes, social networks, and mobilising institutions. While these four key mechanisms can and often do include the activities and skills of individual actors, the concepts themselves foreground the importance of relational processes and network dynamics as a prerequisite to any movement for change.

Drawing on an impressive body of academic research on social movements, as well as on a long-running MBA course on how to effect change inside organisations, Davis and co-author Christopher J. White have recently published *Changing your company from the inside out: A guide for social entrepreneurs* (Davis & White, 2015). In closing, I can only encourage all leadership scholars to read this book. In fact, I will be working through the book with a new crop of MBA students in a course on Organizational Behavior and Leadership at the Copenhagen Business School starting this fall. If we can encourage our students and ourselves to reconceive of leadership as a form of social movement, we can help to bring about the kind of transformation of business education that Ken Parry and Brad Jackson propose; we can build on the romantic impulse towards protest and change; we can respect the plurality of interests and co-responsibilities in a democratic society; and we can hopefully contribute to meaningful and productive change in the face of pressing societal and global challenges.

References

Bolman, L. G., & Deal, T. E. (2001). *Leading with soul: An uncommon journey of spirit* (2nd edn). San Francisco: Jossey-Bass.

Campbell, C. (1997). Romanticism, introspection and consumption: A response to Professor Holbrook. *Consumption Markets & Culture, 1*(2), 165–173.

Campbell, C. (2005). *The Romantic ethic and the spirit of modern consumerism* (3rd edn). York: Alcuin Academics.

Case, P., & Gosling, J. (2010). The spiritual organization: Critical reflections on the instrumentality of workplace spirituality. *Journal of Management, Spirituality & Religion, 7*(4): 257–282.

Cloud, D. L. (1998). *Control and consolation in american culture and politics: Rhetoric of therapy.* Thousand Oaks, CA: Sage.

Davis, G. F., & McAdam, D. (2000). Corporations, classes, and social movements after managerialism. *Research in Organizational Behavior, 22,* 193–236.

Davis, G. F., McAdam, D., Scott, W. R., & Zald, M. N. (2005). *Social movements and organization theory.* Cambridge: Cambridge University Press.

Davis, G. F., & White, C. (2015). *Changing your company from the inside out: A guide for social intrapreneurs.* Boston, MA: Harvard Business Review Press.

Fry, L. (2003). Toward a theory of spiritual leadership. *The Leadership Quarterly, 14*(6): 693–727.

Goffee, R., & Jones, G. (2006). *Why should anyone be led by you? What it takes to be an authentic leader.* Boston, MA: Harvard Business School Press.

Guthey, E. (2004). New economy romanticism, narratives of corporate personhood, and the antimanagerial impulse. In K. Lipartito & D. B. Sicilia (Eds.), *Constructing corporate America: History, politics, culture* (pp. 321–342). Oxford: Oxford University Press.

International Institute for Spiritual Leadership. (2011). *The spiritual leadership online survey.* Retrieved from www.iispiritualleadership.com/products_services/survey.php.

Lears, T. J. J. (1994). *No place of grace: Antimodernism and the transformation of American culture, 1880–1920* (University of Chicago Press ed.). Chicago: University of Chicago Press.

Löwy, M., & Sayre, R. (2001). *Romanticism against the tide of modernity.* Durham: Duke University Press.

Maak, T., & Pless, N. M. (2006). Responsible leadership in a stakeholder society: A relational perspective. *Journal of Business Ethics, 66*(1): 99–115.

Streeter, T. (2011). *The net effect: Romanticism, capitalism, and the internet.* New York: New York University Press.

Uhl-Bien, M. (2006). Relational leadership theory: Exploring the social processes of leadership and organizing. *The Leadership Quarterly, 17*(6): 654–676.

Index

Page numbers in **bold** indicate figures.

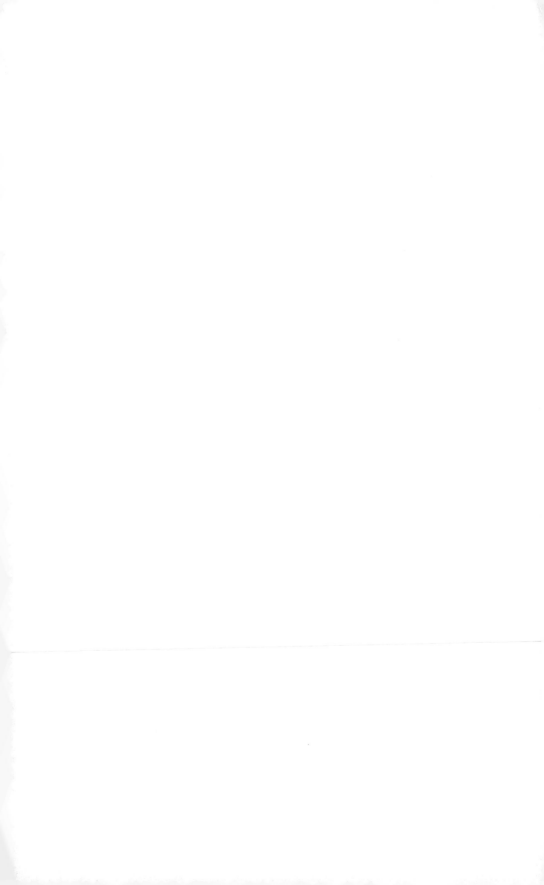